Visions for Teacher Educators

Perspectives on the Association of Teacher Educators' Standards

Edited by
Cari L. Klecka, Sandra J. Odell,
W. Robert Houston, and Robin Haskell McBee

Association of Teacher Educators
and
Rowman & Littlefield Education
Lanham • New York • Toronto • Plymouth, UK

Published in cooperation with the Association of Teacher Educators (ATE)
Published in the United States of America
by Rowman & Littlefield Education
A Division of Rowman & Littlefield Publishers, Inc.
A wholly owned subsidiary of The Rowman & Littlefield Publishing Group, Inc.
4501 Forbes Boulevard, Suite 200, Lanham, Maryland 20706
www.rowmaneducation.com

Estover Road
Plymouth PL6 7PY
United Kingdom

British Library Cataloguing in Publication Information Available

Library of Congress Cataloging-in-Publication Data

Visions for teacher educators : perspectives on the Association of Teacher
Educators' standards / edited by Cari L. Klecka . . . [et al.].
   p. cm.
  "Published in cooperation with the Association of Teacher Educators (ATE)."
  ISBN 978-1-60709-127-1 (cloth : alk. paper) — ISBN 978-1-60709-128-8
(pbk. : alk. paper) — ISBN 978-1-60709-129-5 (electronic : alk. paper)
  1. Teachers—Certification—Standards—United States. 2. Association of
Teacher Educators. I. Klecka, Cari L. II. Association of Teacher Educators.
  LB1771.V57 2009
  379.1'57—dc22   2008048714

∞™ The paper used in this publication meets the minimum requirements of
American National Standard for Information Sciences—Permanence of
Paper for Printed Library Materials, ANSI/NISO Z39.48-1992.
Manufactured in the United States of America.

Contents

Foreword

Cari L. Klecka, Sandra J. Odell, W. Robert Houston,
and Robin Haskell McBee, Editors

The Association of Teacher Educators (ATE) revised its Standards for Teacher Educators in 2007. Revisiting the standards by members of ATE generated dialogue about the notion of professional standards for teacher educators. In a desire to expand the dialogue about standards for teacher educators, the Association's Commission on the Assessment of the Teacher Educator Standards conceptualized this book to give voice to many of the issues and perspectives on standards for teacher educators. We view the role of standards for teacher educators as a vehicle for articulating a vision for our profession. At the same time, we recognize that the standards muddy the waters; just the term "standards" raises red flags for some and communicates very different messages in diverse contexts for various people.

The purpose of this book is not only to articulate a vision for the profession through Standards for Teacher Educators but also to provide a historical perspective on standards in our profession and to explore the issues and questions surrounding these particular standards. To accomplish this, D. John McIntyre sets the stage in the first chapter by establishing the history of teacher education as a discipline. Robert Fisher follows this with a discussion of the debate about who is a teacher educator—an issue that has dominated the conversation around the standards. W. Robert Houston concludes this section by establishing the historical foundation for standards themselves.

In the following section, the reader is presented with a set of chapters designed to conceptualize a vision for the teacher education profession. In these nine chapters, members of the Commission on the Assessment of the Teacher Educator Standards flesh out the theoretical and empirical underpinnings of each standard. In these chapters, much of the language of the standards and of the indicators and artifacts is excerpted from the standards document itself to maintain the integrity of the standards. Much of this reflects the work that the Commission accomplished in its expanded vision and subsequent revision of the Standards for Teacher Educators.

The third section focuses on broadening our vision for the teacher education profession by understanding better the implications of the Standards for Teacher Educators in diverse educational fields. Voices of educators in varied roles and areas of study are highlighted in this section to expand our thinking about the standards. An examination of the application of the standards to individuals' work in diverse areas of education is included. The section ends with a discussion of the perspective of the National Council for Accreditation of Teacher Education (NCATE) on the interplay between standards for teacher educators and accreditation of teacher education programs.

The final section provides unique points of view on the vision for teacher education that can be generated through careful crafting of standards for teacher educators and the potential impact of such standards on the profession. Scott Imig and David Imig open this section with an examination of the role of standards in the educational landscape. Then Roy Edelfelt considers what standards can do for teacher educators. Emily Lin and Cari Klecka follow this with a chapter focusing on how the standards may be used as a framework for professional growth through self-study in teacher education. Renée Clift completes this section with a critical view of teacher educator standards, suggesting that there may be a number of issues and questions generated by establishing these standards.

Our intended audience for this book is teacher educators and those who work in teacher education and who may not primarily identify themselves as teacher educators. A central feature of our exploration is to raise the tough questions and issues that emerge as a result of introducing standards to the profession and putting them into use. Ultimately, ours is not a question of whether or not teacher educators should have standards because these standards have been in existence for over a decade. Rather, we view this book as an invitation for conversation, particularly among those who educate teachers. We hope that people read this book and ask the questions, raise the issues, and consider the implications of standards for the teacher education profession. Our goal is to provide many voices and views within these pages that encourage our audience to think creatively, rather than finitely, about standards for teacher educators.

Part I

FOUNDATIONS FOR TEACHER EDUCATOR STANDARDS

CHAPTER 1

The History of Teacher Education as a Discipline

D. John McIntyre, Southern Illinois University, Carbondale

Wikipedia, the online encyclopedia, defines an academic discipline as a body of knowledge that is being given to, or received by, a student of that discipline. The term also denotes a 'sphere of knowledge' in which an individual has chosen to specialize (2007). The purpose of this chapter is not to argue whether or not the field of teacher education is a discipline or that there is a knowledge base to support it as a discipline. The fact that teacher education is a discipline worthy of study with an evolving knowledge base has been established by a series of publications that have both described and critiqued the scientific foundation for teacher education (Howsam, Corrigan, Denemark, & Nash, 1976; Reynolds, 1989; Houston, Haberman, & Sikula, 1990; Sikula, Buttery, & Guyton, 1996; Cochran-Smith & Zeichner, 2005; Cochran-Smith, Feiman-Nemser, McIntyre, & Demers, 2008).

Instead, this chapter examines the discipline of teacher education as it has evolved throughout history. In addition, this chapter describes the evolution of the curriculum of teacher education and of the professional standards that guide formal teacher education. Johnson (1968) noted that while schools have existed for over four thousand years, formal teacher education has existed for only a little over three hundred years. It was not until the late seventeenth century that much interest was given to the formal preparation of teachers. In fact, teacher education did not exist in any formal or structured manner for the first 200 years of American history (Urban, 1990).

THE EMERGENCE OF FORMAL TEACHER
EDUCATION IN EUROPE

Johnson (1968) states that from approximately 100 A.D. until 1700, education was primarily the responsibility of the church. In general, the purpose of education was to transmit religious beliefs and culture and the clergy, who had religious training but no formal teacher training, conducted teaching.

There is debate as to the originators of formal teacher preparation. McGucken (1932) claims that the Jesuits began professional teacher preparation, including student teaching, in the mid-1500s in Europe. He claims that the Jesuit priests selected to be teachers had to prove their ability by teaching in the presence of experienced teachers in classes similar to the one they were to be assigned. The Jesuits focused their educational programs on what is today commonly known as secondary education. On the other hand, many educational historians believe that Jean Baptiste de la Salle established the first normal school in approximately 1685 in Rheims, France (Cubberly, 1920). In addition, he opened a second school in Paris that contained an elementary laboratory school for the sole purpose of promoting "practice teaching" (Battersby, 1949). Johnson (1968) states that de la Salle is often known as the "Father of Student Teaching."

The normal school concept established by de la Salle quickly spread and a Lutheran clergyman, August Hermann Francke, established the first professional teacher training institution in Germany in 1696 (Johnson, 1968). At first, Francke only prepared elementary education teachers but later established a school for the training of secondary teachers. In addition, he provided room and board for students who were poor and needed assistance.

Little is known about the curriculum studied by prospective teachers of that period. However, Barnard (1851) states that teacher trainees received separate instruction for two years and obtained a "practical knowledge" of methods. In addition, prospective teachers had to possess the right basis of piety, knowledge, skill, and desire for teaching. Perhaps this was the first precursor to the National Council for the Accreditation of Teacher Education's (NCATE) standards for knowledge, skills and dispositions.

In the mid-1700s, it was a philosopher and writer, not an educator, who made a large contribution to teacher preparation, not only at that time but also to future educational considerations. Jean-Jacques Rousseau published *Emile* in 1762 and challenged the manner that schooling was being conducted in Europe. Johnson (1968) claimed that Rousseau was very vocal in his opposition to classrooms being places where teachers talked and pupils merely listened as the sole means of gaining knowledge. Rousseau exhorted schools to allow children to be children. He urged schools to make games an education and education a game and that teachers should teach less from books and more from nature (Cole, 1950). In essence, Rousseau was urging schools to become places where students "experienced" learning as active participants rather than being passive vessels. This philosophy would later influence the thinking of such American educators as John Dewey and Jerome Bruner.

The first state supported school for teacher preparation was the Gymnasial Seminary established in Berlin in 1788 (Johnson, 1968). Johnson described a "student teaching" experience that is remarkably unchanged from today in its outward appearances. The teacher trainees taught under a director and three other appointed teachers. They were required to teach a minimum of ten hours per week as well as assisting their supervising teachers in correcting written work. In addition, the teacher trainees were required to attend a monthly conference for the purpose of receiving criticism and engaging in pedagogical discussions. This monthly conference was open to all of the teachers in the school.

Again, there is very little known about the curriculum utilized for preparing these teachers in the late 1700s in Germany. Barnard (1851) wrote that completing a teacher-training program took two years. During the first year, the prospective teachers learned the content needed to teach others. Throughout this initial year, the trainees assisted in classrooms of a school attached to the normal school. The second year was devoted almost solely to "practice" as the teacher trainee practiced his or her "craft" in a school for an entire year. It is easy to note similarities between these early programs and the structure of modern teacher preparation programs.

Another educator who had considerable influence on the early preparation of teachers was Johann Heinrich Pestalozzi. According to Johnson (1968), Pestalozzi was critical of the mode of instruction conducted in most European schools in the early 1880s as it almost singularly consisted of memorization and recitation. Pestalozzi introduced reasoning and individual judgment to the teaching process and, for the first time, initiated teaching as a science to reflect the emerging role of psychology as an important component of the teaching and learning process. This resulted in a new approach to the preparation of classroom teachers.

Johann Friedrich Herbart and Friedrich Froebel were influenced by and extended the work of Pestalozzi. Herbart helped to further establish the concept of teaching as a science by formulating his principles of psychology and adapting them to the teaching/learning process (Johnson, 1968). He advocated that teachers utilize a methodology with five formal steps (Hilgenheger, 1993):

1. Prepare the pupils to be ready for the new lesson.
2. Present the new lesson.
3. Associate the new lesson with ideas studied earlier.
4. Use examples to illustrate the lesson's major points.
5. Test pupils to ensure they had learned the new lesson.

In order to appeal to pupils' interests, Herbart suggested using literature and historical stories instead of the basal readers that were prevalent during the time. In addition, he established a pedagogy seminar and laboratory school at Norway's Kongsberg University.

Friedrich Froebel, the founder of the kindergarten, also established a number of teacher training classes that emphasized appropriate teaching methods for young children (Johnson, 1968). He established "play" as a central theme in the development of young children. In addition, Johnson (1968) claims that Froebel is often given credit for originating the proposition that women make the best teachers for young children.

As teacher education evolved in Europe through the late 1700s and early 1800s, ideas were beginning to emerge that would lay the foundation for the modern preparation of teachers. Teacher education as a science was being espoused by a number of early educators as the field of psychology began to develop. As a result, teaching methods became an integral part of most teacher preparation programs. In fact, Froebel helped to establish the notion that certain methodologies and approaches to instruction might be more conducive to certain age groups than other methodologies. In addition to the emergence of courses focusing on teaching methods, student teaching and laboratory schools began to emerge in Europe. Eventually, these would be the precursors to our normal schools. Still, this period was not defined by a comprehensive curriculum for teacher education, nor were standards developed that would guide the teacher education profession.

EARLY TEACHER EDUCATION IN AMERICA

Although teacher education was beginning to emerge in Europe during the seventeenth and eighteenth centuries, it is fairly clear that formal preparation of teachers did not exist during this period in colonial America. Urban (1990) pointed out that those who taught at this time were usually not people who viewed teaching as their primary role or their primary occupation in life. For most of this period, teachers were hired as tutors or taught elementary subjects in their homes. Cremin (1970) stated that these types of schools were called "dame schools" since the teachers employed in such schools were often older, mature women. These teachers often had very little, if any, teacher preparation (Urban, 1990).

Secondary schools emerged during the later colonial period and were mostly sites to prepare students for college. Secondary school or academy teachers had usually attended college but typically did not intend to make teaching their career (Urban, 1990). It was not until the early nineteenth century when common schools began to emerge in New England that the preparation of teachers also began to emerge (Urban, 1990). Common schools were the foreshadowing of our public school system, just as teacher preparation started in public normal schools. As a result, the link between the nation's public schools and teacher education was established a little over 200 years ago. However, the curriculum established for teacher preparation as well as any professional standards required for teachers was still woefully lacking.

THE EMERGENCE OF NORMAL SCHOOLS

Urban (1990) reported that the common school movement experienced a considerable increase in enrollment during the mid-1800s. As a result, there was a parallel need for an increased number of teachers to staff classrooms. Thus, the normal school was created for the purpose of preparing teachers for common schools. Again, Urban (1990) stresses that most students entering normal schools had only an elementary education background. It was believed that this was appropriate since most of the students would eventually teach at the elementary level only. However, this lack of an education at the secondary level caused normal schools to adopt a curriculum that not only stressed technical training of teachers but also included academic subjects in order to bolster their content knowledge.

Urban's (1990) chapter in the first edition of the *Handbook of Research on Teacher Education* did a wonderful job of presenting the history of normal schools. However, a glance at the curriculum of normal schools reveals a relatively stable situation. In fact, as Pangburn (1932) points out, the curriculum of the normal school remained relatively unchanged during most of its duration. For the most part, the academic subjects studied by future teachers were those that were studied in elementary schools. She also relates that the professional education component of the curriculum consisted of courses in the history of education, science of education, teaching methods in elementary schools, field observation, and practice teaching.

Normal schools would continue to thrive as the major source for the preparation of elementary teachers into the twentieth century. However, their ability to prepare secondary teachers was challenged by the emergence of university-based teacher preparation programs designed to prepare high school teachers. Until this time, normal schools existed with a fairly basic curriculum for teacher preparation and virtually no standards established for those who wished to become teachers.

Furthermore, as high schools became more prevalent in the United States, the curriculum of the normal school was being challenged. Although Tyack (1967) states that it was well into the twentieth century before certification requirements and professional standards became established for future teachers, it was this divergence of teacher preparation from the normal school concept to the universities that served as an initial spark for a radically different teacher education curriculum and the eventual emergence of standards to guide the profession.

THE EMERGENCE OF UNIVERSITY-BASED TEACHER EDUCATION

Urban (1990) points out that the emergence of departments of education in universities came shortly after the end of the Civil War. This post-Civil War period found colleges and universities being established throughout the United States. The first chair of pedagogy in a university, John Milton Gregory, was at the University of Michigan in 1879. He then moved to the University of Illinois to begin the education program (Urban, 1990).

Urban's (1990) treatise on the history of teacher education described this era as the point at which the curriculum of the normal school and the emerging university-based teacher education curriculum began to diverge. Whereas the normal school's curriculum was focused primarily on subjects specific to the elementary school, university teacher preparation programs adopted a more scientific approach and began to align themselves with the emerging fields of psychology and philosophy. This divergence would eventually lead to the common perception of a great divide between the practice of the public schools and the theory of the university teacher education programs.

The establishment of science as a foundation for teacher preparation accompanied by the distancing from the practice in the classroom was done for a number of reasons. For example, in order for university teacher educators to gain credibility and acceptance for themselves and their programs on the university campus, they had to align themselves with the more respected scientific knowledge of higher education. It was also perceived that future teachers graduating from a university would then be better prepared and more competitive in the market than those completing their preparation at a normal school.

Urban (1990) stressed that the emphasis on science, especially psychology, in the early twentieth century led to the estrangement between many entrenched education programs, such as at the University of

Chicago, Harvard University, Teachers College, Stanford University and the University of California at Berkeley, and practice in public schools. In many instances, teacher education faculty at these types of institutions became more concerned with their own research than with the reality of the public school classroom. As a result, courses in educational psychology, cultural and social foundations, and measurement were incorporated into the curriculum in many major universities. Thus, many teacher education programs and their faculty began moving their curriculum in the direction of a scientifically oriented practice and away from the practical problems and issues embedded in the school classrooms.

This dichotomy was true not only for the major research universities but also for the teachers colleges that evolved out of the normal schools. Urban (1990) points out that many faculty in teachers colleges were trained in universities so they brought the value of their disciplines to the teachers college settings. This value did not always honor the preparation of teachers as the ultimate goal of their professional work. Students often were encouraged to major in particular disciplines and their preparation, as teachers became less of a priority than having mastered a given body of knowledge within the discipline.

The evolution in the early twentieth century of teacher education programs with a more scientifically oriented curriculum did not mean that teacher education programs had totally abandoned any focus on the work of the schools. For example, the first recognized internship in teacher education was implemented at Brown University in 1909. Graduates of the university were placed in the Providence Public Schools for one full year as half-time salaried teachers under the supervision of a professor of education and supervising teacher. At the same time, they were required to complete course work at the university designed to prepare for teaching positions in a secondary classroom (Gardner, 1968).

The internship, much like the apprenticeships of the seventeenth through nineteenth centuries, were developed with the philosophy of providing teacher candidates with opportunities to test the educational theory learned at the university with practice in the classroom. Gardner (1968) cites the five underlying principles established by the National

Society of Colleges of Teachers of Education as guiding internship practices at that time:

1. Serve as a professional laboratory facility for observations and participation by prospective teachers.
2. Conduct research and experimentation in child growth and development and in the use of instructional materials and teaching procedures.
3. Test and demonstrate forward-looking school practices.
4. Enrich the program of graduate studies in education.
5. Exercise leadership in in-service education programs for teachers.

(Gardner, 1968, p.2)

It is clear that the National Society of Colleges of Teachers of Education's intent to provide direction for the development of internship programs closely resembles the foundations for many current programs such as alternative routes to certification, Masters of Arts in Teaching (MAT), and, to a degree, some professional development schools. One might even note some similarities to the current standards for professional development schools developed by the National Council for the Accreditation of Teacher Education (NCATE).

The scientifically oriented teacher education curriculum of the early twentieth century combined with the need for teachers to be prepared to meet the challenges of the classroom would, by the late 1920s, result in a countermovement that would have a major impact on the evolving field of teacher education.

TEACHER EDUCATION'S SOCIAL FOUNDATIONS MOVEMENT

In the late 1920s, a group of educators led by John Dewey, William Kirkpatrick, Harold Rugg, and Boyd Bode began a series of discussions that eventually led to the development of the "foundations of education" as practiced in many teacher education programs today (Tozer & McAninch, 1986; Urban, 1990). As Urban (1990) points out, these educators were unhappy with the then current state of teacher education for two reasons. First, the emphasis on the scientific basis of teaching and learning was based on the concerns of particular disciplines rather than on the real problems of teaching. Second, the curriculum practiced by most teacher education programs accepted the current social reality as a given and, thus, attempted to adjust the actions of teachers and schools to meet that reality. Led by Dewey, these educators proposed an approach that encouraged teachers and students to reflect upon and question American society and schools, and to encourage a more democratic process in the education of students.

The social foundations movement was important for helping to shift the teacher education curriculum away from the strict discipline-oriented approach advocated earlier in the 1900s to a more balanced view of preparing teachers that would include not only subject matter content and foundations courses but also instructional methods and field experiences in schools. As a result, the curriculum of teacher education programs began to include courses within one's academic discipline as well as courses in educational psychology, educational philosophy, history of education, teaching methodology, and field experiences. The curriculum established by the mid-1900s was considerably more sophisticated and rigorous than the teacher education curriculum offered by normal schools at the beginning of the century.

THE ERA OF STANDARDS AND ACCOUNTABILITY IN TEACHER EDUCATION

Although currently more prolific than at perhaps any other time in our history, standards are not new in teacher education. For example, at their 1870 meeting, the American Normal School Association developed criteria for admission to teacher education programs and a two-year course of study for normal schools (Edelfelt & Raths, 1999). Much like many of today's standards, these also were apparently met with fierce opposition.

Edelfelt and Raths (1999) stated that standards emerged from two assumptions. First, it was assumed that teacher educators could develop a code that would define "best practice." Second, it was assumed that some approaches to teaching and teacher education are better than others. By setting standards, the profession would identify the better practices and eradicate the weaker ones. I would add a third assumption that recently has arisen as a rationale for establishing standards in teacher education. The third rationale is based on the faulty assumption by state and national legislators as well as policy makers that teacher education is in a state of disarray and that teacher educators cannot be trusted to develop standards that would guide their own profession.

As stated previously, attempts to create standards for teaching and teacher education are not new and often emerge from studies or reports about teaching and/or teacher education. Edelfelt and Raths (1999) reported that one of the first major studies involving a critical analysis of teacher education was the *Commonwealth Teacher-Training Study of 1929*. The study examined what "excellent" teachers actually did in the classroom and then attempted to determine what the teacher candidate must know and be able to do in order to perform these tasks effectively. One of the significant contributions of this study was the emphasis for the first time on actually collecting data on effective teaching. As a result, the topics of teacher behavior and performance began and, to a great extent, are still being studied today.

The Improvement of Teacher Education Report was published in 1946 and recommended standards for eleven areas in teacher education (American Council on Education, Commission on Teacher Education, 1946). These areas within teacher education were: personnel services, selection and recruitment of teacher candidates, placement and follow-up, curriculum, general education, subject-matter preparation, professional education, student teaching, and preparation and in-service growth of college teachers. Edelfelt and Raths (1999) report that many of the standards set by the Commission have been pursued successfully while others have not.

Historically, one of the most influential reports in teacher education was the publication *School and Community Laboratory Experiences in Teacher Education,* published in 1948 by the Sub-Committee of the Standards and Surveys Committee of the American Association of Teachers Colleges (Johnson, 1968; Edelfelt & Raths, 1999). Commonly known as the Flowers Report (named after John Flowers, chair of the subcommittee and former president of the Association for Student Teaching), it established standards for professional laboratory experiences, including student teaching, which would eventually become part of the NCATE standards. These standards specified that:

(1) laboratory experiences be an integral part of work in each of the four years of college; (2) before student teaching, laboratory experiences be integrated into other parts of the college program; (3) provisions be made for pre-student teaching experiences; (4) provisions be made for full-time student teaching; (5) assignments be made cooperatively by the people most acquainted with the student and his or her needs and the opportunities in the laboratory situation, and (6) the college faculty member and the cooperating teacher share in supervision.

(Edelfelt & Raths, 1999, p.8)

One can see that 60 years later, these standards continue to influence most teacher education programs' laboratory and student teaching experiences. With the ascension of a teacher education curriculum from the early to mid-1900s and the renewed emphasis on field experiences emitting from the Flowers Report, teacher education programs were continuing their evolution from the days as normal schools.

As standards for the teaching and teacher education professions continued to be adopted, teacher educators believed there was a need to develop an accrediting system that would provide some type of regulation of teacher education programs. As early as the late 1800s, the American Normal School Association (the precursor to the American Association of Colleges for Teacher Education—AACTE) petitioned the regional associations for accreditation of their programs but was rebuffed as being not worthy of their efforts (Edelfelt & Raths, 1999). As a result, teacher educators eventually began to accredit themselves through self-study of the then established standards proposed by professional organizations and various commission reports. However, this was viewed as suspect since no governance system was universally accepted (Edelfelt & Raths, 1999).

From these early accreditation efforts, several stakeholders developed the National Council for the Accreditation of Teacher Education in 1952. Since its inception, NCATE has undergone several redesigns and changes, but it has consistently examined the nation's teacher education programs through the lenses of these standards, including knowledge, skills, and dispositions of teacher candidates; assessment system; teacher education candidates; professional education faculty; diversity; and governance and resources.

In the 1980s, NCATE required all teacher education programs to develop a conceptual framework, basically a philosophical thread—based on the knowledge base that tied all elements of their program together. Edelfelt & Raths (1999) pointed out that most teacher educators missed the irony that such insight also motivated the 1870s reports on teacher preparation. McIntyre, Byrd, and Foxx (1996) credit the adoption of conceptual frameworks for enabling teacher education programs to narrow the gap between theory and practice and experiences of campus courses with those during field experiences and student teaching.

Most recently, NCATE has come under much criticism because of its assessment of candidates' dispositions. Opponents of this criterion claim that it is merely an attempt by teacher education programs to thrust their political agendas upon their candidates. An in-depth discussion of the debate over dispositions in teacher education can be found in articles by Borko, Liston, and Whitcomb (2007); Damon (2007); Villegas (2007); Murray (2007); and Diez (2007). However, despite this criticism, there are studies that indicate that NCATE-accredited institutions appear to prepare more effective teacher candidates than non-NCATE-accredited programs (Gitomer, Latham, & Ziomek, 1999; Darling-Hammond & Youngs, 2002).

In 2003, the Teacher Education Accrediting Council (TEAC) was instituted as an alternative to NCATE (Murray, 2005). This has sparked a debate within teacher education regarding standards, accountability, and whether or not two accrediting bodies is a strength or weakness for our profession. In 2008, NCATE and TEAC began discussing a merger organized by AACTE.

The advent of a new accrediting body for teacher education did not abolish the publication of reports and studies that resulted in recommendations for changes in teacher education. In 1974, AACTE appointed the Commission on Education for the Profession of Teaching chaired by Robert Howsam (1976). The Commission examined the characteristics of professions and whether or not teaching met these criteria. In addition, the Commission examined several topics not often considered by other groups or past reports. These included: the role of governance in teacher education, the lack of autonomy of schools and colleges of education in the university, the lack of political or institutional support of teacher education, and the need to extend teacher preparation beyond the university.

One of the major contributions of the Commission was its frank assertion of teacher education's status in the profession. In brief, the Commission noted that teacher education was being virtually ignored in the professional literature and that there was no professional language, taxonomy of terms, and standards that would enable teacher educators to effectively communicate with others (Edelfelt & Raths, 1999). These assertions contributed to a new debate among teacher educators about their role within the university and society.

In 1986, the Carnegie Forum of Education and the Economy issued *A Nation Prepared: Teachers for the 21st Century*. The purpose of this report was to respond to the Forum's task of linking the nation's economic growth with the skills of its citizens. Edelfelt and Raths (1999) stated that the report issued mandates rather than standards. These included:

1. All teacher education degrees should be abolished by all states, and teacher education should become a graduate program.
2. Admission into teacher education programs should be contingent on an applicant's mastery of basic skills and knowledge.
3. Graduate programs should allow candidates to make up work missed in their undergraduate programs.
4. States should offer incentives to attend graduate teacher education programs to students of exceptional academic background.
5. A National Board for Professional Teaching Standards (NBPTS) should be created to establish standards to high levels of professional competence and to issue certificates to teachers meeting those standards.
6. State and local policy should encourage institutions of higher education to develop programs of continuing education to keep teachers abreast of the field and to prepare teachers to meet the NBPTS standards.

Although most institutions generally ignored the recommendations regarding teacher education as a graduate education enterprise, the National Board for Professional Teaching Standards was established and has awarded thousands of teachers with national board certification. The second recommendation also was influential in helping to establish the numerous entrance and exit exams teacher candidates must now successfully complete to be licensed to teach.

The Association of Teacher Educators (ATE) established the Commission on the Education of Teachers into the 21st Century (1991) that examined factors influencing the quality of teacher education. The Commission lamented the fact that many past reform movements and recommendations had not yielded major improvements in the profession and cited reasons for this lack of progress. In addition, the Commission emphasized the need to prepare teachers for students who were at risk, minority, and poor, especially those in urban areas. As a result, the Commission made strong recommendations for recruiting and retaining teachers of color who would be prepared to teach in urban schools.

Perhaps two of the most influential reports in the past two decades have been those issued by the Interstate New Teacher Assessment and Support Consortium (INTASC) (1992) and the National Commission on Teaching and America's Future (NCTAF) (1996). INTASC's primary constituency is state education agencies responsible for teacher licensing, program approval, and professional development. INTASC stresses that all students can learn and perform at high levels when teachers integrate content knowledge with the specific strengths and needs of their students. Perhaps the cornerstone of INTASC's efforts is their belief that all education policy should be driven by what we want P–12 students to know and be able to do. As a result, INTASC has promoted the notion that a state's education system, including its teacher licensing system, should be aligned with its P–12 student standards.

Many of the INTASC standards, including the core beginning teacher standards as well as content standards in such disciplines as mathematics, English language arts, science, special education, and foreign languages, have been adopted or adapted by state education agencies to guide not only their P–12 classroom but also their teacher education programs. The proliferation of standards that now guide the teaching profession is a far cry from the past when little to no standards existed to guide the preparation of teachers.

The National Commission on Teaching and America's Future (NCTAF) published *What Matters Most: Teaching for America's Future* (1996). This report caused policy makers and educators to once again place the issue of teacher quality at the center of the nation's education agenda. NCTAF called for a national initiative to provide every child with competent, caring, qualified teachers in schools organized for success by 2006. However, the commission identified a number of barriers to achieving that goal. These included low expectations for student performance, unenforced standards for teachers, major flaws in teacher preparation, inadequate teacher recruitment, inadequate induction for beginning teachers, lack of professional rewards for knowledge and skills, and schools that are structured for failure rather than success.

In order to address these concerns, the report offered the following recommendations:

(1) get serious about standards, both for students and teachers
(2) reinvent teacher preparation and development
(3) fix teacher recruitment and put qualified teachers in every classroom
(4) encourage teacher knowledge and skills
(5) create schools that are organized for student and teacher success

Within these recommendations, NCTAF stressed the need for teacher tests in content knowledge, teaching knowledge and teaching skills, yearlong internships in professional development schools, mentoring programs for beginning teachers, using the NBPTS as the benchmark for accomplished teaching, and accreditation for all schools of education. These recommendations led to much debate among educators, legislators, and policy makers and continue to influence change within many teacher education programs and state agencies.

Other than the Flowers Report in 1948, the majority of recommendations emanating from the myriad of commission reports during the past fifty years or more have focused on teacher education curriculum, teacher quality, teacher recruitment, and teacher development. However, in 1970, the Association of Teacher Educators first published *Guidelines for Professional Experiences in Teacher Education* (1986). This major report focused on what many teacher candidates and teachers consider to be the most important aspect of their teacher preparation program—their field experiences, including student teaching (McIntyre, Byrd, & Foxx, 1996).

This report recommended guidelines to provide direction for the most promising practices in professional experiences. The guidelines covered numerous aspects of the professional experiences in teacher education, including defining roles; organizational structures for professional experiences; planning of professional experiences; qualifications, responsibilities, and loads of college and university supervisory personnel; qualifications and responsibilities of affiliated supervisory personnel; in-service education programs for supervisors; and evaluation of personnel and programs of professional experiences.

In 2000, ATE published a revised set of guidelines for field experiences that responded to a maturing knowledge base within teacher education (Guyton & Byrd, 2000). These standards were intended to correspond with, complement, and extend the NCATE accreditation standards on field experiences. Although some of the original guidelines remained, most were much more specific and reflected the evolving nature of teacher education. For example, the current standards provide much more emphasis on collaboration with P–12 school partners, working in diverse school settings, reflective practice on the part of field supervisors and teacher candidates, best practices based on current research on teaching and pupil learning, and alignment of standards with INTASC standards.

In 1996, the Association of Teacher Educators published the first set of national standards aimed at establishing expectations for the professoriate involved in teacher education. The national standards for teacher educators are an attempt to guide those who are aspiring to be teacher educators as well as those who are currently engaged in the profession. In addition, these standards can assist in the development of graduate programs in teacher education and teacher leadership so that future teacher educators understand the standards deemed necessary by their peers if they are to become effective teacher educators. These standards include indicators and suggested artifacts that can accommodate both school-based teacher educators as well as those in university settings.

These standards, amended in 2008, are discussed in detail in other chapters of this book. However, it is important to note that the amended standards for teacher educators emphasize issues that have emerged since 1996. For example, teacher educators are now expected to meet a standard that addresses their cultural competence as well as their ability to promote social justice in the classroom. Our classrooms reflect the changing demographics of our nation and make this standard an essential one to be addressed by those preparing future and current teachers. As more pupils from diverse cultures and learning needs, as well as those where English is their second language, enter our public school systems, teacher educators must possess the skills, knowledge, and dispositions to meet their academic and social needs.

The era of accountability and standards for education and teacher education do not appear to be ebbing in the near future. The *No Child Left Behind Act* was purposively not addressed in this section because there has been, and will continue to be, much written about it and its impact on teaching, learning, schooling, and teacher education. Although not always viewed as positive, the advocacy for accountability and the promotion of standards have prompted a national dialogue about expectations for teacher education and teacher educators, and have assisted in the development of programs and assessments. This dialogue has resulted in a more common thread across the profession as to what teachers should know and be able to do. The fact that there is still debate regarding particular standards and their impact, or lack thereof, on the profession assures that this topic will remain an important one.

THE CURRENT STATUS OF TEACHER EDUCATION

Perhaps now more than any other time, teacher education is central to the discussions of state and national legislators, policy makers, and other educators. Cochran-Smith (2004) asserted that these are "dangerous times for teacher education." She described three major developments that are driving practice, policy, and research in teacher education. These are an intense focus on teacher quality, an emergence of "tightly regulated deregulation" as a federally mandated reform agenda, and the ascendance of science (once again) as the solution to educational problems. Taken separately, these developments should pose no threat to our profession, but she believed that their convergence is pushing the profession towards a technical view of teaching that equates learning with testing.

Others echo Cochran-Smith's assertion about the precarious position of teacher education in the early twenty-first century. Ravitch (2007) linked the future of public education with that of teacher education, as we currently know it. She believes that today's critics of public education do not want to reform it, but to dismantle it as an obsolete institution. Many of today's critics, such as the New Commission on the Skills of the American Workforce (2006), call for the privatization of our nation's schools as a means for dealing with our educational problems. How does this impact teacher education? A number of the same groups also advocate the privatization of teacher education. As stated earlier in this chapter, there has been a long history of a relationship between our nation's public schools and teacher education. Ravitch (2007) believes that elimination of public education would seriously undermine our country's democratic principles.

Lois Weiner (2007) also raised this alarm in her discussion of the perceived threat to public education and teacher education posed by the growing neo-liberalism movement in this country and beyond. Without involving this chapter in a discussion about the pros or cons of neo-liberalism, Weiner (2007) perceived this movement as advocating the elimination of publicly funded teacher education programs, reducing education to no more than vocational schooling, viewing teaching as no more than preparing students for tests, and eliminating the need for substantial investment in teacher education's role in promoting democracy and social justice. In agreement with Ravitch, Weiner views that these positions not only threaten teacher education and public schooling, but also our democratic foundation.

As stated earlier by Cochran-Smith (2004), science has reemerged as a potent force in teacher education. The scientific, evidence-based research agenda that currently dominates educational discussions in our nation's and state capitols is based on similar approaches in medicine. However, as Cochran-Smith (2004) asserted, this model that uses mostly experimental, process-product research designs is often not appropriate for the more complex interaction between teaching and learning and the many variables that contribute to this interaction. She continues by pointing out that the emerging evidence focus on research in teacher education has much to offer as long as it does not get reduced to causal studies only. As we develop more sophisticated approaches to research that are able to gather reliable data and evidence on the teaching and learning process and the qualities and behaviors that contribute to effective teaching, we will improve the quality and effectiveness of our schools as well as our teacher education programs.

Given this emphasis on data-driven research, the question should be asked, "What do we know about the preparation of effective teachers?" This question is far too complex to be addressed adequately by this chapter. However, it is safe to say that we know far more today about what contributes to the preparation and development of effective teachers than at any other time in our history. Quality studies exist that shed light on the effects of teacher education programs (Cochran-Smith & Fries, 2005; Cochran-Smith & Zeichner, 2005; Cochran-Smith, Feiman-Nemser, McIntyre, & Demers, 2008; Darling-Hammond, 2000; Houston, Haberman, & Sikula, 1990; Kennedy, 1999; Sikula, Buttery, & Guyton, 1996).

However, Cochran-Smith (2002) asserted that scientific, evidence-based research could only provide some of the answers to the research questions in teacher education. Ideas, values, and beliefs about teaching and learning, community resources, and the purposes of education in a democratic society must all be considered if we are to understand the qualities supporting an effective teacher and teacher education program.

What of the future of teacher education? What will our profession look like in ten years?

Several prominent teacher educators have proposed a variety of measures—some in contrast to each other—for the future of teacher education. For example, Zeichner (2006) proposed four measures for addressing the future of university-based teacher education:

(1) work to reduce the debate about the relative merits of alternative and traditional certification programs; (2) work to broaden the goals of teacher education beyond simply raising scores on standardized achievement tests; (3) change the center of gravity in teacher education to provide a stronger role for schools and communities in the education of teachers; and (4) take teacher education seriously as an institutional responsibility or do not do it. (2006, p. 326)

Zeichner (2006) also warns critics of teacher education, who equate a concern for social justice with a lowering of quality, that they need to consider more seriously the purpose of public education in a democratic society. He warns that we must move beyond territorial debates and focus, instead, on the needs of children.

Berry (2005) expressed his vision for the future of teacher education by advocating the following strategies:

(1) continue to collect data on the effectiveness of teacher education
(2) enforce tougher teacher education standards
(3) develop and disseminate model program designs and costs
(4) eliminate duplicating programs within states and reallocate investments
(5) build public engagement

He also believes that teacher educators must design, validate, and use a broader set of indicators that can better illustrate the effects of teacher education programs on student learning than the current use of standardized test scores.

Darling-Hammond (2006) described three critical components for teacher education programs in the twenty-first century. These include a tight coherence and integration among courses and between coursework and clinical experiences in schools, extensive and intensely supervised clinical work using pedagogies that link theory and practice, and closer, proactive relationships with schools that effectively serve diverse learners. She also urged universities and state education agencies not to water down teacher preparation programs by adopting alternative delivery routes for teacher certification that circumvent minimal standards for effective teachers and the needs of children.

In recognition of the growing diversity in our classrooms—academic, ethnic, socioeconomic, language, family structure, sexual orientation—Grant and Gillette (2006) offered their suggestions to teacher educators for preparing teachers to meet the needs of these diverse classrooms. First, they echoed Haberman's (1995) claim that not everyone who wants to be a teacher should be allowed to proceed through our teacher education programs. Teacher candidates must have the knowledge, skills, and dispositions to be able to meet the needs of all children, especially those in high need schools.

Grant and Gillette (2006) recommended that teachers possess the following skills to be successful in a twenty-first century classroom. First, teachers must be able to "put it all together." In other words, teachers must be able to apply their skills and knowledge from multiple perspectives with recognition of the world in which their students live. Second, teachers must possess reflective skills so that they are able to analyze and act on teacher-generated data. Third, teacher education programs must build collaborations that not only demonstrate to teacher candidates how to work with each other but also to build commitment and understanding across lines of ethnicity, gender, academic ability, socioeconomic status, language, and sexual orientation. Fourth, teacher education programs must develop strategies and approaches for teacher candidates to learn to effectively manage classrooms and to arrange engaging learning environments. Finally, all teacher candidates must possess the ability to use technology as a teaching-learning tool.

CONCLUSION

The discipline of teacher education has been on an interesting journey since the Jesuits and de la Salle in the sixteenth and seventeenth centuries began the first formal approaches to the preparation of teachers. What began as more of an apprenticeship venture with little formal curriculum has emerged in the twenty-first century as a discipline that has a growing knowledge base with national accrediting bodies and state education agencies making judgments on the worthiness of a college or university's teacher education program.

Today teacher education has emerged as a political issue that often can be narrowed down not only to who will control the preparation of teachers but also the very existence of publicly supported university teacher education as well as the potential elimination of our public school system. As the stakes have become higher, teacher education must continue to mature as a discipline or cease to exist, as we know it. In conclusion, it will be interesting to read a chapter on the history of teacher education as a discipline in ten or twenty years to see how it will emerge from the pressures currently being applied to it both from within and outside of the profession.

REFERENCES

American Council on Education, Commission on Teacher Education. (1946). *The improvement of teacher education*. Washington, DC: American Council on Education.

Association of Teacher Educators. (1986). *Guidelines for professional experiences in teacher education: A policy statement*. Reston, VA: Association of Teacher Educators.

Association of Teacher Educators. (1991). *Restructuring the education of teachers* (Report of the Commission on the Education of Teachers into the 21st Century). Reston, VA: Association of Teacher Educators.

Association of Teacher Educators. (1996). *National standards for teacher educators*. Reston, VA: Association of Teacher Educators.

Association of Teacher Educators. (2008). *National standards for teacher educators (revised)*. Manassas Park, VA: Association of Teacher Educators.

Author. (2007) Discipline. Wikipedia. The free encyclopedia. wikipedia.org/wiki/Discipline. Retrieved December 3, 2007

Barnard, H. (1851). *On normal schools*. Hartford, CT: Case, Tiffany & Company, Reprinted by Colorado State Teachers College, 1929.

Battersby, W. J. (1949). *de la Salle: A pioneer of modern education*. New York: Longman.

Berry, B. (2005). The future of teacher education. *Journal of Teacher Education, 56*(3), 272–278.

Borko, H., Liston, D., & Whitcomb, J. (2007). Editorial: Apples and fishes: The need for a more rigorous definition. *Journal of Teacher Education, 58*(5), 359–364.

Carnegie Forum on Education and the Economy, Task Force on Teaching as a Profession. (1986). *A nation prepared: Teachers for the 21st century*. New York: Carnegie Forum on Education and the Economy.

Cochran-Smith, M. (2002). Editorial, The research base for teacher education: Metaphors we live by. *Journal of Teacher Education, 53*(4), 283–285.

Cochran-Smith, M. (2004). Editorial, Taking stock in 2004: Teacher education in dangerous times. *Journal of Teacher Education, 55*(1), 3–7.

Cochran-Smith, M., Feiman-Nemser, S., McIntyre, J., & Demers, K. (Eds.). (2008). *Handbook of research on teacher education: Enduring questions in changing contexts*. (3rd ed.). Mahwah, NJ: Taylor & Francis Publishing.

Cochran-Smith, M., & Fries, K. (2005). The AERA Panel on research and teacher education: Context and goals. In M. Cochran-Smith & K. M. Zeichner (Eds.), *Studying teacher education: The report of the AERA panel on research and teacher education* (pp. 37–68). Mahwah, NJ: Lawrence Erlbaum Associates.

Cochran-Smith, M., & Zeichner, K. M. (Eds.). (2005). *Studying teacher education: The report of the AERA panel on research and teacher education.* Mahwah, NJ: Lawrence Erlbaum Associates.

Cole, L. (1950). *A history of education: Socrates to Montessori.* New York: Holt, Rinehart & Winston.

Cremin, L. A. (1970). *American education: The colonial experience, 1607–1783.* New York: Harper & Row.

Cubberly, E. (1920). *The history of education.* Boston, MA: Houghton Mifflin Co.

Damon, W. (2007). Dispositions and teacher assessment: The need for a more rigorous definition. *Journal of Teacher Education, 58*(4), 365–369.

Darling-Hammond, L. (Ed.). (2000). *Studies of excellence in teacher education.* Washington, DC: American Association of Colleges for Teacher Education and National Commission on Teaching and America's Future.

Darling-Hammond, L. (2006). Constructing 21st century teacher education. *Journal of Teacher Education, 57*(3), 300–314.

Darling-Hammond, L., & Youngs, P. (2002). Defining highly qualified teachers: What does scientifically based research tell us? *Educational Researcher, 31*(9), 13–25.

Diez, M. (2007). Looking back and moving forward: Three tensions in the teacher dispositions discourse. *Journal of Teacher Education, 58*(5), 388–396.

Edelfelt, R., & Raths, J. (1999). *A brief history of standards in teacher education.* Reston, VA: Association of Teacher Educators.

Gardner, H. (1968). The teacher education internship in historical perspective. In H. Southworth (Ed.), *Internships in teacher education: Forty-seventh yearbook* (pp. 1–16). Washington, DC: Association for Student Teaching.

Gitomer, D. H., Latham, A. S., & Ziomek, R. (1999). *The academic quality of prospective teachers: The impact of admissions and licensure testing.* Princeton, NJ: Educational Testing Service.

Grant, C., & Gillette, M. (2006). A candid talk to teacher educators about effectively preparing teachers who can teach everyone's children. *Journal of Teacher Education, 57*(3), 292–299.

Guyton, E., & Byrd, D. (2000). *Standards for field experiences in teacher education.* Reston, VA: Association of Teacher Educators.

Haberman, M. (1995). *Star teachers of children in poverty*. Bloomington, IN: Kappa Delta Pi.

Hilgenheger, N. (1993). Johann Friederich Herbart (1776–1841), *Prospects: The Quarterly Review of Comparative Education, 23*, 649–664.

Houston, W. R., Haberman, M., & Sikula, J. (Eds.). (1990). *Handbook of research on teacher education*. New York: Macmillan.

Howsam, R., Corrigan, D., Denemark, G., & Nash, R. (Eds.). (1976). *Educating a profession*. Washington, DC: American Association of Colleges for Teacher Education.

Interstate New Teacher Assessment and Support Consortium. (1992*). Model standards for beginning teacher licensing, assessment and development: A resource for state dialogue*. Washington, DC: Council of Chief State School Officers.

Johnson, J. (1968). *A brief history of student teaching*. DeKalb, IL: Creative Educational Materials.

Kennedy, M. (1999). The problem of evidence in teacher education. In R. Roth (Ed.), *The role of the university in the preparation of teachers* (pp. 87–107). London: Falmer.

McGucken, W. (1932). *The Jesuits and education*. New York: Bruce Publishing Company.

McIntyre, D. J., Byrd, D. M., & Foxx, S. M. (1996). Field and laboratory experiences. In J. Sikula, T. J. Buttery, & E. Guyton (Eds.), *Handbook of research in teacher education* (2nd ed., pp. 171–193). New York: Macmillan.

Murray, F. B. (2005). On building a unified system of accreditation in teacher education. *Journal of Teacher Education, 56*(4), 307–317.

Murray, F. B. (2007). Disposition: A superfluous construct in teacher education. *Journal of Teacher Education, 58*(5), 381–387.

National Center on Education and the Economy. (2006). *Tough choices or tough times: The report of the New Commission on the Skills of the American Workforce*. San Francisco: Jossey-Bass.

National Commission on Teaching and America's Future. (1996). *What matters most: Teaching for America's future*. Washington, DC: Author.

Pangburn, J. M. (1932). *The evolution of the American teachers college*. New York: Columbia University, Teachers College, Bureau of Publications.

Ravitch, D. (2007). Major address, Challenges to teacher education. *Journal of Teacher Education, 58*(4), 269–273.

Reynolds, M. C. (Ed.). (1989). *Knowledge base for the beginning teacher*. Oxford, UK: Pergamon.

Sikula, J., Buttery, T. J., & Guyton, E. (Eds.). (1996). *Handbook of research on teacher education*. 2nd ed. New York: Macmillan.

Tozer, S., & McAninch, A. (1986). Social foundations of education in historical perspective. *Educational Foundations*, *1*, 5–32.

Tyack, D. B. (1967). *Turning points in American educational history.* Waltham, MA: Blaisdell.

Urban, W. (1990). Historical studies of teacher education. In W. R. Houston, M. Haberman, & J. Sikula, (Eds.). *Handbook of Research on Teacher Education* (pp. 59–71). New York: Macmillan.

Villegas, A. M. (2007). Dispositions in teacher education. *Journal of Teacher Education*, *58*(5), 370–380.

Weiner, L. (2007). A lethal threat to U.S. teacher education. *Journal of Teacher Education*, *58*(5), 274–286.

Zeichner, K. (2006). Reflections of a university-based teacher educator on the future of college- and university-based teacher education. *Journal of Teacher Education*, *57*(3), 326–340.

CHAPTER 2

Who is a Teacher Educator?

Robert L. Fisher, Illinois State University

OVERVIEW

The established route to becoming an effective teacher is through a formal pre-service program together with continued professional development. Although teaching has an intuitive component, it is necessary to learn appropriate subject matter and teaching strategies, how to assess success in student learning, and how to revise teaching strategies and practice based on student performance.

Who are the individuals or *teacher educators* who provide that formal instruction for both pre-service preparation and continued professional growth? This chapter explores this question as well as the issues and tensions surrounding the possible answers. The discussion distinguishes those who are responsible for the instruction of teaching content and strategies from those who provide significant support roles for teacher education or professional development programs. The issues explored in this chapter demonstrate that the concept of teacher educator is not widely accepted, is under continual rethinking, and is impacted by changes in teacher education programs. The ultimate goal is to support improved education of teachers by those who provide that education.

INTRODUCTION

When a teacher is asked why he or she decided to be a teacher, the answer often is based on experiences while a student: admiration for a teacher from the early grades, a teacher's apparent enjoyment of working with young people, the anticipation of working with a particular subject matter, and/or the quality of life a teacher appears to have. These experiences in schools have a significant influence on the perception of the role of the teacher and also ultimately shape how the teacher teaches.

Also influencing how teachers teach are formal programs that prepare future teachers. To earn a teaching certificate requires completion of a traditional or an alternative-route teacher preparation program. The individuals who teach, supervise, and mentor in these programs, appropriately identified as teacher educators, are the primary influence on future teachers in teacher preparation programs. In traditional teacher preparation programs, these individuals are usually faculty members in higher education institutions; in alternative certification programs, they may come from a variety of other institutions. It is these individuals who would logically be termed teacher educators and constitute the answer to the question posed in this chapter. The more complete answer to the question, however, is not that direct or simple.

The Association of Teacher Educators (ATE) took on the challenge of defining the work of those who are responsible for the education of teachers. The members of the first commission to develop teacher educator standards were surprised by the reactions of teacher educators who attended a workshop sponsored by ATE to introduce the then new teacher educator standards. Many responded that the standards were unrealistic for all of the individuals who they considered to be teacher educators. When pressed to explain, many rationalized that almost anyone who influences how a teacher teaches deserves the title of teacher educator. The individuals mentioned included the following:

- a primary teacher who first inspired the child to become an elementary teacher
- the middle school or high school teacher who first introduced their students to an exciting discipline of study
- the teacher in the classroom in which student teaching took place

Clearly the developers of the standards did not have in mind such a wide range of individuals to carry the title of teacher educator.

Defining the role of teacher educators is not limited to the United States. While ATE's first Commission on Teacher Educator Standards created an operational definition of teacher educators, individuals in the Netherlands were also engaged in similar activity (Houston, Dengerink, Fisher, Koster, & McIntyre, 2002). As the authors discovered, there were striking similarities in the process and in the findings of the two groups. Specifically, the two groups struggled with defining who is actually in the role of a teacher educator, should carry that title, and is the audience for these standards.

In the years since the first efforts to disseminate the standards for teacher educators, many conversations have taken place that have helped distinguish the role of teacher educators from the role of other professionals in the education of teachers. This chapter explores the meaning and use of the term *teacher educator*.

WHO ARE TEACHER EDUCATORS?

Teacher educators can be defined by the work they do. For example, the term teacher educator can be applied to individuals who do the following:

1. Provide instruction for teacher candidates or practicing teachers.
2. Demonstrate the knowledge, skills, and dispositions for becoming effective teachers and share those with novices.
3. Provide instruction for teacher candidates or practicing teachers that applies cultural competence and promotes social justice.
4. Engage in systematic inquiry about the effective education of teachers.
5. Engage in activities that increase their own professional development leading toward more effective education of teachers.
6. Contribute to the development and implementation of programs for effective preparation of teachers and their continued professional growth.
7. Work with others to improve teaching, research, and student learning.
8. Advocate for improved learning through more effective teaching.
9. Participate in professional organizations that lead to improved teachers.

10. Contribute to looking for improvements in education of teachers that take advantage of current theory, research, and technology.

Not all teacher educators do all of these activities. In actuality, rather than identifying an individual as either a teacher educator or not, it is more realistic to see the role on a continuum. There are educators, perhaps very effective educators, who teach or administer without any regard for helping others learn to teach. On the other end of the continuum are the individuals who devote their entire career to facilitating the learning and development of teachers.

Ducharme, in a 1986 review of what was known about teacher educators, equated the term to university faculty members responsible for the preparation of teachers. At that time teacher education was generally equated to programs in a higher education institution that prepared individuals for initial certification. In subsequent years, the view of learning to teach has changed dramatically. It is now recognized that learning to teach is influenced by many factors, formally begins in a pre-service program, and continues throughout the teaching career. This means that those individuals who provide direction and instruction for the continuing education of teachers are also teacher educators.

Institutions other than those in higher education frequently conduct alternative teacher education programs. In both of these instances, personnel in schools and other agencies play a significant role in the initial and/or continuing education of teachers.

Using this view, teacher educator falls into the following categories:

- faculty members in higher education who provide coursework and conduct research described by the National Council for Accreditation of Teacher Education (NCATE) as professional studies, including clinical experiences
- personnel in schools and higher education institutions who provide instruction or supervision of clinical experiences of prospective teachers
- personnel in schools and higher education institutions who administer or conduct instructional activities designed to provide advanced professional study for teachers

- personnel from other agencies who design, implement, and evaluate professional study for teachers (e.g., state department certification officers, U.S. Department of Education personnel, researchers in research and development centers, and professional association leaders)

THE TEACHER EDUCATOR STANDARDS
DEFINE TEACHER EDUCATORS

The ATE Standards for Teacher Educators are directed at those educators who provide formal instruction or conduct research and development for educating prospective and practicing teachers. Teacher educators provide the professional education component of pre-service programs and the staff development component of in-service programs. Teacher educators utilize other individuals in the education of teachers who may not be described by these standards. These individuals may not be teacher educators. For example, staff members in a public school who have little involvement in teacher preparation and no preparation themselves as teacher educators may interact with and serve as role models for teacher education students who are placed in their school as student teachers, but would not necessarily be considered teacher educators.

The emphasis in this chapter on the definition and role of teacher educator as those primarily responsible for teacher education is not intended to diminish the role of other personnel who contribute to the education of teachers. The purpose of distinguishing between these roles is to suggest that individuals who do not provide formal instruction or conduct research and development for educating prospective and practicing teachers would not be expected to be compliant with the standards for teacher educators.

Rather than debate where to draw the distinction among the many individuals who influence the way teachers teach, the standards can be used to guide the selection and continued professional development of these personnel. It is not the institution or the position title that distinguishes one as a teacher educator. Rather it is how individuals approach their work, how they are prepared to do their work, and how their work influences teachers' development. The following sections address various roles in higher education and the schools and how each may relate to being a teacher educator.

Higher Education Personnel

Faculty members in higher education who have primary responsibility for the instruction of teacher candidates are the ones most typically referred to as teacher educators. They teach courses about learning, child development, curriculum development, as well as methods of instruction and assessment, and they supervise and mentor teacher candidates in field experiences and student teaching. They also provide graduate coursework for experienced teachers for advanced preparation in the areas listed above. They may specialize in areas such as literacy, special education, and teaching non-English speakers. These faculty members are involved in professional activities that relate to many, if not all, of the areas specified in the teacher education standards.

Other higher education faculty members teach such courses as educational psychology, history and social foundations of education, and multicultural education. These faculty members also see themselves as teacher educators and are likely to be involved in professional activities described by the standards.

It should be noted that faculty members in the two groups above may not hold a position in a department or college of education. The educational psychology instructor might be in the psychology department; the pedagogical expert in a content field could be housed in the respective content department; or the instructor could hold a regular position in a school district and teach the course for higher education as an adjunct faculty member. If these individuals are responsible for a component of teacher education, they could, perhaps should, align their professional interests with the role of being a teacher educator.

Another group of faculty members in higher education provide the content that will be taught by the teacher candidates in their respective fields of preparation. Some of the content faculty members may see themselves as teacher educators while others, perhaps the majority, may not. Some content faculty members may have taught in the P–12 schools and held an appropriate teaching certificate and, as a result, have extensive involvement in the preparation of teachers. In their professional lives they may or may not align their professional activity with being a teacher educator. Let's look at this group more closely.

Ducharme (1986) pointed to the issue of identifying the role in teacher education for a faculty member who delivers the content for teacher preparation. There is great concern for the quality of the content preparation of teachers. For example, what is the appropriate mathematics content preparation for an elementary teacher or a secondary teacher of mathematics?

Although a pre-service teacher education program typically specifies a number of credit hours, the concern for quality teaching of mathematics is about the quality of that instruction. The concerns generally delve into the content of the mathematics courses as well as the way mathematics is taught to the prospective teacher. To be successful, the future teacher of mathematics needs to understand the appropriate content of mathematics as well as the appropriate pedagogy for the teaching of mathematics. Although the content is dealt with in a mathematics methods course, the influence of the mathematics professor's way of teaching mathematics is a major influence on the way the prospective teacher will teach mathematics.

If the content is not presented in the way advocated in the methods course, there is a conflict in the mind of the prospective teacher: teach in the way the pedagogy was presented, not in the way the mathematics was taught in the college classroom. This dilemma also exists for other fields such as science, social science, and literacy.

Are the content preparation faculty members teacher educators? The response is specific to the individual and depends on their orientation to their professional work. The promotion and tenure of a content faculty member may conflict with being a teacher educator. This orientation does not diminish their contribution to teacher education by modeling effective content instruction.

School Personnel

Few personnel employed in the schools would initially call themselves teacher educators or find their interests aligned with the teacher educator standards. Their primary work is providing instruction for

P–12 students, not teachers. They associate the term teacher educator with higher education personnel.

Most would agree, however, that teachers continue the process of learning to teach throughout their careers, both informally through experience and formally through staff development programs. They are likely to refer to this continued learning as professional development rather than teacher education. In recent years most school districts have instituted formal teacher induction programs to assist teachers in the initial years of teaching to continue learning beyond their initial preparation program.

In addition, all schools operate professional development days during the year. Teachers who have completed the National Board for Professional Teaching Standards Certification generally agree that it was a learning process. So who are the people who conduct all of these learning activities? They fulfill at least some of the characteristics listed above and often provide formal instruction or conduct research and development for educating prospective and practicing teachers, so they are, to at least some extent, teacher educators in the schools.

The personnel who provide the instruction for professional development are teacher educators, even though they may not regard themselves in that light. These individuals conduct activities that are included in the teacher educator standards. The following paragraphs explore categories of individuals employed by schools that are, to varying degrees, educating teachers. In each category the individuals and the context of their work allow them to choose the extent of their role as defined by the ATE teacher educator standards.

The most obvious individuals in the role of teacher educator are those employed in school districts as professional development personnel. Their primary role is instructing teachers in various aspects of curriculum, instruction, assessment, and other teaching related areas. They design programs of instruction for teachers or implement professional development programs provided by other organizations. The goal may be initiating a new curriculum, learning a new instructional method, or working on some aspect of teacher assessment. The learning might be integrated with addressing an issue about student learning. The positions of those responsible for professional development in school districts could be enhanced through reflection about their work using the ATE teacher educator standards.

Many teachers volunteer to accept a student teacher in their classrooms. The "cooperating teacher" is ostensibly chosen for his or her ability to model effective teaching. In the optimum student teaching experience, cooperating teachers exhibit at least some of the aspects of teacher educators. In addition to teaching the children in the classroom, they teach student teachers about teaching, learning, and curriculum and instruction. They do formative assessment of student teachers' lessons, and coordinate the work of other professionals who can further support their student teachers' development.

There was a time when the student teaching experience was considered "practice teaching," where it was assumed the teacher education candidate knew what to do and he or she just needed to practice it under the observation of a professional. Fortunately, this unrealistic view of teacher education is not the norm today.

However, given the actual realities of the student teaching learning experience, not all classroom teachers are comfortable, prepared, or even able to provide this type of adult instruction or teacher education. Those who are comfortable with this role make a significant contribution to the education of the student teacher by mentoring novices toward effective teaching, guiding novices as they learn to teach, providing a good model of effective teaching, working with parents, and being involved as a professional. Over time, classroom teachers can improve their role in working with student teachers by using the standards for teacher educators and viewing themselves as site-based teacher educators.

In today's schools, the demands placed on the principal may mean that they are not working directly on the professional development of teachers, either in groups or one-on-one. Those who make it a priority to be involved in the professional development of teachers may develop an affinity with some aspects of teacher education. Depending on their level of involvement in teacher education, principals may find the standards for teacher educators helpful as a guide in contributing to the development of teachers in their schools.

The Professional Development School (PDS) initiative is based on the premise that initial and continuing education of teachers is best when it is conducted as a partnership of higher education and schools. PDS partnerships with colleges and universities provide more school-based activities for pre-service teacher education candidates with a greater involvement of school personnel working alongside higher education personnel. In the collaborative planning and implementation, school personnel can take on aspects of being teacher educators. Similarly, the university personnel are involved in the continuing education of school personnel. This education can include instruction in areas that propel the school faculty members into leadership positions in which they can assume responsibilities for education of their peers.

There is truth to the adage that teachers teach as they have been taught. Learning how to teach by observing effective teachers is found to be appropriate in pre-service programs as well as throughout teachers' careers. For example, literature on the student teaching experience suggests that taking time to observe and discuss teaching with other teachers is beneficial (Guyton & McIntyre, 1990). Similarly, recommendations for effective teacher induction programs suggest that new teachers spend time observing their mentors and other effective teachers (Odell & Huling, 2000). Are the teachers who are observed teacher educators? They are effective teachers, but not necessarily teacher educators unless they view part of their primary role as helping educate teachers.

ISSUES RELATED TO THE ROLE OF TEACHER EDUCATOR

It is often stated that the most important element in the P–12 classroom is the teacher. Historically, there is much literature about the need to develop the quality of teachers to improve learning in the P–12 schools (i.e., Grossman, 1990; Holmes Group, 1986; Levine, 1996; Lortie, 1975). It is surprising that there is a lack of such literature on improving the quality of teacher educators as a way to improve learning by teacher candidates and in-service teachers. This section explores the issue of improving the quality of teacher educators as a component of improving the education of teachers.

Changes in Teacher Education Impacts Teacher Educators

Changes in teacher education have led to changes in teacher educators. The evolution in student teaching provides a simple example of this perspective. There are individuals teaching today who culminated their pre-service teacher preparation program by engaging in a few weeks of "practice teaching." This was often a very casual experience, with limited supervision, limited assessment, and almost always a grade of *A*.

There were few criteria for the teacher in the school or the supervisor from the university. Through the years this experience has matured to be longer, to have standards-based assessments, to reflect greater concern for diversity of the students taught, to generate higher expectations of performance by the teacher candidate, and to require increased frequency and duration of classroom experiences prior to the culminating experience. The change in student teaching has also placed more emphasis on the qualifications of those who supervise the experience, both in higher education and the schools.

Knowledge about teacher education has vastly matured in the past three decades. The evolution of research in teacher education was benchmarked in 1990 by the publication of the first *Handbook on Research in Teacher Education*. This massive tome provided 925 pages and 48 chapters on critical issues in teacher education, such as purposes of teacher education, settings and roles in teacher education, and the recruitment, selection, and retention of teachers. Since then second and third editions of the Handbook were published in 1996 and 2008, respectively. Indeed, each of the Handbooks illuminates the important knowledge base in teacher education. To be a teacher educator also implies having an understanding of the literature of teacher education.

The role of teacher educator has evolved through the years as the process of educating teachers has matured. In 1996, Murray edited a publication with the provocative title *The Teacher Educator's Handbook: Building a Knowledge Base for the Preparation of Teachers*. The 28 chapters dealt with a wide range of knowledge about the education of teachers, including the need for a knowledge base in teacher education, issues related to subject matter knowledge, information on education as a discipline, various program structures and design in teacher education, and a discussion of teacher education faculty and their work. There were no chapters, however, on how individuals would acquire this knowledge to become a teacher educator.

Clift and others (2008) conducted a longitudinal study of teacher education graduates. Their study documents that beginning teachers can and should continue their professional education in the beginning years of teaching. They conclude, as have many others, that it is short sighted to seek improvements in the preparation of teachers by focusing only on the pre-service experience. Teacher education is a career-long experience (Odell & Huling, 2000), and those who provide that instruction are all potentially teacher educators.

Learning to Be a Teacher Educator

The popular opinion that "anyone can teach" led to a comparable phrase that "anyone who teaches can be a teacher educator." A faculty member hired for a college department of education is most likely to be selected for their experience in a field such as literacy or curriculum rather than for their preparation to be a teacher educator. Over the past few decades, it has been common for an experienced faculty member in a content department to be given the assignment to provide the teacher preparation programs in that field. In schools, it is common for an experienced classroom teacher to be promoted to a staff development position in the school or central office.

When teacher education was primarily associated with higher education, it was common to equate receiving a doctoral degree in education with preparation to be a teacher educator. For example, when this author wanted to prepare for a career in teacher preparation, the institution provided an Ed.D. program that included courses such as curriculum and instructional design, psychology of education, and research methods.

There were no courses that focused on how adults learn; how teacher education programs are designed, managed, and evaluated; how to conduct and evaluate teacher candidates in clinical experiences; how to relate pre-service teacher education to in-service professional development; or how to consult effectively with schools to improve teaching and learning. When I interviewed for my first higher education position, I was not asked to explain my expertise in teacher education. Instead, my interviewers were (apparently) impressed with my experience in several teaching positions in secondary schools and other related experiences.

Years later, when I was involved in projects related to teacher education, I realized that it was the other experiences that provided valuable contributions to learning to be a teacher educator. These included being a consultant to schools and attempting to help teachers learn to use new curriculum materials. It was also apparent that some colleagues were limited by not having had such school-based experiences.

There are now doctoral programs that specifically deal with learning to be a teacher educator. The University of Nevada Las Vegas has designed a doctoral program for the specific preparation of teacher educators (UNLV, 2006). This program incorporates the ATE Standards for Teacher Educators as a basis for planning the program and for candidate self-assessment.

Knowledge about teacher education has also evolved in recent years, as evidenced by the handbooks referenced above. However, there still remains a lack of research on the role and practice of teacher educators. Early research on teacher educators referred to them as professors of education (Wisniewski, 1986) since the reference was typically for pre-service teacher preparation. This early research had more to do with the characteristics of a faculty member than the teaching and learning provided by the teacher educator. Information about the teaching load of a higher education faculty member does not inform how that faculty teaches; nor does it inform how the school-based teacher educator contributes to the continuing education of teachers.

FURTHER DEVELOPMENT OF THE ROLE OF TEACHER EDUCATORS

Clearly, there has been inconsistency in the field of teacher education around the use of the term teacher educator. It has been the view of the current ATE Standards Commission that improving the quality of teacher educators requires that a more consistent definition of the role of teacher educators should be used. As research on teacher educators increases our understanding of their role and practices, the standards are likely to evolve. Until then, the ATE Standards for Teacher Educators offers an operational definition that may be useful.

Those who consider themselves teacher educators hold the primary responsibility to define further the role and practices of teacher educators.

Given that many individuals attending a meeting of the Association of Teacher Educators held a broad view of who holds the role of teacher educator, there should be a continued discussion among professionals to clarify the definition.

A valuable contribution to this discussion was made by a group of teacher educators who used the ATE Standards for Teacher Educators to examine their own professional lives. Klecka and others (2008) reported on how the teacher educators developed electronic portfolios and engaged in extended dialogue among themselves, both face-to-face and electronically, to gain greater understanding of the standards and their roles as teacher educators. The authors examined the portfolios and concluded there were five facets of a teacher educator's identity as manifested through work with the teacher educator standards: teacher, scholar in teaching, collaborator, learner, and leader. Perhaps these facets provide a good working framework for further discussions of the role and practices of a teacher educator.

In preparing this chapter, I noted that many publications about initial teacher preparation made very little, if any, reference to the personnel who conduct the programs of teacher preparation. It was rare to find the term *teacher educator* as one of the items listed in the appendix. The three handbooks on research on teacher education (Houston, Haberman, & Sikula, 1990; Sikula, Buttery, & Guyton, 1996; and Cochran-Smith, Feiman-Nemser, McIntyre, & Demers, 2008) did not include significant references to those who provide the education of teachers. The understanding of the role of teacher educator will only be advanced when the role of teacher educator figures more prominently in the presentation of teacher education programs.

Moving teacher education away from the traditional campus setting adds many dimensions to this dialogue about the role and practices of the teacher educator. The development of alternative routes to certification generally involves personnel not associated with a traditional university program. Professional Development Schools and other field-based teacher education alternatives involve school personnel who have demonstrated a high capacity for teaching but may not have had the preparation needed to teach teachers.

The concern for the role of teacher educator is just as vital in the continuing education of teachers. Those who provide professional development are educating teachers and, using the definitions listed above, are teacher educators. The rapid expansion of school-based teacher induction programs to support beginning teachers has produced a new role of school leaders that directly relates to teacher preparation. Activities of teacher educator organizations should expand the dialogue on teacher educator to include these individuals as well as associations that focus on the continuing education of teachers.

Research on teacher education, both initial and continuing, should include a component that focuses on the role and practices of those individuals who provide the instruction in the program. The ATE Standards for Teacher Educators could provide a very useful framework for building the common terminology necessary to add clarity to this research.

REFERENCES

Clift, R. T., Mora, R.A., & Brady, P. (2008). The categories that bind: Connecting teacher education to teaching practice. In C. J. Craig, L. F. Dretchin, (Eds.), *Imagining a renaissance in teacher education*. Teacher Education Yearbook XVI, Lanham, MD: Rowan and Littlefield Education.

Cochran-Smith, M., Feiman-Nemser, S., McIntyre, J., & Demers, K. (Eds.). (2008). *Handbook of research on teacher education: Enduring questions in changing contexts*. (3rd ed.). Mahwah, NJ: Taylor & Francis Publishing.

Ducharme, E. R. (1986). *Teacher educators: What do we know?* ERIC Digest 15.ED 279642. Washington, DC: ERIC Clearinghouse on Teacher Education.

Grossman, P. L. (1990). *The making of a teacher: Teacher knowledge and teacher education*. New York: Teachers College Press.

Guyton, E., & McIntyre, D. J. (1990). Student teaching and school experiences. In W. R. Houston (Ed.), *Handbook of research on teacher education* (pp. 514–534). New York: Macmillan.

Holmes Group. (1986). *Tomorrow's teachers: A report of the Holmes Group*. East Lansing, MI: Author.

Houston, W. R., Dengerink, J. J., Fisher, R., Koster, B., & McIntyre, D. J. (2002). National standards for teacher educators: The story of two nations. In J. Rainer & E. Guyton (Eds.), *Research on Meeting and Using Standards in the Preparation of Teachers* (pp. 25–52). Dubuque, IA: Kendall-Hunt.

Houston, W. R., Haberman, M., & Sikula, J. (Eds.) (1990). *Handbook of research on teacher education*. New York: Macmillan.

Klecka, C. L., Donovan, L., Venditti, K. J., & Short, B. (2008). Who is a teacher educator? Enactment of teacher educator identity through electronic portfolio development. *Action in Teacher Education*, *29*(4), 83–91.

Levine, M. (1996). Educating teachers for restructured schools. In F. B. Murray (Ed.), *The teacher educator's handbook: Building a knowledge base for the preparation of teachers* (pp. 620–647). San Francisco: Jossey-Bass.

Lortie, D. C. (1975). *Schoolteacher: A sociological study*. University of Chicago Press.

Murray, F. B. (Ed.). (1996). *The teacher educator's handbook: Building a knowledge base for the preparation of teachers*. San Francisco: Jossey-Bass Publishers.

Odell, S. J., & Huling, L. (2000). *Quality mentoring for novice teachers*. Indianapolis: Kappa Delta Pi.

Sikula, J., Buttery, T. J., & Guyton, E. (Eds.). (1996). *Handbook of research on teacher education*. 2nd ed. New York: Macmillan.

University of Nevada, Las Vegas. (2006). Department of curriculum and instruction: Doctoral studies guide. Retrieved July 7, 2008 from http://ci.unlv.edu/files/doctoral/handbook.pdf

Wisniewski, R. (1986). The ideal professor of education. *Phi Delta Kappan*, *68*, 288–292.

CHAPTER 3

Conceptualizing, Developing, and Testing Standards for Teacher Educators

W. Robert Houston, University of Houston

Education in Western culture has become an objectives-based system. Based on some organizer such as exemplars of effective educational practice, structure of a discipline, or theoretical construct, objectives are identified first and then instruction and assessment are constructed based on those objectives. The movement evolved during the twentieth century from general ideas and practices to very specific algorithms and contents. This evolution resulted in rubrics or "guidelines" for writing and testing sets of standards that has even become a discipline itself. Standards for professional practice are part of this movement. Stated as both objectives to achieve and criteria for judging professional quality, standards have evolved over the past century to become a major force in determining and judging the quality of education.

ROOTS OF STANDARDS FOR TEACHER EDUCATORS

Standards for teacher educators have roots and practices going back 300 years in France. The purpose of normal schools was to establish teaching standards or *norms*; hence its name, *normal school*, after which all other schools and teaching practices would be modeled. One of the first schools so named, the *école normale*, meaning "model school," was established in Paris in 1794 to serve as a model for other teacher-training schools (De Landsheere, 1987). The normal school provided "model" classrooms in which prospective teachers could observe and practice teaching children under the direction of faculty members who themselves had demonstrated their own competence as teachers, thus establishing the criterion measures for the standard.

One of the first normal schools in the United States was organized in 1839 in Lexington, Massachusetts. Like its French counterpart, its purpose was to model effective educational practice and in the process it became a harbinger of teacher educator standards. Rather than written standards, prospective teachers observed effective practice, modeled it, and were evaluated on their performance. The schools' faculties (teacher educators) were expected to emulate effective instruction, sometimes stated as moral imperatives as well as educational excellence.

The industrial revolution and increased urbanization resulted in major changes in schools including longer school years, availability of secondary education, need for more and improved education, and increased time for children to attend school. This created the need for additional teachers who were better qualified. As a result, normal schools evolved into teachers colleges then universities with much broader missions and curricula. Content fields such as mathematics, history, and biology became independent departments in the university, and grew more and more isolated from the education department.

The university I attended serves as an example of this evolution: beginning as the Denton County Normal School, it became North Texas State Teachers College, then North Texas State College, North Texas State University, and finally, the University of North Texas. With each name change, the mission broadened and teacher education became a less dominant part of its curriculum.

THE CLIMATE AND RATIONALE FOR STANDARDS

Standards for teacher educators mirror those for teachers in schools. Ralph Tyler was one of the first to propose a model of learning and accountability that included three phases: objectives or statements of knowledge, attitudes, and skills to be achieved; instructional activities or learning experiences; and evaluation to measure achievement of objectives (Tyler, 1949).

Robert Mager's book, *Preparing Instructional Objectives* (1962), established a model that influenced instruction for decades. He recommended that objectives should be specific and measurable and include three parts: (1) a measurable verb (an action verb), (2) specification of what is given to the learner, and (3) criteria for success.

While the general approach has been consistent, the terminology has changed from Mager's criterion-referenced objectives to Outcomes-Based Education, Mastery Learning (Bloom, 1980), and objectives renamed as Intentions, Educational Objectives, Enabling Objectives, Competencies, and Performances. It has been applied to business (management by objectives or MBO), to process/product assessment of programs, and, in behavioral psychology, to intentional and incidental learning. As each term was hailed and then maligned, it fell into disuse as new educators desired to put their own imprimatur on basically the same tenets.

Teacher education became a focus of standards-based teacher preparation in 1968, when the United States (U.S.) Office of Education's Bureau of Research funded nine institutions to design model teacher education programs for elementary school teachers (Burdin, 1969).[1] The models were based on practices of effective teachers and supported by educational research. The Elementary Models Project became the harbinger of the Competency-Based Teacher Education (CBTE) or Performance-Based Teacher Education (PBTE) movement in the 1970s (Houston & Howsam, 1973).

CBTE/PBTE programs had four characteristics that distinguished them from earlier teacher education programs:

(1) Program requirements were derived from, and based on, the practices of effective teachers.

(2) Requirements were stated as competencies (objectives, standards, goals).

(3) Competencies were classified as cognitive objectives (what a teacher knew), performance objectives (what the teacher could do with what was known); consequence objectives (what was accomplished as a result of a teacher's actions, such as increased student achievement or more positive student attitudes), and affective objectives (the teacher's attitudes or values).

(4) Both instruction and assessment were specifically derived from the identified competencies.
(5) Learner progress was determined by demonstration of competencies.

By 1980, at its apogee, more than 400 institutions used CBTE/PBTE as the conceptual basis for their teacher education programs (Sandefur & Nicklas, 1981). But the movement had run its course; later surveys indicated fewer institutions were referring to their programs as based on CBTE/PBTE principles, but most continued to use objectives as the basis for program design and student assessment. Their names had changed, for example, to outcomes-based teacher education, standards-focused teacher education, or inquiry-based teacher education, but the underlying conceptual basis remained essentially the same.

This goals-oriented or objectives-based concept continues to dominate education. Course syllabi, requirements for certification, textbook chapters, and specification of standards continue to this day. When translated from statements of objectives or competencies into lists of standards, statements typically are not so specific and generally do not identify the criteria or levels of success.

Specific standards for teachers and teacher educators emerged in this cultural environment or educational climate. Trends in educational movements such as CBTE, other innovations, or new trends seem to follow similar pathways from conception to advocacy and renown to abandonment.

The ebb and flow of educational thought has been shaped by and has in turn spawned a series of educational movements and trends. Each movement has reflected a general societal climate, technological advances, research, innovations, and the dreams of educators. As each movement has matured, it has come under increasingly close scrutiny by educators and the general public. Implemented programs never quite achieve the idealized models. Critics point out basic structural flaws in the model and inherent weaknesses in the operational programs. The ensuing debate between advocates and critics causes both to focus more clearly on basic issues, and from the analysis is derived a more viable educational enterprise. Of such is progress (Houston, 1974, p. xvi).

This paragraph, written over thirty years ago, could have been written about the development of the ATE Standards for Teacher Educators over the past decade.

STANDARDS AS THE BASIS FOR IMPROVED QUALITY OF PRACTICE AND OUTCOMES

Standards have become the indicator of quality in products, professionals, services, and organizations. They form the basis for the school curriculum, for teacher licenses, and for the organization of schools and universities. Agencies such as state departments of education and the Southern Association of Colleges and Schools monitor schools on the basis of standards; the National Council for the Accreditation of Teacher Education (NCATE) accredits teacher education programs based on standards.

The Interstate New Teacher Assessment and Support Consortium (INTASC) identified assessments for first-year teachers and worked with states to implement standards and assessments. The National Board of Professional Teaching Standards (NBPTS) specified standards for accomplished teachers. Professional associations and learned societies linked with the Alliance for Curriculum Reform developed standards (both content- and pedagogy-based) that apply both to P–12 students and to new and experienced teachers.

Standards of different professional groups, agencies, and businesses, both in the United States and abroad, reflect their needs and perspectives. Best known to educators are those that specifically relate to their own discipline (e.g., National Council of Teachers of Mathematics [www.nctm.org]; National Council for the Social Studies [www.ncss.org]; International Reading Association [www.reading.org]). The Association of Teacher Educators-Europe developed a set of standards based on their educational needs and conditions, and related to those in the Netherlands (Houston et al., 2002). Standards from several organizations are summarized in the following paragraphs to indicate the wide range of rationales and perspectives. Based on their membership and needs, the standards are very divergent; there is no single model for conceptualizing standards, stating them, or implementing them.

The standards of the American Historical Association (www.historians .org) address "questions and dilemmas, professional misconduct, and identify a core of shared values that professional historians strive to honor in the course of their work: plagiarism, scholarship, teaching, reputation and trust." Note the difference in purpose from the ATE Standards.

Standards of the National Association of Social Workers (NASW) and the International Reading Association (IRA) have been tailored to the varied roles of their members. Each role has its own set of qualifications and standards. NASW (www.socialworkers.org) specifies standards for professionals working with substance use disorders, clinical social work, child welfare, cultural competence, school social work, and genetics, among others.

The International Reading Association (www.reading.org) targets four roles: paraprofessional, classroom teacher, reading specialist, and teacher educator. Each role has its own list of qualifications and standards for practice specifically tailored for that role:

(1) Knowledge of foundations of reading and writing processes and instruction
(2) Use a wide range of instructional practices
(3) Use a variety of assessment tools and practices
(4) Create a literate environment
(5) View professional development as a career-long effort and responsibility.

Four of the reviewed organizations are specifically concerned with the ethics of practice. Their varied practices are reflected in the ways that they have specified their standards and the language used with them. The Code of Ethics of the National Association of Realtors (www.realtor.org) assists appropriate regulatory bodies to eliminate practices that may damage the public or might discredit or bring dishonor to the real estate profession. Standards are organized around duties to clients and customers, duties to the public, and duties to realtors.

The Standards of the Association of Computing Machinery (www.acm .org) concern the fundamental imperatives that apply to the conduct of computing professionals. Standards are organized in four areas: general moral imperatives, more specific professional responsibilities, organizational leadership imperatives, and compliance with the code.

The New York Lawyer's Code of Professional Responsibility (www.law.cornell.edu/ethics/ny/code) consists of three parts written in the legal language of their profession: canons, ethical considerations, and disciplinary rules. "The Code is designed to be both an inspirational guide to the members of the profession and a basis for disciplinary action when the conduct of a lawyer falls below the required minimum standards stated in the Disciplinary Rules."

The Archaeological Institute of America (www.archaeological.org) in 1997 defined its Code of Professional Standards as responsibilities to the archaeological record, to the public, and to colleagues. It encourages all professional archaeologists to keep ethical considerations in mind as they plan and conduct research.

Like several of the other professional associations, the International Association of Conference Interpreters' Professional Standards (www.aiic.net) states as its purpose "to ensure an optimum quality of work performed with due consideration being given to the physical and mental constraints inherent in the exercise of the profession." Its standards are organized around the roles and responsibilities of its members: recruitment, canceling contracts, remuneration, length of the workday, and travel.

The Association of American Medical Colleges (www.aamc.org) and the American Medical Association (www.ama-assn.org) since 1994 have jointly approved Standards for Accreditation of Medical Education Programs Leading to the MD degree. The language and organization of their standards are unique to the medical profession as they define the structure of a medical school and its professionals.

The standards of the Australian School Library Association (www.asla.org.au) are similar in perspective and purpose to the ATE Standards for Teacher Educators though they are half a world apart. Its standards "describe the professional knowledge, skills, and commitment demonstrated by teacher librarians working at a level of excellence. The standards are organized in several sections: Professional Knowledge, Professional Practice, and Professional Commitment . . . The major aim of the Standards project is to achieve national consensus on standards of excellence for teacher librarians."

The Council for the Advancement of Standards in Higher Education (CAS; www.cas.edu) promotes standards in student affairs, student services, and student development programs in the United States. Its standards are concerned with thirty-four functional areas in student affairs.

These and all other standards were developed and honed based on a conceptual basis by an association or agency that reflected its objectives and needs. The organization supported the development of standards and later publicized its usefulness. The validity of any set of standards depends on the process upon which it was developed, its relevance and usefulness to those being assessed, and the value placed on the standards by all those involved.

EXPLORING STANDARDS FOR TEACHER EDUCATORS

It was inevitable that the standards movement would be applied to those who educate teachers. The Association of Teacher Educators (ATE) explored standards for teacher educators and their use in certification beginning in 1992 with the appointment of a national task force on the certification of master teacher educators, and continued through 2000 with the publication of a set of standards for teacher educators.[2]

The task force spent its first year studying the use of teacher educator standards as a basis for certification. Other groups such as the National Board for Professional Teaching Standards (www.nbpts.org) were developing a professional certification that identified professional teachers. The ATE Commission explored the feasibility of this approach. It distinguished between a *license*, which is a permit to teach issued by state agencies, and *certification*, which is a recognition of special expertise by professional bodies. The standards and processes of other professional groups were explored, and a process adopted to study and make recommendations concerning certification of teacher educators.

The charge to the task force was to focus on certification of teacher educators that would recognize expert teacher educators—persons with recognized contributions to the development of teacher education. The certification considered was comparable to the *diplomate* in some fields, membership in academies in science and medicine, and the *ac-*

complished teacher described in the National Board for Professional
Teacher Standards.

Several principles guided the early work of the task force. First, this
certification should be desirable and voluntary. Second, it should recognize that the expertise of teacher educators goes beyond that of teachers
and requires specialized study of teacher education. Third, it should apply to teacher educators employed in a wide range of institutions (e.g.,
schools, universities, state and national agencies, private firms, and research organizations). Fourth, such certification should apply to those
teacher educators who contribute to any phase of teacher development
including pre-service preparation and in-service education. Fifth, standards and criteria should contribute to both assessments of teacher educators by external bodies and their own personal development.

DEVELOPMENT OF STANDARDS

The task force, renamed the National Commission on Teacher Educator
Standards, developed the initial set of standards, and then circulated it
to the professional community for comment. The initial draft of the standards was conceptualized during the fall of 1993, formulated at the ATE
Conference in February 1994, and refined during the following months.

Over one hundred educators participated in a two-round Delphi to
analyze and recommend changes in the standards in 1994. The first
round was devoted to editing the standards for relevance, fidelity to established concepts of effective teacher educators, clarity, and significance. The second round of the Delphi was devoted to reviewing and
approving the revised standards and analyzing draft indicators of
achievement and modes of assessment for each standard. These analy-
ses became the first iteration of revised standards, indicators, accept-
able evidence, and modes of assessment.

A preliminary report of findings, *Certification of Teacher Educators*
distributed in 1995, provided the substance for a long working session
by the ATE Delegate Assembly. The delegate assembly voted to accept
the standards in principle and charged the task force to continue refining them, hold open hearings during the following year across the
country, and explore ways to extend the standards.

Open Hearings and Conferences

During 1995–1996, open hearings were held in about one third of the states, and presentations with audience feedback were made at national conferences including the National Association of State Directors of Teacher Education and Certification (NASDTEC) conferences, ATE annual meetings, and the American Association of Colleges of Teacher Education (AACTE) conferences. The standards were publicized nationally in three articles. Two appeared in *Teacher Education Reports* newsletters, "ATE Circulates First Draft National Standards For Master Teacher Educators" on March 9, 1996 and "Final Report Issued by ATE Task Force on Certification of Teacher Educators" on May 2, 1996. The third appeared in *Education Week*, titled "Teacher educators implored to 'lead' in improving training" (Bradley, 1991).

Refined Standards

In refining the standards, the commission analyzed the recommendations of the various groups and individuals in a series of summative evaluation sessions. Consistently, participants in the open hearings spoke against developing another certificate based on the standards, noting that many teacher educators were already certified as teachers and administrators, and that most were subject to NCATE standards, state certification standards, accreditation agencies such as the Southern Association of Colleges and Schools, and expectations from their particular national content-based professional associations. They further pointed out that their employing university or school district had its own set of expectations and that they were subject to them for salary purposes and promotion and tenure.

The ATE standards could not replace any of these expectations. During development of the standards, then, strong and consistent recommendations resulted in three major changes in the standards. One standard was deleted, most were edited for clarity, and the purpose of the standards was broadened beyond certification to include teacher educator initial and advanced study, awards and honors, and job descriptions.

USE OF THE STANDARDS

During the development and adoption of the standards, the commission recognized the need not only to publish the standards, but also to identify ways the standards could be used to influence the preparation, performance, and evaluation of teacher educators. The commission was no longer dedicated to use the standards primarily for certification. To help teacher educators examine the variety of purposes for the standards, Robert Fisher developed a simulation that was used in several workshops to explore the implications of the standards. The simulation identified a number of uses and approaches to which the standards could be applied, and challenged participants to explore the implications of each approach.

ATE initiated a special award, the *Distinguished Teacher Educator*, in conjunction with Wadsworth/ITP Publishing "to recognize and honor those individuals in higher education or state departments of education who have advanced the profession of teacher education." The standards were used as the basis for making decisions about the award. Initiated in February, 1997, the award has been presented annually at the ATE national meeting.

In June 1998 the commission initiated in Washington, D.C. the *National Academy on Alignment of Standards for Teacher Education*, co-sponsored with NCATE and AACTE and attended by over 300 participants. The conference brought together the organizations that were developing standards for professional educators and those implementing programs based on standards. The purpose of the two-day conference was to stimulate the alignment of teacher education programs at the institutional and state levels with national standards and with teacher education research. Participants examined the ATE standards as part of the conference.

The ATE Commission on Standards and its members were active in a number of related contributions growing out of commission activities. Roy Edelfelt and James Raths authored *A Brief History of Standards in Teacher Education* (1999) that was published by ATE. Joseph Vaughan of the U.S. Office of Education wrote a stimulating conceptual paper on teacher educator standards that formed the basis for commission discussions. When revising its standards for accreditation, NCATE used the ATE standards as a basis for its faculty standards.

Two teams, Ronnie Stanford of the University of Alabama and Peggy Ishler of the University of Northern Iowa, and Ralph Fessler and Rochelle Ingram of Carnegie Mellon University, designed doctoral programs based on the standards. Other educators have proposed and initiated other innovative ways to base improved education on the standards. None were immediately implemented although they formed the basis for several program revisions.

EXTENDING THE CONCEPT OF TEACHER EDUCATOR STANDARDS

In 2003, ATE President Frances van Tassell appointed a second national commission[3] to expand and refine the work of the initial task force and commission. The commission's charge was broadened and its membership expanded in 2006 when it was reappointed for an additional three-year term. The purpose of the second commission, according to its charge, was "to further develop and implement the excellent teacher educator standards prepared by the previous ATE Commission on Teacher Educator Standards." The commission initiated three strategies: first, establish a Teacher Educator Standards Cohort (TESC) to test the viability of the standards; second, survey teacher education institutions to determine the extent to which the ATE standards were being used and were viable; and third, refine the current standards based on recent educational developments and research.

Teacher Educator Standards Cohort

The Teacher Educator Standards Cohort (TESC) was organized in 2004 with leadership from Cari Klecka. Understanding the purpose and processes of TESC can best be understood from a brochure on the program.

The Teacher Educator Standards Cohort (TESC) is designed to support teacher educators representing a cross section of the profession, including university-based and school-based personnel, in the development of their own professional portfolios using the ATE Standards. Participants will interact around the standards and the development of their electronic portfolios. During the portfolio development phase, participants will have the opportunity to learn together and to communicate at the ATE annual meetings and via the Internet to reflect on practice and to facilitate further development of the ATE Standards for Teacher Educators. The experiences of the cohort will inform the work of the National ATE Commission to refine the ATE Teacher Educator Standards. (Association of Teacher Educators, 2004).

In the following year, sixteen professionals developed electronic portfolios based on the ATE standards. Expenses of participants were supported by a generous grant from National Evaluation Systems, Inc., Richard Allan, vice president. The electronic portfolios were based on a system designed by *TaskStream*, which also sponsored TESC. During the year, small groups met together to explore the system while Cari Klecka engaged TESC members in conference calls to discuss feedback on their portfolio drafts. TESC members met for a full day at the 2005 and 2006 ATE national conferences, participating in focus groups, analyzing their experiences with the standards using computers for communication, and interacting with members of the commission.

Several commission members served as readers to provide feedback on the standards to the authors. Robert Fisher, in organizing the assessment, identified three aspects of the framework for feedback: (1) Mechanical— is it readable, organized, user friendly? (2) Quality judgment—is individual making a good case for meeting the standards? Do the artifacts support (or not) each standard? and (3) Are there recommendations for making the case for being a quality teacher educator?

Research Committee Results

The commission established a research committee, chaired by Edith Guyton. Committee member Mary Harris conducted a survey about use of the standards. To secure feedback from the widest range of participants, 940 surveys were mailed to AACTE members and NCATE accredited institutions. As of January 1, 2004 when the committee reported to the ATE National Commission on Standards, 226 surveys had been returned, a 24 percent return rate. Responses were received from institutions in forty-six states and the District of Columbia. Twenty-one institutions used the ATE standards in their master's level programs, ten at the doctoral level, four at the postdoctoral level, and fifteen institutions in their certificate or nondegree programs. Some used the standards explicitly while others indicated they relied on them informally.

Twenty institutions indicated they used the standards in assessing professional needs of teacher educators and fifteen institutions in organizing their faculty's professional portfolios. Eighteen institutions used them as part of exit interviews of teacher educator candidates, eighteen others as part of employment criteria, thirteen institutions as criteria for tenure and promotion, fifteen institutions in their annual reviews, and eleven as the basis for awards recognition.

The survey results indicated that fifty-six institutions were aligned with other standards and eighteen respondents clearly rejected the use of standards of any type. When those institutions not using the standards were asked about potential use of standards, more than half (58 percent) responded with one of eight circumstances under which standards might be implemented. Their answers included: with more information/awareness/consideration; standards need credibility/power; if required by NCATE/state/AACTE; for faculty renewal/development; for faculty employment/review; for program review/development; for candidate assessment; and used implicitly rather than explicitly in their programs.

Publications

Multiple national presentations and publications have resulted from this work. This includes three publications focused on the work of TESC (Klecka, Donovan, & Fisher, 2007; Klecka, Donovan, Venditti, & Short, 2008; Short, Donovan, Klecka, & Venditti, 2007). Additionally, the commission has made numerous presentations on the standards to share the conceptualization of, and the potential uses for, the standards (e.g., Fisher, Arisman, Dorton, Harris, Houston, Klecka, Odell, McIntyre, & Williams, 2005; Klecka, Fisher, Allen, Clift, & Sowder, 2007).

A technical assistance guide or manual currently is being developed to provide specific information and advice on the use of the standards. Chaired by Susan Arisman, the committee plans a short, succinct document to be included with the standards. Another publication of the commission is the one you currently are reading. Its purpose is to place the standards in a broader context, to describe the development of the standards, and to provide a broader perspective on standards in American education.

Standards Revision

The initial set of standards, adopted in 1997, was subjected to extensive review by members of the second commission. A featured panel at the February 2003 ATE annual conference responded to questions such as, "What do the standards communicate about a vision for teacher educators?" "Who do these standards serve and what role, if any, should they play in teacher education?" "What are the options to standards and to what extent do they inhibit or facilitate teacher educator competence?" Open hearings were held at the ATE national conferences and each standard's meaning, merits, and research support were questioned and debated.

Potential standards were explored, such as the political and social responsibilities of teacher educators, technology in teacher education, and the responsibility of teacher educators to think of future needs, opportunities, and movements in preparing prospective teachers. In refining the standards, the commission recognized the need for specificity, for definitions of key terminology, and for specific assessments or rubrics. Commission members were cautioned in revising the standards to keep in mind the ultimate outcomes of teacher educators' work—improved learning of the pupils of prospective and in-service teachers.

Emerson Elliott, renowned specialist in professional standards and member of the staff of NCATE, was invited to respond to several questions related to the standards. His first recommendation was that the standards be written in more specific terms so as to reduce questions about the interpretation of evidence; "we should strive to be explicit about the knowledge and professional behaviors we expect from teacher educators in terms of evidence measures—what kind of evidence and how much is enough" (Elliott, 2004).

A century earlier, Abraham Flexner had proposed striking changes in medical education, including the expectation that physicians would "complete biology, chemistry, and physics courses prior to medical school; focusing medical school training on basic laboratory sciences of anatomy, physiology, bacteriology, pathology, and pharmacology; and then providing two years of supervised clinical practice" (Flexner,

1910). Referring to Flexner's commitment to "firmly grounded medical education in scientific and medical knowledge of the day," Elliott recommended that teachers be scholars in their fields (Elliott, 2004). The implication of this recommendation for assessing prospective teacher educators involves four specific requirements: (a) some kind of demonstration of subject knowledge such as the Graduate Record Exam (GRE) subject content test; (b) demonstration of knowledge of research; (c) knowledge of the practice of teaching; and (d) collaboration to improve the profession.

Following extensive reviews by the research team, discussions by the commission, and editing of standards for congruence with current conditions in 2005–07, the seven original standards were revised and extended. Nine standards were identified by the commission in February 2007, adopted by the ATE Executive Board in November 2007, and ratified by the ATE Delegate Assembly in February 2008.

These are described in greater detail in the following chapters. Each standard in these chapters is specified, an *introduction* or rationale stated; its *theoretical or empirical base* described; the *focus of each standard* contrasted with the other standards; and several paragraphs related to the *demonstration of the standard*, including *examples of its accomplishment, indicators and artifacts* supporting achievement of the standard, and *references* supporting the standard.

PROLOGUE AND EPILOGUE

During the past decade, members of two commissions have worked with the development of standards for teacher educators. Much has been accomplished, yet much still needs to be done. That is our profession's challenge.

The standards remain a "work in progress," and this chapter chronicles activities through 2007. Yet plans have already been initiated for continued development. As noted above, the ATE Delegate Assembly will discuss the standards and ratify them, based on a recommendation by the executive board. Two clinics have been organized for the 2008 national ATE meeting. A recommendation has been made to the program planning committee that every presentation be linked to one of the standards to demonstrate relevance and continuity.

A proposal is being made to the ATE Executive Board and Delegate Assembly that the commission be re-formed as a standing committee in ATE to signal the importance of standards in ATE. The description of the Teacher Educator Standards will continue to be included on the ATE Web site. The commission plans to continue meeting with other committees and commissions to collaborate on joint planning. Open hearings to explore uses of the standards are planned in conjunction with state and regional ATE meetings. A second cohort of the Teacher Educator Standards Cohort (TESC) is being planned.

Teacher educators have an obligation to be precise about what is entailed in being a teacher educator. The standards included herein are designed to foment a continuing dialogue designed to sharpen our understanding of the multiple roles of teacher educators and the qualities that make them effective.

NOTES

1. The nine models were located at the following institutions, with their directors identified in parentheses: Columbia University Teachers College (Bruce Joyce), Florida State University (Wesley Sowards and Norm Dodl), Michigan State University (W. Robert Houston), Northwest Regional Educational Laboratory (Del Schalock), Syracuse University (William Benjamin and Wilford Weber), University of Georgia (Charles Johnson), University of Massachusetts (Dwight Allen and James Cooper), University of Pittsburgh (Horton Southworth), University of Toledo (George Dickson).

2. Members of the Task Force and the first Commission on Teacher Educator Standards, appointed by ATE Presidents John McIntyre, Leonard Kaplan, and Peggy Ishler, were: W. Robert Houston (University of Houston), Chair, Robert Alley (Wichita State University), Susan Arisman (Frostburg State University), Beverly Busching (University of South Carolina), Evelyn DiTosto (College of Notre Dame), Sheliah Allen Dorton (Delaware Community School Corp.), Rose Duhon-Sells (McNeese State University), Roy Edelfelt (Chapel Hill, NC), Robert Fisher (Illinois State University), Richard E. Ishler (University of South Carolina), Leonard Kaplan (Wayne State University), Phyllis H. Lamb (University of Toledo), John McIntyre (Southern Illinois University), Dale Scannell (Indiana University-Purdue), and Joseph Vaughan (Hammond, LA).

3. Members of the Assessment of Teacher Education Standards Commission appointed by President Francis van Tassell (2003–2006 and 2006–2009): Robert

Fisher (Illinois State University), Chair, Susan Arisman (Frostburg State University), Sylvia Auton (Fairfax County Public Schools), Elizabeth D. Dore (Radford University), Sheliah Dorton (Delaware Community School Corp.), Mary Harris (University of North Texas), W. Robert Houston (University of Houston), Thomas A. Kessinger (Xavier University), Cari Klecka (University of Nevada-Las Vegas), Jane Carol Manner (East Carolina University), John McIntyre (Southern Illinois University), Robin Haskell McBee (Rowan University), Sandra Odell (University of Nevada-Las Vegas), Anne Grall Reichel (Reichel's Essential Curriculum), Barbara Short Carthage College), Mary Sowder (University of Nevada-Las Vegas), Francis van Tassell (University of North Texas), Karen J. Venditti (St. Joseph's College), Gary L. Willhite (Southern Illinois University), Boyce C. Williams (NCATE).

REFERENCES

Association of Teacher Educators, Commission on Teacher Educator Standards. (2004). *Teacher educator standards cohort (TESC)*. Reston, VA: Author.

Bloom, B. S. (1980). *All our children learning*. New York: McGraw-Hill.

Bradley, A. (February 20, 1991). Teacher educators implored to 'lead' in improving training. *Education Week*. Retrieved January 15, 2008 from www.edweek.org/ew/articles/1991/02/20/10150003.h10.html

Burdin, J. L. (1969). *A reader's guide to the comprehensive models for preparing elementary teachers*. Washington, DC: ERIC Clearinghouse on Teacher Education and the American Association of Colleges for Teacher Education.

De Landsheere, G. (1987). Teacher education. In Dunkin, M. J., *The International Encyclopedia of Teaching and Teacher Education* (pp. 77–83). Oxford: Pergamon.

Edelfelt, R. A., & Raths, J. D. (1999). *A brief history of standards in teacher education*. Reston, VA: Association of Teacher Educators.

Elliott, E. J. (2004). *Responses to four questions about teacher educator standards*. Invited Presentation to the Commission, Annual Meeting of the Association of Teacher Educators, Dallas, TX.

Fisher, R., Arisman, S., Dorton, S., Harris, M., Houston, R., Klecka, C. L., Odell, S. J., McIntyre, D. J., & Williams, B. (2005). *Promoting quality and professionalism for teacher educators through standards and assessment*. Featured Panel at the Annual Meeting of the Association of Teacher Educators, Chicago, IL.

Flexner, A. (1910). *Medical education in the United States and Canada: A report to the Carnegie Foundation for the Advancement of Teaching*. Bulletin Number Four. Boston: D. B. Updike, The Merrymont Press.

Houston, W. R. (Ed.) (1974). *Exploring competency based education*. Berkeley, CA: McCutchan.

Houston, W. R., & Howsam, R. B. (Eds.) (1973). *Competency-based teacher education: Progress, problems, and prospects*. Chicago, IL: Science Research Associates.

Houston, W. R., Dengerink, J. J., Fisher, R., Koster, B., & McIntyre, D. J. (2002). National standards for teacher educators: The story of two nations. In J. Rainer & E. Guyton (Eds.), *Research on Meeting and Using Standards in the Preparation of Teachers* (pp. 25–52). Dubuque, IA: Kendall-Hunt.

Klecka, C. L., Donovan, L., Venditti, K., & Short, B. (2008). Who is a teacher educator? Enactment of teacher educator identity through electronic portfolio development. *Action in Teacher Education*, 29(4), 83–91.

Klecka, C. L., Donovan, L., & Fisher, R. (2007). In their shoes: Teacher educators' reframing portfolio development from the students' perspective. *Journal of Computing in Teacher Education*, 24(1), 31–36.

Klecka, C. L., Fisher, R., Allen, R., Clift, R. T., & Sowder, M. (2007). *A vision for teacher educators*. Featured panel presented at the Annual Meeting of the Association of Teacher Educators, San Diego, CA.

Mager, R. (1962). *Preparing instructional objectives*. Palo Alto, CA: Fearon Publishers.

Sandefur, W. S., & Nicklas, W. L. (1981). Competency-based teacher education in AACTE institutions: An update. *Phi Delta Kappan*, 62, 747–48.

Short, B., Donovan, L., Klecka, C., & Venditti, K. (2007). Teacher educator portfolios: The how, the what, and the why. *Proceedings of the Society for Information Technology and Teacher Education International Conference*, 1892–1897.

Tyler, R. (1949). *Basic Principles of Curriculum and Instruction*. Chicago: University of Chicago Press.

Part II

CONCEPTUALIZING VISIONS
FOR TEACHER EDUCATORS
THROUGH STANDARDS

CHAPTER 4

Standard One: Teaching

Thomas A. Kessinger, Xavier University

Accomplished Teacher Educators . . .

Model teaching that demonstrates content and professional knowledge, skills, and dispositions reflecting research, proficiency with technology and assessment, and accepted best practices.

RATIONALE

Education is continuous and lifelong, and it focuses on teaching, learning, and caring for the whole person. Teaching and learning are mutually inclusive terms located at the heart of education. For many, teaching is a passion. *Docendo discimus*, or we learn by teaching! In fact, Darling-Hammond and Sykes (1999) indicated that "teaching (can be viewed) as the learning profession."

Teacher educators prepare teachers. Consequently, it is imperative that teachers and teacher educators seek, and continuously prepare themselves, to become better at their craft and its concomitant responsibilities. Moreover, modeling effective learning is critical to teaching others to be lifelong learners.

THEORETICAL OR EMPIRICAL BASE

As noted by Darling-Hammond (2007), in 1996 the National Commission on Teaching and America's Future summarized its challenge to the American public with these words:

> We propose an audacious goal. . . . By the year 2006, America will provide every student with what should be his or her educational birthright: access to competent, caring and qualified teaching. (p. 65)

According to Danielson (2002), "The capstone of any school improvement effort is the quality of teaching, which represents the single most important aspect of any school's program for ensuring student success" (p. 106). The preparation of teachers and their continual improvement throughout their careers are the responsibilities of teacher educators. However, as indicated in *A Nation at Risk* (National Commission on Excellence in Education, 1983), "teacher preparation programs need substantial improvement" (p. 22).

Every teacher and all teacher educators have (or should have) a philosophy of education by which they live their professional lives. According to Knight (2008), "[e]ach of us has a philosophy of life that we carry into the classroom" (p. 159). Thus, there should be a close connection between one's philosophy and one's adopted educational theory in order to avoid "mindlessness" (pp. 159–166). In other words, it is important for one's philosophy of education to reflect and manifest what one thinks about education *and* how one acts or behaves or teaches in a classroom.

Teaching today is different from a few years ago; in fact, teaching is a rather daunting task. With the dawn of the twenty-first century, it is critical that teacher educators have a well-defined philosophy of education and are well prepared to work with both pre-service and in-service teachers. Various educational reform reports address the need for improvements in the preparation of teachers (e.g., *A Nation at Risk*, National Commission on Excellence in Education, 1983; *What Matters Most*, National Commission on Teaching & America's Future, 1996). Further, national and state legislative enactments, such as the *No Child Left Behind Act* of 2001, often reflect the urgency for improvements in teacher preparation programs. In terms of recommendations for teaching, *A Nation at Risk* (National Commission on Excellence in Education, 1983) stated:

> Persons preparing to teach should be required to meet high educational standards, to demonstrate an aptitude for teaching, and to demonstrate competence in an academic discipline. Colleges and universities offering

teacher preparation programs should be judged by how well their graduates meet these criteria. (p. 30)

Recall that the *No Child Left Behind Act* insists that teachers are highly qualified and offers strategies for improving teacher quality. Darling-Hammond and Baratz-Snowden (2005) were specific about what teachers need to know and be able to do to ensure that all their students learn. These same criteria apply to teachers of teachers—to teacher educators. Teacher educators, like teachers, should model the knowledge and skills, the attributes and dispositions, and the performances of effective teachers. What applies to effective teachers is equally relevant to teacher educators.

In order for teacher educators to impact the profession, they must successfully model appropriate behaviors in order for those behaviors to be observed, adjusted, replicated, internalized, and applied appropriately to all learners. According to Kauchak and Eggen (2005), "Modeling means exhibiting behavior that is observed and imitated by others" (p. 396). Boyer (1990) linked good or effective teaching with scholarship; and Valente (2008) cited one of Boyer's key ingredients as "mentors who defined their work so compellingly that it became, for them, a lifelong challenge" (p. 24).

Darling-Hammond (2006a) stated: "The importance of powerful teaching is increasingly important in contemporary society. Standards for learning are now higher than they have ever been before. . . ." (p. 300). Bandura (1989) and Darling-Hammond (2006b) indicated that teachers are powerful and meaningful role models for students at all levels in affecting learning and motivation. Consequently, Darling-Hammond and Bransford (2005) state that "[a]bove all, teachers need to keep what is best for the child at the center of their decision making" (pp. 1–2). This applies to teacher educators as well.

FOCUS OF THIS STANDARD

This standard particularly emphasizes the importance of teacher educators as model teachers who are exemplars in content and pedagogy and who use technology, reflection, and other research-based practices in continuously seeking to improve and share their craft.

DEMONSTRATING THE STANDARD

Examples of Standard One Accomplishment:

Teacher educators draw on a deep and developing knowledge of the content of their discipline as well as their knowledge and use of effective instruction.

- Receiving favorable teaching evaluations and completing successful mentoring experiences are examples of accomplished work under this standard.
- Mentoring as part of a university or college program
- Pursuing advanced degrees, receipt of appropriate credentials in content and/or in pedagogy, special training in content fields, and awards in teacher training
- Making presentations on effective and/or innovative teaching practices to teachers and to other teacher educators

Indicators for Standard One Include:

- Model effective instruction to meet the needs of diverse learners
- Demonstrate and promote critical thinking and problem solving among teacher educators, teachers, and/or prospective teachers
- Revise course content and delivery to incorporate current research and/or best practices
- Model reflective practice to foster student reflection
- Demonstrate appropriate subject matter content
- Demonstrate appropriate and accurate professional content in the teaching field
- Demonstrate a variety of instructional and assessment methods including use of technology
- Mentor novice teachers and/or teacher educators
- Facilitate professional development experiences related to effective teaching practices
- Ground practice in current policy and research related to education and teacher education

Artifacts for Standard One Include:

- Evaluations from superiors, colleagues, students, or others
- Course syllabi
- Video and/or audiotapes of teaching
- Developed instructional materials (e.g., lessons, units, courses of study, presentations)
- Testimonials
- Teaching awards and/or other forms of recognition
- Logs or other documentation of classroom activities
- Journals of reflective practice
- Philosophical statement that reflects underlying knowledge and values of teacher education
- Relevant credentials (e.g., certificates, licenses)
- Evidence of technology-based teaching and learning
- Advanced degrees or special training in content field and in education

REFERENCES

Bandura, A. (1989). Social cognitive theory. In R. Vasta (Ed.), *Annals of Child Development* (Vol. 6, pp. 1–60). Greenwich, CT: JAI Press.

Boyer, E. L. (1990). *Scholarship reconsidered: Priorities of the professoriate.* San Francisco, CA: The Carnegie Foundation for the Advancement of Teaching.

Danielson, C. (2002). *Enhancing student achievement: A framework for school improvement.* Alexandria, VA: Association for Supervision and Curriculum Development.

Darling-Hammond, L. (2007). Building a system for powerful teaching and learning. In B. Wehling (Ed.), *Building a 21st century U.S. educational system* (pp. 65–74). Washington, DC: National Commission on Teaching and America's Future.

Darling-Hammond, L. (2006a). Constructing 21st-century teacher education. *Journal of Teacher Education*, 57(3), 300–314.

Darling-Hammond, L. (2006b). *Powerful teacher education: Lessons from exemplary programs.* San Francisco, CA: Jossey-Bass.

Darling-Hammond, L., & Baratz-Snowden, J. (Eds.). (2005). *A good teacher in every classroom: Preparing the highly qualified teachers our children deserve.* [Sponsored by the National Academy of Education Committee on Teacher Education] San Francisco, CA: Jossey-Bass.

Darling-Hammond, L., & Bransford, J. (Eds.). (2005). *Preparing teachers for a changing world: What teachers should learn and be able to do.* San Francisco, CA: Jossey-Bass.

Darling-Hammond, L., & Sykes, G. (Eds.) (1999). *Teaching as the learning profession: Handbook of policy and practice.* San Francisco, CA: Jossey-Bass.

Kauchak, D., & Eggen, P. (2005). *Introduction to teaching: Becoming a professional.* Upper Saddle River, NJ: Pearson Education.

Knight, G. (2008). *Issues and alternatives in educational philosophy* (4th ed.). Berrien Springs, MI: Andrews University Press.

National Commission on Excellence in Education. (1983). *A nation at risk.* Washington, DC: Author.

National Commission on Teaching & America's Future. (1996). *What matters most: Teaching for America's future.* Washington, DC: Author.

Valente, S. (2008). The heart of the scholarship of teaching and learning— Lifelong mentoring. [Presidential Address]. In *Mid-Western Educational Researcher, 21*(1), 4–7.

CHAPTER 5

Standard Two: Cultural Competence

Susan Arisman, Coppin State University
and Frostburg State University

Accomplished Teacher Educators . . .

Apply cultural competence and promote social justice in teacher education.

RATIONALE

The population of America is increasingly diverse, thus enhancing the need for cultural competence. Cultural competence is the ability to meet the academic and developmental needs of students of different genders, races, ethnic backgrounds, sexual orientations, learning styles and abilities, and values. While the need has always existed, it has never been felt as keenly as today. Schools are held responsible for the achievement of *all* students, a huge change in priorities that educators struggle with today. During the early twentieth century, diversity was less evident in a particular school because of the homogeneity of students in individual communities. Diversity was less obvious to teachers who tended to teach in their home communities and to students similar to themselves.

Communities today are less isolated as a result of television, instant communication, and the worldwide distribution of goods and ideas. Students with a wide range of lifestyles and values attend the same schools. Schools must meet the widely dispersed and shifting needs of increasingly more diverse students. Teachers tend to teach children of cultures other than their own and must learn new customs and behaviors. Teacher educators now must prepare prospective teachers who understand and can meet the needs of an increasingly wider range of diverse learners. Therefore, teacher educators must demonstrate that they themselves are culturally competent and can promote social justice.

THEORETICAL OR EMPIRICAL BASE

The rationale for cultural competence is rooted in the research focused on connecting with all learners. In her monograph, *A Synthesis of Scholarship in Multicultural Education*, Gay (2005) stated that the research on learning and development concludes that the needs of students must be addressed, personal meaning and relevance facilitate learning, and the procedural rules and routines embedded in school life should be understood by all learners. Furthermore, educators know that learning is best facilitated when the content to be learned is connected to the students' prior knowledge. Such connections are grounded in the assumption that educators understand the cultures and backgrounds of their students, which is a basic component of cultural competence.

In a recent review of research on teacher education, Darling-Hammond and Bransford (2005) concluded that teacher education should prepare teachers to connect and communicate with diverse learners. They contended teachers needed to accomplish the following in order to meet the needs of diverse learners:

- know their own cultures
- hold high expectations for all students
- understand developmental levels and what is common and unique among different groups
- reach out to families and communities to expand their knowledge about cultures different than their own
- select inclusive curriculum materials
- use a range of assessment methods
- be proficient in a variety of pedagogical methods that make content accessible to all learners

Gay (2005) supported that establishing a closer fit between teaching style and the needs of culturally different students has positive social and academic results. She concluded that a wide range of instructional strategies could be used to achieve common outcomes without compromising educational standards and quality.

Ladson-Billings (1995) asserted that culturally relevant pedagogy "not only addresses student achievement but also helps students to accept and affirm their cultural identity while developing critical perspectives that challenge inequities that schools (and other institutions) perpetuate" (p. 469). To prepare prospective teachers who embody these qualities, teacher educators must work collaboratively with arts and science faculty, school faculty, and community groups to provide the breadth of experiences that assures that all candidates possess the qualities necessary to meet the needs of today's children.

Teacher educators assume responsibility for helping pre-service and in-service teachers understand concepts underlying cultural competence and how they are applied successfully in their classrooms. It is not merely a matter of understanding the concepts underlying the definitions of cultural competence. Teacher educators must also clearly demonstrate how these concepts are applied in their own teaching and in that of their students.

To be culturally competent, teacher educators themselves should possess the qualities that they strive to instill in their students. Just as is expected of their students, they need to know their own cultures and share their backgrounds with them; to hold high expectations for all their students; and to talk about cultural differences, which includes making transparent their own prejudices and stereotypes. Additionally, they make visible the relationship between teacher expectations and student achievement.

Accomplished teacher educators are steeped in the research on developmental levels and learning theory as related to cultural differences. Teacher educators have the responsibility to reach out to different families and communities to further develop their knowledge about diverse cultures. If teacher educators isolate themselves from diversity, they cannot possibly prepare candidates to address diversity in practice. Accordingly, examples of differences and similarities permeate teaching. Teacher educators model both culturally sophisticated pedagogy and assessment that enable prospective teachers to value and use such a range in their classrooms.

FOCUS OF THIS STANDARD

Although there are elements of standard two in standard six, which focuses on collaboration, standard two is unique because it envisions collaboration or connections with learners and their families and communities as a means to meet the needs of diverse learners and achieve cultural competence. Standard two is critical in the rapidly changing cultural context of schools, a condition that is likely to expand in coming years based on projections of population changes in the United States.

DEMONSTRATING THE STANDARD

Examples of Standard Two Accomplishment:

- Including the elements cited above in the design and execution of syllabi
- Participating in diverse communities, workshops, and conferences that bring together people not part of the background of the teacher educator.
- Writing materials or developing audiovisual materials that develop an understanding of diversity

Indicators for Standard Two Include:

- Exhibit practices that enhance both an understanding of diversity and instruction that meets the needs of society
- Engage in culturally responsive pedagogy
- Professionally participate in diverse communities
- Model ways to reduce prejudice for pre-service and in-service teachers and/or other educational professionals
- Engage in activities that promote social justice
- Demonstrate connecting instruction to students' families, cultures, and communities
- Model how to identify and design instruction appropriate to students' stages of development, learning styles, linguistic skills, strengths, and needs
- Foster a positive regard for individual students and their families regardless of differences such as culture, religion, gender, native language, sexual orientation, and varying abilities

- Demonstrate knowledge of their own culture and aspects common to all cultures and foster such knowledge in others
- Promote inquiry into cultures and differences
- Teach a variety of assessment tools that meet the needs of diverse learners
- Recruit diverse teachers and teacher educators

Artifacts for Standard Two Include:

- Course syllabi
- Instructional materials
- Evidence of involvement in schools and other organizations with diverse populations
- Video and/or audiotapes of teaching
- Course assignments
- Student work samples
- Evidence of involvement in school-based projects and/or service learning
- Evidence of providing professional development to others at all levels
- Philosophical statement that reflects underlying attention to diversity
- Assessment tools appropriate for use with diverse learners

REFERENCES

Darling-Hammond, L., & Bransford, J. (2005). *Preparing teachers for a changing world: What teachers should learn and be able to do.* San Francisco, CA: Jossey-Bass.

Gay, G. (2005). *A synthesis of scholarship in multicultural education.* Naperville, IL: North Central Regional Educational Laboratory.

Ladson-Billings, G. (1995). Toward a theory of culturally relevant pedagogy. *American Educational Research Journal, 32*(3), 465–491.

CHAPTER 6

Standard Three: Scholarship

Cari L. Klecka, University of Nevada, Las Vegas

Accomplished Teacher Educators . . .

Engage in inquiry and contribute to scholarship that expands the knowledge base related to teacher education.

RATIONALE

Scholarship is central to the work of teacher educators, especially since teacher educators, by definition, are teachers of teachers and students of teaching (Loughran, 2006). Scholarship indicates engagement in research that leads to new knowledge, yet it also bridges theory and practice to enhance teaching and learning (Boyer, 1990). The research on teacher education needs to be conducted by those who are engaged in the work of teaching teachers not only to inform teaching, but also to improve teacher education programs (Zeichner, 1999).

Recognizing that teacher educators concurrently take on roles of practitioners and researchers, Cochran-Smith (2005) emphasized that accomplished teacher educators need to personalize research by:

> taking our own professional work as educators as a research site and learning by systematically investigating our own practice and interpretative frameworks in ways that are critical, rigorous, and intended to generate both local knowledge and knowledge that is useful in more public spheres (p. 220).

Thus, an important aspect of scholarship is how new knowledge is used and, in the end, what results occur from applying knowledge that accomplished teacher educators bring to their teaching and to the profession more broadly.

THEORETICAL BASE

The scholarship of an accomplished teacher educator is conceptualized through Boyer's model of scholarship (1990), which includes four foci: discovery, integration, application, and teaching. Discovery involves systematic inquiry leading to new knowledge that is developed and supported. There are multiple frameworks for research in teacher education. Although there are fewer quantitative studies approached from a positivist perspective, the recent trend in scholarship in teacher education takes into account the complexity of teacher education and many times incorporates qualitative methodology to capture this (Zeichner, 1999).

Such approaches encompass naturalistic and interpretative frameworks that focus on learning about teaching and "self-study that is crucial in understanding this methodology embedded in the desire of teacher educators to better align their teaching intents with their teaching actions" (Loughran, 2007, p. 12). Integration extends beyond discovery to include making connections and synthesizing conceptual and empirical ideas through emphasis on interpretation of research related to interdisciplinary contexts both educational and academic.

These first two functions of scholarship, discovery and integration, emphasize the generation of new knowledge through inquiry or synthesis; whereas the third function, application, underscores scholarship in the form of service directly related to an individual's area of expertise. It is through application that theory and practice inform one another and make it possible for new knowledge to be discovered and extended in practical applications of research.

The final function of scholarship, teaching, is central to what teacher educators do. "When defined as scholarship, however, teaching both educates and entices future scholars. Indeed as Aristotle said, 'Teaching is the highest form of understanding.'" (Boyer, 1990, p. 23). This requires deep knowledge of the field and intense study to provide a foundation for the scholarship of teaching. Further, engagement in the scholarship of teaching is an intellectual endeavor that calls for accomplished teacher educators to position themselves as learners in the teaching situation (Loughran, 2006). Thus the teaching-learning paradigm comes full circle as teacher educators investigate and uncover new insights about the impact of teaching practices on students' learning.

FOCUS OF THIS STANDARD

Accomplished teacher educators continually ask questions to deepen existing knowledge and to create new knowledge in teaching, learning, and teacher education. This is achieved through systematic inquiry and the subsequent sharing and/or dissemination of the results. Teacher educators engage in discourse within a community about the quest for new knowledge. This community, for example, can be broadly defined as a community of academics whose discourse takes place within publications or a community of inquirers who dialogue around their "reflection on action" (Schön, 1983).

In addition to discourse around new knowledge, teacher educators integrate their learning about practice within the field of teacher education together with their knowledge across disciplines and contexts in order to elucidate connections between their own work and the broader educational landscape. Teacher educators bridge their theoretical and practical knowledge to create new understandings and interpretations in theory and practice of teaching and teacher education. Finally, accomplished teacher educators strive to teach others and to foster learning about teaching and teacher education.

DEMONSTRATING THIS STANDARD

Examples of Standard Three Accomplishment:

- Engaging in research to generate new knowledge and disseminating that knowledge through publications and/or presentations
- Participating in self-study through formalized processes such as National Board Certification, or through program evaluation to improve the teacher education programs
- Acquiring research-based grants or engaging in service related to area(s) of expertise

Ultimately, engaging in activities framed as scholarship result in new understandings for teacher educators, their programs, and/or the field more generally.

Indicators for Standard Three Include:

- Investigate theoretical and practical problems in teaching, learning, and/or teacher education
- Pursue new knowledge in relation to teaching, learning, and/or teacher education
- Connect new knowledge to existing contexts and perspectives
- Engage in research and development projects
- Apply research to teaching practice and/or program or curriculum development
- Acquire research-based and service-based grants
- Disseminate research findings to the broader teacher education community
- Engage in action research

Artifacts for Standard Three Include:

- Publications
- Presentations at meetings of learned societies or specialized professional associations
- Citations by other scholars
- Professional development workshops and/or seminars
- Speaking engagements that focus on issues of teacher education
- Evidence of improved teaching practice
- Evidence of increased student learning
- Research-based program development
- Funded grant proposals
- Research awards or recognitions
- National Board Certification

REFERENCES

Boyer, E.L. (1990). *Scholarship reconsidered: Priorities of the professoriate*. San Francisco: The Carnegie Foundation for the Advancement of Teaching.

Cochran-Smith, M. (2005). Teacher educators as researchers: Multiple perspectives. *Teaching and Teacher Education*, *21*, 219–25.

Loughran, J. (2006). *Pedagogy of teacher education: Understanding teaching and learning about teaching*. New York: Routledge.

Loughran, J. (2007). Researching teacher education practices: Responding to the challenges, demands, and expectations of self-study. *Journal of Teacher Education*, *58*(1), 12–20.

Schön, D.A. (1983). *The reflective practitioner: How professionals think in action*. New York: Basic Books.

Zeichner, K. (1999). The new scholarship in teacher education. *Educational Researcher*, *28*(9), 4–15.

CHAPTER 7

Standard Four: Professional Development

Barbara J. Short, Carthage College

Accomplished Teacher Educators . . .

Inquire systematically into, reflect on, and improve their own practice and demonstrate commitment to continuous professional development.

RATIONALE

Accomplished teacher educators provide pre-service and in-service teachers with professional development and foster their reflection on practice. They draw on their own development examples to model professional growth including goal setting and collecting data to inform their teaching. Teacher educators examine their practice, which begins with their belief system about effective teaching and learning and deepens with reflection on life experiences. This demonstrates the important connection between beliefs and action (Vygotsky, 1978). Teacher educators model the notion that reflective practice is transformative in various ways and that when one is proactive about the reflection, new learning opportunities occur (Farrell, 2004).

Professional growth transpires as reflective practice promotes self-actualization (Pedro, 2006). The process is enriched through collaboration with others and intertwines experiences with practice (Schön, 1996). Experience is essential to develop thinking (Dewey, 1916), which provides the foundation to create knowledge, collect data, reflect, and change practice.

THEORETICAL OR EMPIRICAL BASE

Accomplished teacher educators are motivated to engage in their own professional development for various reasons. Many confront critical questions about teaching (Greene, Kim, & Marioni, 2007; Genor, 2005), become more conscious of teaching realities in order to refine practices (Singer, 2005; Zeichner & Liston, 1996), and help students with reflective practice by addressing needs of the changing contexts of teacher educator classrooms and the classrooms of their students (Genor, 2005). Through this, they strive to understand better the processes initiated historically and that continue to be important parts of teacher improvement (Lyons, 2006) as well as to merge new ways of thinking and conducting scholarship in higher education with daily teaching interactions (Boyer, 1990).

Educational knowledge evolves and emerges into new ways of thinking resulting from reflection and/or self-study. Teacher educators think about what they know about themselves based on schema, experience, and professional knowledge, then reconceptualize new frameworks onto which they can construct concepts and lead to new ways of reaching students. Experiential thinking allows teachers to reform beliefs and philosophies about teaching and learning over time through examination of practice through multiple lenses (Dewey, 1902, 1933). These new ways of thinking about self and practice start with examining old experiences and knowledge (Vazir, 2006). The development of self-knowledge (Beattie, 2001) focuses on the whole person and how this information about self is constructed.

FOCUS OF THIS STANDARD

The focus of this standard emphasizes the importance of professional development for teacher educators and the need to serve as excellent models for their students concerning professional development. This standard implies that teacher educators seek opportunities to enrich their knowledge and understanding to remain current on research and best practice in order to engage in their work. To accomplish this, they learn, use, and model emerging technologies, methodologies, and approaches suited for learning environments that reflect the needs of an increasingly diverse society.

DEMONSTRATING THE STANDARD

Examples of Standard Four Accomplishment:

Teacher educators report various methods that they use to engage in their professional development grounded in reflection, which may be facilitated through self-study or action research.

- Addressing questions through critical self-reflection that may evolve into action
- Working with colleagues as critical friends to help reframe and clarify perspectives
- Telling and retelling professional stories in narratives, journals, logs, and multidimensional diaries and using inquiry to examine these
- Developing a professional portfolio, which examines professional work and how it addresses a given set of institutional, association, or other performance standards
- Participating in professional conferences or workshops which provide ways to learn about emerging research and technologies in teacher education
- Taking part in a university's faculty development offerings allows participants to interact locally with colleagues
- Learning a new skill not directly related to the classroom, such as how to speak a foreign language

Indicators for Standard Four Include:

- Systematically reflect on own practice and learning
- Engage in purposeful professional development focused on professional learning goals
- Develop and maintain a philosophy of teaching and learning that is continuously reviewed based on a deepening understanding of research and practice
- Participate in and reflect on learning activities in professional associations and learned societies
- Apply life experiences to teaching and learning

Artifacts for Standard Four Include:

- Statement of philosophy of teaching and learning
- Evidence of professional development goals and activities

- Self-assessment
- Evidence of documented professional growth
- Evidence of participation in professional development experiences
- Letter of support
- Reflective journals

REFERENCES

Beattie, M. (2001). *The art of learning to teach: Pre-service teachers' narratives*. Columbus, OH: Prentice Hall.

Boyer, E. L. (1990). *Scholarship reconsidered: Priorities of the professoriate*. San Francisco, CA: The Carnegie Foundation for the Advancement of Teaching.

Dewey, J. (1902). *The child and the curriculum*. Chicago: University of Chicago Press.

Dewey, J. (1916). *Democracy and education*. New York: Macmillan.

Dewey, J. (1933). *How we think: A restatement of the relation of reflective thinking to the educative process*. New York: D.C. Heath and Company.

Farrell, T. (2004). *Reflective practice in action: 80 reflection breaks for busy teachers*. Thousand Oaks, CA: Corwin Press.

Genor, M. (2005). A social reconstructionist framework for reflection: The problematizing of teaching. *Issues in Teacher Education, 14*(2), 45–62.

Greene, W., Kim, Y., & Marioni, J. (2007). The reflective trio: A model for collaborative self-study in teacher education. *Journal of Educational Policy, 4*(1), 41–58.

Lyons, N. (2006). Reflective engagement as professional development in the lives of university teachers. *Teachers and Teaching, 12*(2), 151–168.

Pedro, J. (2006). Taking reflection into the real world of teaching. *Kappa Delta Pi Record, 42*(3), 129–133.

Schön, D. (1996). *Educating the reflective practitioner: Toward a new design for teaching and learning in the professions*. San Francisco: Jossey-Bass.

Singer, J. (2005). Finding and framing teacher research questions: Moving from reflective practice to teacher research. *Teaching and Learning, 19*(3), 144–155.

Vazir, N. (2006). Reflection in action: Constructing narratives of experience. *Reflective Practice, 7*(4), 445–454.

Vygotsky, L. (1978). *Mind in society: The development of higher psychological processes*. Cambridge, MA: Harvard University Press.

Zeichner, K. & Liston, D. (1996). *Reflective teaching*. Mahwah, NJ: Lawrence Erlbaum.

CHAPTER 8

Standard Five: Program Development

Robin Haskell Mcbee, Rowan University
W. Robert Houston, University of Houston

Accomplished Teacher Educators . . .

Provide leadership in developing, implementing, and evaluating teacher education programs that are rigorous, relevant, and grounded in theory, research, and best practice.

RATIONALE

The quality of programs that prepare beginning teachers and provide for teachers' continuing professional development are the foundation of the professional work of teacher educators. The "development of quality programs to prepare teachers" and extending teacher preparation through the "career-long professional development of teachers" lie at the core of the mission of the Association of Teacher Educators (Selke & Alouf, 2004). It is through the programs developed by teacher educators that teachers learn and further expand the content knowledge, understandings, and skills they need in "subject matter content, foundational studies, multicultural and multilingual education, and sound pedagogical practice at all levels of the professional development continuum" (ibid).

Therefore, accomplished teacher educators are regular contributors to and often leaders in the development, refinement, and revision of programs and portions of programs focused on initial teacher preparation and ongoing teacher professional development. Through this, they engage as researchers and evaluators of such programs as well.

THEORETICAL OR EMPIRICAL BASE

In her foreword to the eighth *Teacher Education Yearbook, Research on Effective Models for Effective Teacher Education* (2000), Guyton described effective teacher education as a "complex academic enterprise" in which "powerful programs" carefully connect nested layers of children's and teachers' cognitive development, content knowledge, and contextual experience and understanding (pp. ix–x). Effective teacher education, then, develops beginning teachers and changes experienced teachers so that their work leads to powerful learning for all children in their classrooms. Accomplished teacher educators develop, implement, and evaluate such powerful teacher education programs or components of those programs.

Effective teacher education programs vary in size, structure, time frame, and sponsorship. Examples might include liberal arts colleges, state and private research universities and universities with strong teacher education roots, state governments and local districts, and for-profit institutions. They typically are standards-based in all aspects of coursework, fieldwork, and outcomes; girded by strong research to support their approaches and practices; grounded in content knowledge, child development, pedagogy, and social context; integrative of theory, practice, and content; reflective of the collaborative dynamics of the educational enterprise; and steeped in the content and practice that reflect and respond to the diverse nature and characteristics of learners in our classrooms and of our American populace in general (Darling-Hammond, 2006; Darling-Hammond et al., 2005; Hammerness et al., 2005; Kochan, 2000; Zeichner & Conklin, 2005).

Linda Darling-Hammond built a whole thesis around the idea of powerful teacher education (2006). Her study of seven highly successful teacher education programs of varying types indicated that such highly successful, effective, and powerful teacher education programs share certain common characteristics. These include what is outlined above, along with a "clear vision" that frames and guides all the work of the program, "extended clinical experiences" that are closely interwoven with the courses students take, "strong relationships" between university and school faculty, and the use of "case study methods, teacher research, performance assessments, and portfolio evaluation" in the program's methodology (p. 41).

Two other characteristics often described in the literature on effective teacher education programs are what Houston and Warner (2000) referred to as the "twin needs" of reflection and inquiry. The authors asserted that these two practices ought to become professional habits that are developed through repeated use throughout teacher education programs in order that teachers learn to regularly employ them as a part of their own professional self-monitoring.

In summary, accomplished teacher educators are major players and often leaders of programmatic development in teacher education. Based on an understanding of research and effective practices in the education of pre- and in-service teachers, they contribute in significant ways to the development, implementation, and evaluation of rigorous and effective teacher education programs.

FOCUS OF THIS STANDARD

This standard focuses particularly on providing leadership to the development of, obtaining approval for, and evaluating teacher education programs or components of those programs. Work in program development naturally incorporates many of the characteristics of other standards, such as collaboration, cultural competence, scholarship, and service to the profession; however, the primary focus here is on the actual program development and evaluation of programs in teacher education.

DEMONSTRATING THE STANDARD

Examples of Standard Five Accomplishment:

- Contributing to the design or modification of a teacher education program or courses in need of update would be examples of work under this standard. This might include authoring or coauthoring individual courses, multiple courses, fieldwork for the program, or even the program's rationale and general framework.
- Constructing school-based seminars to instruct and support novice or veteran teachers might also serve as an example of program development in teacher education. These might be oriented toward general induction or toward implementing a major curricular innovation.

- Developing training modules for university and school-based instructors who will deliver a teacher education program would also be an example of providing leadership in teacher education program development. Similarly, research on and evaluation of teacher education programs or components of those programs would also be examples of leadership under this standard.

Indicators for Standard Five Include:

- Design, develop, or modify teacher education programs based on theory, research, and best practice
- Provide leadership in obtaining approval or accreditation for new or modified teacher education programs
- Lead or actively contribute to the ongoing assessment of teacher education courses or programs
- Provide leadership that focuses on establishing standards for teacher education programs or on developing, approving, and accrediting teacher education programs at the local, state, national, or international level
- Contribute to research that focuses on effective teacher education programs

Artifacts for Standard Five Include:

Course or program proposal

Revision to Course or Program

- New materials developed to meet course or program requirements
- Evidence of participation in program development, revision, or evaluation
- Documentation of leadership in program accreditation process (state or national)
- Program recognition or award
- Evidence of participation in research on or evaluation study of a teacher education program
- Publications, handouts, or other documentation of conference presentations on program development

REFERENCES

Darling-Hammond, L. (2006). *Powerful teacher education: Lessons from exemplary programs*. San Francisco: Jossey-Bass.

Darling-Hammond, L., Pacheco, A., Michelli, N., Lepage, P., Hammerness, K., & Youngs, P. (2005). Implementing curriculum renewal in teacher education: Managing organizational change. In L. Darling-Hammond & J. Bransford (Eds.), *Preparing teachers for a changing world: What teachers should learn and be able to do* (pp. 442–479). San Francisco: Jossey-Bass.

Guyton, E. (2000). Foreword: Research on effective models for teacher education: Powerful teacher education programs. In D. J. McIntyre & D. Byrd (Eds.), *Research on effective models for teacher education: Teacher education yearbook VIII* (pp. ix–xii). Thousand Oaks, CA: Corwin Press.

Hammerness, K., Darling-Hammond, L., Bransford, J., Berliner, D., Cochran-Smith, M., McDonald, M., & Zeichner, K. (2005). How teachers learn and develop. In L. Darling-Hammond & J. Bransford (Eds.), *Preparing teachers for a changing world: What teachers should learn and be able to do* (pp. 358–389). San Francisco: Jossey-Bass.

Houston, W. R., & Warner, A. R. (2000). Twin needs for improved teacher education. In D. J. McIntyre & D. Byrd (Eds.), *Research on effective models for teacher education: Teacher education yearbook VIII* (pp. 72–77). Thousand Oaks, CA: Corwin Press.

Kochan, F. K. (2000). Division I: Models for enhancing the professional development of teachers, Overview and framework. In D. J. McIntyre & D. Byrd (Eds.), *Research on effective models for teacher education: Teacher education yearbook VIII* (pp. 1–9). Thousand Oaks, CA: Corwin Press.

Selke, M., & Alouf, J. (2004). *Position framework: ATE*. Retrieved June 8, 2006 from www.ate1.org/pubs/ATE_Position_Frame.cfm.

Zeichner, K. M., & Conklin, H. G. (2005). Teacher education programs. In M. Cochran-Smith & K. M. Zeichner (Eds.), *Studying teacher education: The report of the AERA panel on research and teacher education* (pp. 645–735). Mahwah, NJ: Lawrence Erlbaum Associates.

CHAPTER 9

Standard Six: Collaboration

Jane Carol Manner, East Carolina University

Accomplished Teacher Educators . . .

Collaborate regularly and in significant ways with relevant stakeholders to improve teaching, research, and student learning.

RATIONALE

The very nature of teacher education presupposes collaboration, as its
purpose and functions require the essential intersection between teachers and learners. While this fundamental nexus is at the core of a
teacher educator's professional practice, the wider collaborative network of a teacher educator reflects a complex and reciprocal relationship of many constituencies. Efforts to elaborate the engagements of
teacher education beyond the college and university purview have received particular emphasis since concerns regarding academic achievement were raised in the watershed publication *A Nation at Risk* (Brown
& Jackson, 1983).

The educational community recognized the critical need for many
stakeholders to become involved in promoting excellence in education.
Teacher educators must model collaboration within their institutions
and across many institutions and advocate for involvement with students, families, and personnel in schools; communities at the local,
state, national, and global levels; and through effective participation in
professional organizations.

THEORETICAL AND PRACTICAL PERSPECTIVES

The teacher educator as a collaborative professional has received considerable attention in recent decades. Concerns about academic achievement have developed a climate of accountability that spans the hierarchy of education from the learners in the classrooms of our nation's schools to the programs in higher education that prepare teachers to undertake the critical and daunting responsibilities attendant to public education in contemporary times.

In earlier days, the term "teacher educator" denoted those college and university faculty who were directing the preparation of fledgling teachers. They were concerned primarily with the content and methods that candidates would encounter in the program, and were often isolated and insulated from other disciplines at their universities, actual classroom practice in schools, or involvement with the community at large.

The need to expand that view has become clear. Not only has the definition of the teacher educator developed to encompass a much more inclusive membership, but the requirements and opportunities for collaboration exist on multiple fronts. Freeman (1993) affirmed that, for teacher educators, collaboration is an essential element of educational reform, a tool for involving a wide range of expertise and resources needed by schools. Bartel & Young (1993) supported this view, citing the need to prepare teachers for the realities of contemporary classrooms, schools, and school systems.

There has long been interaction between college faculty and the schools in which candidates have field experiences. However, the nature of that interface was often limited, and frequently represented a kind of one-way relationship in which the university faculty were teaching courses, but not having meaningful involvement with clinical personnel. The need for input from "master teachers" as an essential ingredient to the reform of teacher education emerged as a clear direction from the national commission that declared the nation to be at risk (Johnson, 1999). Trubowitz (1986) described the need for college faculty to avoid the "we the experts" stance in forging partnerships with other constituencies. The mounting demand for higher education to work collaboratively with school-based colleagues is based on the belief that such interaction can produce reciprocal professional development, dissipate isolation, and elevate the relevance of research conducted in schools (Peters, 2002).

But what exactly is collaboration? Numerous definitions relating to teacher education have been offered, and they typically contain certain central characteristics. Collaboration is seen as a situation of working together in which all participants share the common goal of improving America's educational system and the success of school-age students (Jackson, 1999; McNeil, 1999). Collaboration cannot exist as the result of a single institution acting in isolation, but rather has the greatest potential when all parties perceive a clear purpose, have a strong commitment to success, and come to understand and value the different cultures of schools, universities, and communities involved within the target of their work together (Knop, Lemaster, Norris, Raudensky, & Tannehill, 1997).

True collaboration requires positive, meaningful communication between and among members (Raffaele & Knoff, 1999). In the view of Freeman (1993), educational collaboration functions best when involved teacher educators combine knowledge of organizational development with knowledge of global perspectives in a context committed to palpable school improvement.

The benefits of collaboration have implications for teacher educators irrespective of context according to Swain and Dawson (2006) in a protocol they described as a teacher education village. The "village" concept represents the reciprocal interactions of various constituencies in schools and universities, as well as between and among colleges within those universities. Such interactions are not haphazard or occasional, but rather require the allocation of time for negotiation of a common vision for the partnership as well as the provision of appropriate resources and a sustained agenda.

The principal benefit derives from approaching teacher preparation with diverse partnerships. Such an approach elaborates and extends the vision of what education can be for pre-service teachers. Second, when all members of a partnership develop a common vision and sense of trust to accompany that vision, truly powerful partnerships can emerge. As Winn and Blanton (2005) suggested, the context is ripe for collaboration in teacher education.

Simple acceptance of this dictum is not sufficient. It is important for a teacher educator to be aware that meaningful collaboration may not occur quickly nor smoothly. Trubowitz (1986) described a series of stages from *skepticism* to *approval* and *acceptance* through which most partnerships evolve, and Freeman (1993) reminded us that collaboration requires working together over a long period of time.

FOCUS OF THIS STANDARD

This standard focuses on adopting a collaborative approach to teacher education that involves a variety of stakeholders in teaching and learning including, but not limited to, universities, schools, families, communities, foundations, businesses, and museums. Collaboration may be informal or formalized in distinct partnerships forged over an extended period of time, and relating both to pre-service and continuing education of teaching professionals.

DEMONSTRATING THE STANDARD

Examples of Standard Six Accomplishment:

- Initiating a partnership with a school to initiate a collaborative mentor program
- Collaborating with individuals in another department in your institution
- Contributing to a coalition that involves school, university, parents, and others in a community
- Working with international schools or universities to share innovative ideas for improving teacher education (e.g., shared student teaching with part of the experience in one country and part in another)

Indicators for Standard Six Include:

- Engage in cross-institutional and cross-college partnerships
- Support teacher education in the P–12 school environment
- Participate in joint decision making about teacher education
- Foster cross-disciplinary endeavors
- Engage in reciprocal relationships in teacher education

- Initiate collaborative projects that contribute to improved teacher education
- Acquire financial support for teacher education innovation to support collaboration

Artifacts for Standard Six Include:

- Evidence of collaborative activities (e.g., minutes and agenda of meetings)
- Testimonials
- Records of awards, recognition, and financial support for research resulting from collaboration
- Course syllabi that demonstrate collaboration
- Joint publications resulting from collaboration

REFERENCES

Bartel, V., & Young, B. (1993). Redesigning teacher education: Lessons from a school university collaboration. *Education, 114*(1), 85–91.

Brown, S., & Jackson, W. (1983). The cooperative extension service as a model for university-school collaboration. *Education, 104*(1), 3.

Freeman, R. (1993). Collaboration, global perspectives, and teacher education. *Theory into Practice, 32*(1), 33–39.

Jackson, C. (1999). A view from the top on collaboration: School administrators' perspectives on a field-based teacher education program. *Education, 119*(3), 431.

Johnson, E. (1999). Reform in teacher education: the response to accountability is collaboration. *Education, 119*(3), 381–387.

Knop, N., LeMaster, K., Norris, M., Raudensky, & Tannehill, D. (1997). What we have learned through collaboration: A summary report from a national teacher education conference. *The Physical Educator, 54*(4), 170–180.

McNeil Jr., J. (1999). A university and charter school collaboration born out of great need. *Education, 119*(3), 438.

Peters, J. (2002). University-school collaboration: Identifying faulty assumptions. *Asia-Pacific Journal of Teacher Education, 30*(3), 229–242.

Raffaele, R., & Knoff, L. (1999). Improving home-school collaboration with disadvantaged families: Organizational principles. *School Psychology Review, 28*(3), 448.

Swain, C., & Dawson, K. (2006). The teacher education village: Growing partnerships to integrate educational technology into curricula and classrooms. *The Turkish Journal of Educational Technology*, 5(1), 64–70.

Trubowitz, S. (1986). Stages in the development of school-college collaboration. *Educational Leadership*, 43(5), 18–21.

Winn, J., & Blanton, L. (2005). The call for collaboration in teacher education. *Focus on Exceptional Children*, 38(2), 1–10.

CHAPTER 10

Standard Seven: Public Advocacy

Karen J. Venditti, Saint Joseph's College

Accomplished Teacher Educators . . .

Serve as informed, constructive advocates for high quality education for all students.

RATIONALE

Educational reform is a relatively constant movement that requires accomplished teacher educators to facilitate change to support and advance all aspects of the field. In support of reform initiatives, teacher educators must act as role models for both the in-service and pre-service educators whom they serve to promote and encourage advocacy efforts among all stakeholders. It is appropriate to begin that service by understanding and utilizing research as the basis for decisions to drive any actions. Such a focus promotes sound practice, allows the continuation of research-supported improvements which have long been carried out in educational forums (Laitsch et al., 2002), and enables public advocates to support and advance quality improvements that address the changing needs of all students across the globe.

Advocacy built on research-supported improvements to education provides the foundation for moving others to action. It is through collaborative, democratic measures that substantial transformation can occur. Therefore, accomplished teacher educators remain decidedly informed, highly concerned leaders who embrace this role. Through reflection and revision they continue to evaluate their responsibilities as influential change agents who promote sound, evidence-based educational reform.

THEORETICAL OR EMPIRICAL BASE

Public advocacy in teacher education revolves around and necessitates critical investigation of educational reform movements. To continually improve public education, advocacy efforts must examine the ideals that undergird reform movements. Goodlad (1994) suggests that educational reform must be "grounded in a vital component of the mission of our schools: enculturating the young in a social and political democracy" (p. 195). Michelli (2005) supports that assertion while stressing that a primary purpose in education is "to prepare students to be participating citizens in our social and political democracy" (p. 3). To impact those young students, teacher educators need to serve as role models for teachers through their advocacy for changes in the field of education.

Advocacy involves more than promoting obvious pro-education governmental policy initiatives. It also includes the political and social perceptions and challenges the systems that impact education (Cochran-Smith, 2004). Yet, these do not seem to have been on the forefront of teacher education. Public advocacy efforts, generally, are not embedded components in teacher education coursework. Therefore, attempts to promote advocacy at different levels may require venturing into unfamiliar waters.

This shift into uncharted territory may result in inestimable benefits. To encourage future teachers to envision themselves as enfranchised participants in the democratic process, the practice of exploration into and dissemination of public policy and democratic practices should begin in undergraduate education under the guidance of politically savvy, accomplished teacher educators. Teacher educators may choose to integrate measures such as constructed projects, research initiatives, and service learning activities for pre-service and practicing teachers to demonstrate a deeper understanding of the potential political roles they may play. Because there are myriad possibilities where democratic ideals and policy may be investigated and pursued, opportunities abound.

Strategies to involve students at all levels may be incorporated into higher education coursework which should trickle down into P–12 classrooms. Jenlink & Embry Jenlink (2005) advocate for authentically democratic experiences that "prepare future teachers to act responsibly in creating democratic cultures in classrooms and schools through democratic social practice" (p. 96). Promoting such practices encourages each teacher educator to model public advocacy activities for pre-service and practicing educators.

It is desired that this modeling would have an even greater impact on P–12 learners because of the intended outcome, which is that classroom teachers subsequently demonstrate advocacy efforts for their students. This sense of knowledge should propel teachers and their students to the next level. This includes a deeper understanding of the important role collaboration takes in moving public advocacy objectives forward.

Higher education faculty and classroom teachers have many opportunities to support educational reform and influence public policy. Draper et al. (2006) suggest that democratic educational research encourages teacher educators to work alongside practicing classroom teachers to create solutions to relevant issues that are not being adequately addressed through traditional models of research. Research and best practice need to be the basis for advocacy efforts and policy makers' decisions.

Teacher educators need to actively influence the field of research to promote democratic ideals and to formulate real world solutions. This may provide a means for greater influence over those who conceptualize and construct proposed policy. Forming alliances and solidifying a more powerful unified voice enables advocates to be more effective in advancing common goals (Earley, 2005). As a professional group, teacher educators must make conscious and concerted efforts to enlighten and pressure those in decision-making positions.

Effective change agents in teacher education recognize, appreciate, and comprehend countless issues facing educators at every level. Public advocacy promotes this comprehensive understanding of the public education system. This necessitates that one remain current and viable in the field of teacher education. This understanding is contingent upon adopting a personal belief that lifelong learning is paramount in the field and a critical component of the democratic involvement that our country has come to know and expect. Teacher education is a logical venue for those beliefs to be supported. Public advocacy is a means to achieve that end.

FOCUS OF THIS STANDARD

This standard focuses particularly on providing leadership to the development and promotion of public advocacy related to all levels and content areas of education. Work in public advocacy incorporates a deep understanding of all standards because its core work encompasses content and topics relevant to all other standards. Efforts arise from and are built on ideas and issues that permeate these standards. Even though all standards may suffuse public advocacy endeavors, the primary focus is on the support of advocacy initiatives across all areas of education, especially teacher education.

DEMONSTRATING THE STANDARD

Examples of Standard Seven Accomplishment:

- Promoting and supporting education through participation in, or presentations at, community forums or activities with professionals at a variety of levels including professional teachers' associations
- Collaborating with and providing alternative, research-based viewpoints to those involved in the construction of governmental policies and regulations at local, state, and/or national levels to improve teaching and teacher education.
- Canvassing policy makers who determine those policies
- Serving on committees or boards which make proposals for licensing recommendations at local, state, and/or national levels

Indicators for Standard Seven Include:

- Promote quality education for all learners through community forums and work with local policy makers

- Inform and educate those involved in making governmental policies and regulations at local, state, and/or national levels to support and improve teaching and learning
- Actively address policy issues which affect the education profession

Artifacts for Standard Seven Include:

- Evidence of advocacy for high quality teaching and learning in local, state, national, and/or international settings
- Evidence of contributions to educational policy or regulations at local, state, national, and/or international levels
- Papers, presentations, and/or media events designed to enhance the public's understanding of teaching and learning
- Evidence of service to school and university accreditation committees
- Scholarship and/or grant activity promoting education

REFERENCES

Cochran-Smith, M. (2004). Taking stock in 2004: Teacher education in dangerous times. *Journal of Teacher Education, 55*(1), 3–7.

Draper, R., Hall, K. M., & Smith, L. K. (2006). The possibility of democratic educational research to nurture democratic educators. *Action in Teacher Education, 28*(2), 66–72.

Earley, P. (2005). Searching for the common good in federal policy: The missing essence in NCLB and HEA, Title II. In N. M. Michelli & D. L. Keiser (Eds.), *Teacher education for democracy and social justice* (pp. 57–76). New York: Routledge.

Goodlad, J. I. (1994). *Educational renewal: Better teachers, better schools.* San Francisco: Jossey-Bass.

Jenlink, P. M. & Embry Jenlink, K. (2005). *Portraits of teacher preparation: Learning to teach in a changing America.* Lanham, MD: Rowman & Littlefield.

Laitsch, D., Heilman, E., & Shaker, P. (2002). Teacher Education, pro-market policy and advocacy research. *Teaching Education, 13*(3), 251–271.

Michelli, N. (2005). Education for democracy: What can it be? In N. M. Michelli & D. L. Keiser (Eds.), *Teacher education for democracy and social justice* (pp. 3–30). New York: Routledge.

CHAPTER 11

Standard Eight: Teacher Education Profession

Mary M. Harris, University of North Texas

Accomplished Teacher Educators . . .

Contribute to improving the teacher education profession.

RATIONALE

Responsibility for the future of teacher education rests largely with its national, state, and local professional organizations. Without service to teacher education by its members, the profession cannot develop or maintain its moral identity.

Service is an individual as well as a collective virtue. In *The Seven Habits of Highly Effective People: Powerful Lessons in Personal Change* (1989), Covey noted, "One important source (of service) is your work, when you see yourself in a contributing and creative mode, really making a difference" (p. 299). Bellah, Madsen, Sullivan, Swidler, and Tipton (1985), in *Habits of the Heart: Individualism and Commitment in American Life* (1985), noted that although service goes against the grain in much of American culture, "it is most often found among civic-minded professionals as a second language that expresses the civic ideal of friends who sustain one another in pursuit of the common good" (p. 195). Accomplished teacher educators seek the welfare and improvement of the profession through communities of practice and advocacy that include professional organizations.

THEORETICAL OR EMPIRICAL BASE

Discussion of dispositions in teacher education must not exclude the dispositions of the teacher educator. In *Dispositions in Teacher Education* (2007), Wasicsko suggested that teacher educators possess the dispositions expected of teacher candidates. The disposition toward assuring the welfare of others is associated with the helping professions. The professional communities of teacher educators include their students, former students, and colleagues, whose welfare is sought through both individual and collective action.

University-based teacher educators perceive themselves as having greater influence than classroom teachers on the shape and quality of the profession (Isham, Carter, & Stribling, 1981; Reynolds, McCullough, Bendixen-Noe, & Morrow, 1994). They experience dissonance between the professional and institutional values arising from the conflicting demands of teaching and research (Isham et al., 1981). Mager and Myers (1983) found that the list of duties of university-based teacher educators is far longer than is common in higher education, with many of the additional duties falling into the administrative/service cluster. The 1987 RATE study (as cited in Howey and Zimpher, 1990) showed that secondary education methods faculty across all types of institutions spent an average of 22 percent of their time engaged in service, compared to 60 percent in teaching and 15 percent in scholarship.

Within higher education, service to the profession is only one of the types of service rendered. Yet, this type of service is particularly valued because of challenges to institutional collegiality in this field. King, Nystrom, and Wimpleberg (1984) reported that at private colleges and universities, 51 percent of teacher educators held joint appointments, and 90 percent collaborated with others in making decisions about teacher education programs, conditions that may regularly challenge professional focus. Roemer and Martinello (1982) postulated that at research universities, collegiality is further challenged by inclusion of disciplinary and functional studies of education within the same departments. Reaching across institutional contexts, professional organizations offer teacher educators a venue for professional identification, support, and action.

Improvement of the teaching profession is a powerful motivator for teacher educators, but a unified focus on this goal is difficult in their day-to-day work. Professional associations offer accomplished teacher educators support along with opportunities to define and advance professional understandings and values.

FOCUS OF THIS STANDARD

The construct of standard eight enables the work encompassed by many of the other standards. The vulnerabilities of standard eight rest in its assumptions that the profession is vested with authority in teacher education and that technical expertise qualifies the profession for determining the public good. Standard six, with its focus on interaction with other stakeholders, and standard nine, with its focus on envisioning the potential of change, help to counter any illusion that teacher educators may hold about the power of their individual voices. Service to professional communities offers teacher educators an important collective means to influence the direction of societal change.

DEMONSTRATING THE STANDARD

Examples of Standard Eight Accomplishment:

- Presenting records of the successful nomination of a deserving colleague for a state unit's distinguished teacher educator award
- Collaborating with other state professional organizations concerned with issues related to teacher education
- Preparing a white paper to inform stakeholders about proposed legislation; similarly, recommending a policy position to a state unit and provided the groundwork for collaboration with the groups consulted
- Addressing an important professional issue in ways that solidify the profession and enhance its influence

Examples related to standard eight are many and varied, but they share the characteristic of serving to improve the teacher education profession, which can be both a lifeline and a voice for its member teacher educators.

Indicators for Standard Eight Include:

- Actively participate in professional organizations at the local, state, national, or international level
- Edit/review manuscripts for publication or presentation for teacher education organizations
- Review resources designed to advance the profession
- Develop textbook or multimedia resources for use in teacher education
- Recruit promising pre-service teachers
- Recruit future teacher educators
- Mentor colleagues toward professional excellence
- Design and/or implement pre-service and induction programs for teachers
- Support student organizations to advance teacher education
- Advocate for high quality teacher education standards

Artifacts for Standard Eight Include:

- Evidence of active participation in professional organizations
- Conference programs and proceedings
- Books/monographs/periodicals edited or reviewed
- Textbook/multimedia reviews
- Textbooks and multimedia resources developed
- Testimonials
- Evidence of support of student organizations
- Grant proposals
- Reports and evaluations of projects/advancement programs
- Records of awards/recognition for excellence in teacher education

REFERENCES

Bellah, R. N., Madsen, R., Sullivan, W. M., Swidler, A., & Tipton, S. M. (1985). *Habits of the heart: Individualism and commitment in American life*. New York: Harper & Row.

Covey, S. R. (1989). *The seven habits of highly effective people: Powerful lessons for personal change*. New York: Simon & Schuster.

Howey, K. R., & Zimpher, N. L. (1990). Professors and deans of education. In W. R. Houston (Ed.), *Handbook of research on teacher education* (pp. 349–370). New York: Macmillan.

Isham, M., Carter, H., & Stribling, R. (1981). *A study of the entry mechanisms of university based teacher educators.* Report No. 9011. Austin, TX: University of Texas. Research and Development Center for Teacher Education. (ERIC Document Reproduction Service No. ED 230 493).

King, J. A., Nystrom, N. J., & Wimpleton, R. J. (1984). Teacher education in private colleges and universities: Past and present. *Journal of Teacher Education, 35*(2), 27–30.

Mager, G., & Myers, B. (1983). *Developing a career in the academy: New professors in education.* Minneapolis, MN: Society of Professors of Education (ERIC Document Reproduction Service No. ED 236 127).

Reynolds, R. J., McCullough, J. D., Bendixen-Noe, M., & Morrow, L. E. (1994). *The need for knowledge about teacher educators.* Unpublished manuscript, Eastern Connecticut State University. (ERIC Document Reproduction Service No. ED 372 041).

Roemer, R., & Martinello, M. (1982). Divisions in the educational professoriate and the future of professional education. *Educational Studies, 13*(2), 203–223.

Wasicsko, M. M. (2007). The perceptual approach to teacher dispositions: The effective teacher as an effective person. In M. E. Diez & J. Raths (Eds.), *Dispositions in teacher education* (pp. 53–90). Charlotte, NC: Information Age Publishing.

CHAPTER 12

Standard Nine: Vision

W. Robert Houston, University of Houston

Accomplished Teacher Educators . . .

Contribute to creating visions for teaching, learning, and teacher education that take into account such issues as technology, systemic thinking, and worldviews.

RATIONALE

The twenty-first century is characterized by increasingly rapid changes in knowledge, technology, and globalization with changes bordering on *revolution* rather than *evolution* because of their rapidity. Education is at the center of this revolution. Teacher educators need not just understand the impact of revolutionary developments, but translate them for prospective and in-service teachers who work directly with children and youth—who think of the ipod, laptop computer, cell phone, and ready accessibility of the Internet as a normal part of their lives. Knowledge is reported to be doubling and redoubling at an astronomical rate and instantaneous international events a normal part of the 6 p.m. evening news (Hawking, 1988; Naisbitt, 1984; Toffler, 1970).

Education today is very different from that of a quarter century ago, and teacher educators must not only understand and use current innovations, but be prepared to embrace evolving technologies, revised content, and different ways to teach. Change is occurring more rapidly today than ever before. Events, innovations and inventions, wars and religion, economics and poverty, learning theory and brain research, social status and technology all impact almost every aspect of education and teacher education. With rapidly accelerating changes, teacher educators can no longer simply reflect on current conditions; effective teacher educators attempt to lead with experimentation, research, and enhanced program design. They are students of future changes.

Education has traditionally *followed* rather than *led* changes in society, and teacher education has too often lagged behind K–12 innovations. Children and youth tend to be the early adopters of innovations, with teachers needing to translate schooling into the new language of their students, but often they are less adaptable than needed. School districts implement recent trends in classroom management, curriculum content and instructional practices that teachers are expected to use. Teacher educators, assuming roles yet more removed from the learning of children/youth and school procedures, need to embrace their role as change agents, understand the impact teacher education has on classroom practices, and be early adopters of new configurations of learning (Rogers, 2003). Effective teacher educators are firmly in the forefront of educational change.

The rationale supporting this standard is derived from an analysis of the changes in education over the past century, quarter century, or even the past decade. Educational practices of only twenty-five years ago are already almost as extinct as the dinosaur. Compare the ideal classroom of that era (movie projector, slide projector, printed encyclopedia and other reference books) with those of today (power point, digital technology, wireless laptop computers, and online, real-time searches of the World Wide Web). Yet these changes are but harbingers of future developments. Brain-based education (Jenson, 2008), for example, provides a glimpse of potential future educational developments; is it the wave of the future or a false trail in the improvement of education?

Increasingly, education is impacted by changes throughout the world (Gladwell, 2000). Competition for good jobs has increased with globalization. People in India may answer our service calls about problems with technology; the Irish are calculating our financial records; Mexicans are picking our fruit; the Japanese are making an increasing proportion of our automobiles; and many toys and clothes are manufactured in China. Such competition and increased need for advanced education has resulted in greater emphasis in schools on science and mathematics. Thomas L. Friedman's book, *The World is Flat,* paints a compelling picture of the world we currently live in and projects potential future scenarios with serious implications for educators (Friedman, 2005).

In their own practice, teacher educators not only have access to this technology, but a professional obligation to use it in their instruction and research. They also need to rely on valid educational research, brain studies, societal trends, and other valid approaches to a better understanding of learning. While research findings have become more accessible, they often reflect uneven quality and importance. Teacher educators not only contribute to the profession's research base, but also help teachers and other educators cull and interpret findings. They draw not only on summaries of recent research (e.g., Cochran-Smith et al., 2005; Cochran-Smith et al. 2008) and valid individual studies, but also help prospective and experienced teachers to discern between interesting yet invalid findings and those with promise for greater understanding.

THEORETICAL OR EMPIRICAL BASE

Other standards specify needed knowledge of content, learning theory, instructional practices, and social trends—all indicators of the professional teacher educator, but knowing these without applying them to potential future directions, programs, and research makes such knowledge and practice less effective.

Most innovations, particularly in the social sciences, have occurred in the past century when a person examined a problem, issue, or invention from a different perspective. The operant word is *examined*. Teacher educators need to think about current research, innovative practice, needs of constituents, and put them in perspective of evolving social, economic, learning theory, and educational environmental trends. Developing teacher education programs, no matter how interesting they might be, are of no value if they prepare teachers for schools of the past rather than schools and societies of the present and future.

Technology continues to make major strides that influence professional education (for a comprehensive review of the extensiveness of this, see *Education Week,* May 4, 2006). For example, there is an evolving genre of serious technologically based games that provide players with opportunities to learn and understand complex situations or different points of view. These promise new and innovative instructional strategies. While computer-based games were first designed as entertainment for children and young-at-heart (regardless of their age), they are rapidly providing the substance for teacher education.

Societal trends are reshaping America from rural to urban, from isolationism to world power to shared power, from factory-based industrial revolution to postmodern society, from primarily a white and Christian society to one increasingly multicultural, multiethnic, multi-language, and multireligion. No longer can schools deliver a single grade-level-based and industrial-revolution-dominated program that is directed to a narrow portion of the population. Yet many prospective teachers have a limited experience with diversity (Hollins & Guzman, 2005). Turner (2007) identified two major blind spots in prospective teachers' visions of culturally responsive teaching: classroom management and parental involvement, two areas greatly influenced by cultural and ethnic mores.

Haviland (2008) summarized data from a yearlong qualitative study to chronicle ways white teachers used to insulate themselves from implications of social inequality. Sleeter (2008), responding to a request to write a letter to the forty-fourth President of the United States, focused on the need to prepare teachers who "can envision diverse students as constructive participants in a multicultural democracy" (p. 212).

Teacher educators must not only recognize the revolutionary changes in society, education, economics, worldview, and the growing disparity among citizens, but prepare teachers to challenge the status quo and teach for the future, not the past. How? By recognizing the changes that have occurred in the past quarter century and recognize the increasing thrusts of change in technology, and the disparity between the "haves" and "have-nots" in America and the implication of an under-educated populace.

FOCUS OF THIS STANDARD

Standard nine provides a visionary thrust to teacher educator knowledge, understanding, and experience. Effective teacher educators think about future directions and needs of society. While they are students of history so as not to be "destined to relive it," they draw on history and current events to design programs, inform teaching and scholarship, and educate prospective and practicing teachers using the most recent innovations, based on the most viable research in learning theory, sociology, instructional technology, and current events, all in a seamless process. This is not a stand-alone standard, but one that is embedded in every aspect of professional life.

DEMONSTRATING THE STANDARD

Examples of Standard Nine Accomplishment:

- Contributing to the design or modification of a teacher education program or courses needing to be updated. Their contributions, however, should demonstrate knowledge of recent trends in education, technology, and society, and consideration of promising trends and technological innovations. This might include authoring or coauthoring individual courses, multiple courses, fieldwork for the program, or the program's rationale and general framework. The criteria to be applied to these developing instructional strategies and content, however, focus on the extent to which the revised course or experience reflects the most recent research and technology, meets the needs of teachers in schools today, and considers potential changes in the near future.
- Developing educational games or simulations for use in teacher education that effectively change teachers' practices is a second illustration of a way to demonstrate mastery of Standard Nine.
- Constructing school-based seminars to instruct and support novice or experienced teachers might be oriented toward general induction or toward implementing a major curricular innovation. Research on, and evaluation of, teacher education programs or components of programs are examples of leadership under this standard. The key to demonstrating this standard is not only the extent to which the activity involves consideration of recent effective practices and research, but also that it provides for future innovations and changes in society, technology, and globalization.

Indicators for Standard Nine Include:

- Participates actively in learning communities that focus on educational change
- Demonstrates innovation in the field of teacher education

- Demonstrates qualities of an early adopter of technology and new configurations of learning
- Pursues actively new knowledge of global issues
- Supports innovation adoption with research
- Relates new knowledge about global issues to own practice and K–12 classroom teaching

Artifacts for Standard Nine Include:

- Grant writing activity
- Evidence of participation in learning communities
- Reflective journals
- Course syllabi
- Course assignments
- Student work samples
- Evidence of self-directed learning in innovative methodologies
- Evidence of using new and evolving technologies or content in teaching and learning

REFERENCES

Cochran-Smith, M., & Zeichner, K. M. (Eds.). (2005). *Studying teacher education: The report of the AERA panel on research and teacher education.* Mahwah, NJ: Lawrence Erlbaum Associates.

Cochran-Smith, M., Feiman-Nemser, S., McIntyre, J., & Demers, K. (Eds.). (2008). *Handbook of research on teacher education: Enduring questions in changing contexts.* (3rd ed.). Mahwah, NJ: Taylor & Francis Publishing.

Education Week. (2006). *Technology counts 2006: The information edge: Using data to accelerate achievement. 25*(35) Retrieved January 15, 2008 from www.edweek.org/ew/toc/2006/05/04/index.html

Elliott, E. J. (2004). *Responses to Four Questions about Teacher Educator Standards.* Invited Presentation to the Commission, Annual Meeting of the Association of Teacher Educators, Dallas, TX.

Friedman, T. L. (2005). *The world is flat.* New York: Farrar, Straus and Giroux.

Gladwell, M. (2000). *The tipping point.* Boston, MA: Little, Brown and Company.

Haviland, V. S. (2008). "Things get glossed over." Rearticulating the silencing power of whiteness in education. *Journal of Teacher Education, 59*(1), 40–54.

Hawking, S. W. (1988). *A brief history of time*. New York, NY: Bantam Press.

Hollins, E., & Guzman, M. (2005). Research on preparing teachers for diverse populations. In M. Cochran-Smith & K. Zeichner (Eds.), *Studying teacher education* (pp. 477–548). Mahwah, NJ: Lawrence Erlbaum.

Jenson, E. P. (2008). A fresh look at brain-based education. *Phi Delta Kappan, 89*(6), 408–417.

Naisbitt, J. (1984). *Megatrends*. New York, NY: Warner Communications.

Rogers, E. M. (2003). *Diffusion of innovations* (5th ed.). New York, NY: Free Press.

Sleeter, C. (2008). An invitation to support diverse students through teacher education. *Journal of Teacher Education, 59*(3), 212–219.

Toffler, A. (1970). *Future Shock*. New York, NY: Bantam Books.

Turner, J. D. (2007). Beyond cultural awareness: Prospective teachers' visions of culturally responsive literacy teaching. *Action in Teacher Education. 29*(3), 12–24.

Part III

MULTIPLE VOICES:
EXAMPLES OF APPLYING THE
STANDARDS ACROSS DISCIPLINES

CHAPTER 13

A Multicultural Approach to ATE's Standards for Teacher Educators

Carl A. Grant and Melissa Gibson
University of Wisconsin, Madison

As a teacher educator, Carl is a Hoefs Bascom Professor of Teacher Education. He teaches both undergraduate and graduate courses and is the codirector of the elementary/middle school student teacher program. Melissa is a graduate student and university supervisor of K–8 student teachers and recently taught school on Chicago's South Side at Chicago International Charter School, Basil Campus. We both are centrally concerned with helping all teachers better educate all children. As scholars within multicultural education, we recognize that children in schools are changing—classrooms in the United States are increasingly populated by students of color, non-native English speakers, and students from low-income families, while teachers remain overwhelmingly white, middle-class females (for more on the demographic imperative, see Banks et al., 2005; Cochran-Smith, Davis, & Fries, 2004; Gay, 1993).

What is more, we contend that although all children *can* and *should* succeed, they have not always done so, due largely to an inequitable educational system embedded within and the product of a larger, and just as inequitable, social system. Therefore, in order to better educate *all* children, teachers today have to be adept at building cultural bridges (Gay, 1993); they have to be attuned to the unique needs of diverse learners; and they have to be committed to catalyzing equitable educational opportunities for all children, regardless of race, class, gender, or ability. To that end, and in our dual role as teacher educators and multicultural education scholars, we focus on developing in our pre-service teachers the capacity (i.e., knowledge, skills, dispositions) to teach effectively, successfully, and fairly, whoever the students are in their classrooms.

While we want our pre-service teachers to realize success with their diverse students, our ultimate vision is much grander. Multicultural education is about far more than ensuring academic success for all students. In fact, such a simplified statement these days is riddled with the political and implicitly racist underpinnings of *No Child Left Behind*, which declares that all children WILL learn without any acknowledgement of or recourse for systemic barriers to that success (Grant, 2006). What, then, is multicultural education advocating? There are numerous definitions and typologies (see Banks, 2004; Bennett, 2001; Cochran-Smith, 2003; Gollnick & Chin, 2006; Sleeter & Grant, 1999), and the following one by Banks and Banks is representative:

> multicultural education is an idea, an educational reform movement, and a process whose major goal is to change the structure of educational institutions so that male and female students, exceptional students, and students who are members of diverse racial, ethnic, language, and cultural groups will have an equal chance to achieve academically in school. (2001, p. 1)

To this end, multicultural education is explicitly concerned with restructuring schools, teaching, and curriculum to meet the unique needs of racially, linguistically, physically, and socioeconomically diverse learners equitably (Banks, 2004; Gollnick & Chinn, 2006) and, ultimately, promote social justice (Grant & Agosto, 2008; Nieto, 2000; Sleeter, 2004; Grant & Sleeter, 2007). Multicultural education is a philosophy that recognizes and values the diversity of the United States; it is a reform movement advocating structural, systemic change of the American educational enterprise; and it is a process of behaving and thinking in education that promotes equity and justice (Gay, 2004). At its core, multicultural education is concerned with identifying and theorizing practices that will achieve these ends, with an emphasis on humanizing constructivist pedagogies, such as culturally relevant and responsive teaching and multicultural social justice teaching (Bartolome, 1994; Gay, 2000; Ladson-Billings, 1995; Grant & Sleeter, 2007; Villegas & Lucas, 2002.

The implication for teacher education programs, including our own, is that our pre-service teachers are expected to know the histories, cultures, learning preferences, and linguistic challenges of culturally diverse students; to have an extensive and varied pedagogical toolkit that can be adapted to their specific students; to collect and analyze evidence and use that evidence to foster improved learning opportunities; and to question how well schooling is furthering democratic goals and values (McDiarmid & Clevenger-Bright, 2008). Thus, central to our work as both teacher educators and multicultural scholars is equipping teachers with the knowledge, skills, dispositions, and practices to educate all students effectively and fairly. In doing so, it is our ultimate hope that teachers and their students will become advocates, activists, and change agents not merely for fairer schools but also for a fairer and more just society (Anyon, 2006).

RESPONDING TO THE ATE STANDARDS FOR TEACHER EDUCATORS

The Standards as a Whole

In our dual role as scholars and teacher educators, we are guided by both the theoretical underpinnings of multicultural education as well as the practical demands of university teaching. Indeed, we are ultimately concerned with praxis, or the nexus of theory and practice, particularly related to teacher capacity (Grant & Agosto, 2006). The great benefit of the ATE Standards for Teacher Educators is that they give voice to the need for rigor and the pre-eminence of praxis in teacher education; they articulate the multiple layers of our work; and they are a document that all can agree is important. However, these nine standards are primarily a background: It is our job as teacher educators to bring them to life by enriching them with specific practices[1] and to link them to our vision for educational reform. We have selected standards one (teaching), two (cultural competence and social justice), and seven (public advocacy) as a primary focus here using our dual perspective of multicultural and teacher education.

We must note, however, that our selection of these standards is somewhat arbitrary. *All* of the standards speak to our complex and multifaceted work within both fields; unfortunately, we are constrained by space limitations. As the standards are written, it appears that multicultural education has been relegated solely to standard two (cultural competence and social justice), but it is for certain that multicultural education is guided by, implicit in, and sits at the nexus of all nine teacher education standards. We could just as easily have delved into any of the remaining six standards in our multicultural enrichment of the standards. Examples of specific standards follow.

Standard Three: Scholarship

Our work with pre-service teachers is grounded in the original scholarship of multicultural education. From syntheses (e.g., Banks & Banks, 2004; Darling-Hammond & Bransford, 2005; Gibson, 1976; Sleeter & Grant, 1987) to field research (e.g., Grant & Sleeter, 1996; Ladson-Billings, 1995; Sleeter, 1992) and comprehensive pedagogical paradigms (e.g. Gay, 2000; Grant & Sleeter, 2007; Villegas & Lucas, 2002), multicultural scholarship is central to the structure and content of our teacher education courses and student teacher observation and support. As such, and given the current political and educational climate, we recognize the grave importance of (and our personal responsibility in) continuing to document and interrogate effective pedagogy, curriculum, and school structures for diverse learners, as well as to challenge those educational structures and practices that perpetuate inequality and leave unquestioned racism, classism, and other oppressive forces (see Grant, 2006; Grant & Agosto, 2008; Grant & Gillette, 2006a, b).

Standard Four: Professional Development

Among teacher educators, the quest to improve pre-service teachers' multicultural preparation and to catalyze personal and professional growth is driven by constant self-reflection, program evaluation, and sharing of best practices (e.g., King, 1991; Kumashiro, 2002; Ladson-Billings, 2006; Mueller & O'Connor, 2007; Nieto, 2006; Sleeter, 1992; Sleeter, Torres, & Laughlin, 2001). Reflection and documentation of our pedagogical choices is the primary way we improve instruction. In turn, the weaknesses, problems, and questions that arise in our classroom practice drive and inform our scholarship (e.g., Bartolome, 1994).

Standard Five: Program Development

Multicultural educators are centrally concerned with the development and reorganization of comprehensive multicultural and social justice teacher education programs (e.g., Beyer, 2001; Cochran-Smith et al., 1999; Quartz & TEP Research Group, 2003; Sleeter et al., 2005; Zygmunt-Fillwalk & Leitze, 2006). In fact, restructuring teacher education programs, and sharing the successes and struggles of that work, is central to preparing our students systematically to work with diverse student populations.

Standard Six: Collaboration

Particularly because multicultural scholars often work alone or in small numbers within teacher education programs, our work can only thrive through collaboration, whether that be across institutions (most evident in scholarship, e.g., Banks & Banks, 2004), between different disciplines and departments (e.g., Olson, Evans, & Schoenberg, 2007), or between K–12 schools/teachers, teacher associations and universities (e.g., Grant, Agosto, & Jetty, 2007).

Standard Eight: Teacher Education Profession

Multicultural scholars occupy dual positions as teacher educators. We serve as editors of journals, active participants in professional organizations, writers of scholarly and practical materials and other tools for pre-service courses and the entire field of education; and we are leaders in the field. Improving education for all students requires our active advocacy for teacher education and education in general.

Standard Nine: Vision

As we move forward in the twenty-first century, multicultural educators are concerned with our changing world and, in particular, the effects of globalization on classroom learning. To that end, we are in the forefront of conceptualizing the changes that must be made at the K–12 and university level to deal with both negative and positive influences of globalization (e.g., population mobility, cultural, environmental, and social interdependencies).

Clearly, all of the ATE standards guide our work within teacher and multicultural education, and our selection of standards one, two, and seven are arbitrary. These standards, however, speak strongly to our emphases within teacher education.

Standard One: Teaching

While there are certainly practices proven successful with particular students, and while we recognize the importance for teachers to understand cognition, human development, and other professional and content knowledge, we are also wary of the methods fetish in education (Bartolome, 1994). We certainly model best practices in our courses, often in a metacognitive way that makes explicit our lesson design and pedagogical choices. However, we are also aware that there are no silver bullets or magic pedagogies miraculously successful with all students.

Our practice as teacher educators is as much about modeling effective practices as it is about teaching our students to be critical of those very practices (Grant & Gillette, 2006a, b). In addition, effective teaching of diverse students is, at its core, about teacher beliefs and ideologies (see Bartolome, 2004; King, 1991; Ladson-Billings, 1995). Therefore, teacher beliefs and ideologies are the foundations of our courses, from Introduction to Elementary Education to the student teaching seminar. While we may, for example, employ and teach humanizing, student-centered pedagogies that build upon personal knowledge, often quite successful with diverse learners (Bartolome, 1994), their very success reflects the teacher's belief that it is *worth* building on students' knowledge and life experiences, however varied and marginalized they may be (Grant & Sleeter, 2007).

We also believe that, while a toolkit of varied assessments and practices is central to success, whether with pre-service teachers or K–12 students, good teaching most importantly emphasizes higher-order thinking and a critical analytic lens. It is not enough to model teaching to multiple intelligences, to employ the latest technological fad, or to move beyond the blue-book exam to portfolios or journaling. Rather, modeling effective teaching in the pre-service classroom requires a comprehensive, self-conscious pedagogy akin to Ladson-Billings' (1995) notion of culturally relevant pedagogy, which is as much about *good teaching* as it is about cultural competence.[2] Such an approach maintains fluid student-teacher relationships, demonstrates connectedness with all students, develops a community of learners, and encourages collaboration.

Teacher educators explicitly teach, and thereby empower, their pre-service teachers with a pedagogical language that declares knowledge is not static, must be viewed critically, is produced through dialectical relationships; and, as Werstch (1998) argues, human performances are never individual performances but always mediated by other people, cultural tools, and artifacts. Teacher educators must also scaffold learning experiences for their students (Vygotsky, 1978) so that pre-service teachers can become critical and passionate consumers of knowledge committed to the success of all students (Grant & Gillette, 2006a, b). Just as in Ladson-Billings' theory of culturally relevant pedagogy, this approach produces students who achieve academically, demonstrate cultural competence, and understand and critique the social order.

What does such an approach look like in a university classroom of pre-service teachers? There is a rich body of reflective literature documenting various teacher educators' practices, lessons, and projects designed to foster critical thinking and knowledge consumption among their students. For example, in an effort to equip teachers with the tools to critique the viewpoints of curricula and to identify misrepresentations, Gay (2002) advocates engaging pre-service teachers in a critical analysis of cultural representations within pop culture, popular media, and academic textbooks.

In order to foster constructivist approaches among future teachers, Villegas and Lucas (2002) advocate metacognitive approaches where students rank themselves on a constructivist/transmission model continuum and monitor their ideological progress over the course of a class or program. In addition, experiential learning (Olson, Evans, & Schoenberg, 2007) should also play a prominent role in an effective multicultural and constructivist teacher education classroom, whether that be through cultural plunges (Nieto, 2006), study/teaching immersion experiences (e.g. Sleeter, 2001; Zygmunt-Fillwalk & Leitze, 2006), partnerships with diverse and constructivist classrooms (e.g. Villegas & Lucas, 2002), or engaging teachers in action research (Caro-Bruce et al., 2007).

Ultimately, for teacher educators to model effective teaching practices we need to practice what we preach, and this means modeling far more than any single method or fad. If what we're advocating is a high-quality, rigorous education that will be successful for all students, then we must show pre-service teachers what effective teaching looks like and how to make it happen. If we want our students to become rigorous scholar-teachers, agents for social change, and bridge makers not only of cultures but also of theory and practice, then our teacher education programs must be self-consciously designed explicitly to show our students what this looks like in practice.

The reform of a master's program at California State University, Monterey Bay is an excellent example of a teacher education program modeling effective practices for diverse learners (Sleeter et al., 2005). Finally, if we want our pre-service teachers to be able to evaluate critically the effectiveness of teaching and curricula for all students, we must model these practices in our university courses and in all school of education policies and procedures. We teach in an era of evidence; therefore, we must teach our students how to gather, analyze, and interpret evidence, and how to make instructional and pedagogical decisions based on their interpretations of that evidence (McDiarmid & Clevenger-Bright, 2008).

Standard Two: Cultural Competence & Social Justice

Cultural competence is the traditional arena of multicultural education, the often supplementary domain where our work is deemed relevant, and it is certainly central to multiculturalism. In order to teach the increasingly diverse students of America's classrooms effectively and fairly, our overwhelmingly white teacher candidates must recognize themselves as cultural beings benefitting from white privilege and social inequality (see King, 1991; Ladson-Billings, 2006; Mueller & O'Connor, 2007). Also, they must be aware that all teacher candidates, including pre-service teachers of color, have much to learn about diversity and changes introduced to education by global and local conditions.

Pre-service teachers must be knowledgeable about the cultural experiences of other groups, and not simply in terms of food, fairs, and festivals. Rather, they need to honor and value diverse funds of knowledge (Moll et al., 1992; Moll et al., 2004) as well as understand what it means to be marginalized, oppressed, and silenced by language differences, cultural barriers, or hegemonic narratives. This is an arena where scaffolding pre-service teachers' learning experiences is essential and often highly successful (see Cooper, 2007; Nieto, 2006; Rios, Trent, & Castaneda, 2003; Sleeter, Torres, & Laughlin, 2001).

In working to build cultural competence, our hope is to develop teachers' capacity to see from multiple viewpoints; to think, work, and move across multiple boundaries; to seek out multiple perspectives; to become advocates for justice and equity; and to reduce prejudice (Kumashiro, 2002; Olson, Evans, & Schoenberg, 2007). We want our preservice teachers to teach in support of a democratic agenda that values access to knowledge for all learners, a cultivation of democratic values, and a critical consumption of knowledge and education (McDiarmid & Clevenger-Bright, 2008).

It certainly seems, then, that we are promoting social justice. But herein lies a problem: The ATE Standards for Teacher Educators, like most other documents referencing social justice, fail to define exactly what social justice is (Grant & Agosto, 2008; North, 2006). In failing to do so, social justice remains a mirage, as explained by Michael Novak (2000). He references British-born economist and political philosopher Friedrich Hayek's assertion that "whole books and treatises have been written about social justice without ever offering a definition of it. It is allowed to float in the air as if everyone will recognize an instance of it when it appears" (p. 11).

Is social justice, as referenced by the ATE standards, referring to distributive equality and cultural recognition? Is it referring to a social reconstructionist project of transforming schools and society? Or is it merely referring to good human relations and fairness? And what, precisely, does fairness mean? The problem with allowing social justice "to float in the air as if everyone will recognize an instance of it when it appears," by not defining it at all or by narrowly defining it in relation to teacher capacity, is that it leads to superficial, ineffective, and uninformed actions by teacher educators and pre-service teachers (Grant & Agosto, 2008).

Therefore, central to our work as multicultural educators is defining social justice, both in scholarship and in our classroom practice, and in connecting it and teacher capacity to the good of society as a whole. We also advocate for developing tools of adjudication by which to measure and evaluate the social justice efforts of teachers and teacher educators. Too often, teacher education pays lip service to social justice without ever advancing it beyond Hayek's mirage (Grant & Agosto, 2008). By defining social justice substantively and by creating evaluative tools for assessing our actions, we can move social justice from a mirage to an actual guiding principle of education.

Standard Seven: Public Advocacy

While our work as teacher educators is centrally about helping our pre-service students to become more effective and fairer teachers for all students, we also recognize that improving classroom teaching alone is not enough to produce educational or social equity. Classroom teachers can only be as effective and transformational as the educational system within which they are operating. Unfortunately, the educational system they are currently working within is designed to perpetuate inequality.

Educational inequity is not an accident. Rather, it is the product of racist, assimilationist, and unjust policies designed to perpetuate the privileges of the dominant class (Kozol, 1992, 2005; Orfield & Lee, 2005). Therefore, as teacher educators committed to supporting our teacher candidates and as multicultural scholars attuned to the need for policies and practices that equitably support and nurture a diverse polity, we take seriously our role as public advocates, not merely for equitable education but for more just policies in our communities and our nation as a whole.

Particularly in our current political and educational climate that values the market more than individual citizens, that sees inequality as a technical issue rather than a structural one (Grant, 2006; Lipman, 2006), and that ignores our nation's deeply entrenched history of racism and oppression, our work as public advocates for social change is critical. Current educational reforms, such as *No Child Left Behind*, are ostensibly committed to the success of all children, but the on-the-ground reality of twenty-first century school reform is that it is patently not in the public interest, including the interests of diverse children. Rather, it supports private and corporate interests, usually in direct opposition to the needs and interests of nonwhite, low-income individuals (Lipman, 2006).

NCLB and its accompanying accountability, standards, and data-driven reforms not only delegitimize other forms of research, inquiry, and education (Barone, 2006), but they also actively produce differential student outcomes (Cornbleth, 2006; Gillborn, 2006). What makes this particularly tragic is that many in the United States seem oblivious to the ways our current policy makers and politicians ignore and attack our public interests. As Barone (2006) describes:

> The populace seems lost, distracted, largely unconcerned as one of the last bastions of hope for what Dewey called the Great community—the public school—is betrayed by policymakers who are failing to act in the public's interests in ways that most do not fully comprehend (p. 215).

Therefore, teacher educators, as researchers, scholars, and *citizens*, must speak out against the current wave of neoliberal policies that are clearly not in the interest of children or the public. To work within education and to not speak out against them is a moral failing: education researchers have an "obligation to take more courageous and bold steps in the face of retreats from all things public" (Ladson-Billings & Tate, 2006, p. 12). In speaking out in advocacy for those who are marginalized by our political and social systems, it is not enough to call attention to education in isolation. Rather, we must also call attention to greater social inequities, such as structural and systemic racism, and argue for systematic, overarching social change (Ladson-Billings & Tate, 2006; Lipman, 2006). In fact, as Anyon (2006) argues, research in the public interest is fundamentally about things other than education.

Educational researchers need to be advocates for reform in all areas of society. Just as our pre-service teachers can only be as effective and transformative as the schools in which they operate, schools can only be as effective and transformative as the society in which they operate. Comprehensive urban school reform, for example, if it occurred, or even if it seemed to 'succeed' according to accountability measures, would ultimately fail students unless it were coupled with adequate jobs in all sectors of the economy, resources to support college educations, the guarantee of a living wage, and access and support of a flourishing life (Nussbaum, 2000).

In advocating for the public interest, teacher educators must set their sights on the democratic ideals that supposedly guide the American educational project:

> In the Declaration of Independence, the Preamble of the Constitution, the Bill of Rights—are America's ideals: freedom, dignity, equality for all

people, justice, and a fair opportunity. . . . We must begin the conversation at the point where we admit that we have failed to align our practices with [these] democratic ideals; accept that we have a dual society
and a racist discourse; and have done little as a nation to foster intergroup
integration and harmony (Grant, 2006, p.170).

We can then present new visions of what democracy can be, new visions of how schools can further that democratic project, and new visions of educational and social reform.

CONCLUSION

From the perspective of multicultural education, our goal here has been
to elaborate upon the generalities of the ATE Standards for Teacher Educators. We have sought to name our best practices, to outline the ideologies and pedagogical beliefs that support our work, and to problematize
key ideas in our field. In looking at the indicators, the rationale, and
the artifacts called for in the standards, one sees that this is a well-
researched document, inclusive of scholars representing a variety of
viewpoints and addressing the multifaceted work of teacher educators.
This document provides a solid background for our work, and we have
discussed here the ways in which we build upon and give specificity to
this background. The standards themselves are not providing the vision
for our work, but rather, they are the structure and the outline of what
teacher education work is. We have then enriched this background with
a multicultural vision.

However, while the standards are well researched, inclusive, and
comprehensive, they strike us as functioning still as rhetoric. There is
certainly no argument about their validity and importance, but what
happens now that these standards have been added to the teacher education discourse? How well will they accomplish what they set out
to, and how will we evaluate and measure our progress? Where is the
language moving towards action, and then where are the tools of adjudication to measure this action? As so often happens within teacher
education, we have defined good teaching, we have defined our outcomes and objectives, but we have not given consideration to assessing our progress against these outcomes and objectives.

Multicultural education is as guilty of this as any other field (see Cochran-Smith, Davis, & Fries, 2004; Grant & Agosto, 2008; Sleeter, 2001). It is as we explained earlier regarding social justice: By not defining the term and then by not giving tools for assessing our work towards it, most teachers' and teacher educators' efforts are superficial, uninformed, or ineffective. What the ATE Standards for Teacher Educators have going for them is that they have taken the first step, they have defined high-quality teacher educators. Now, we must turn to the next step.

Certainly, tools of adjudication are outside the stated boundaries of this document, but they are definitely within the bounds of the organization. How has ATE dealt with this responsibility? If it has not, we must make this happen, or else the hard work of providing standards for teacher educators threatens to prove meaningless.

NOTES

1. Indeed, by enriching the standards with multiple perspectives, it is possible to resist the oft-hegemonizing force of educational standardization. After all, the very idea of standards is contentious: While we absolutely see merit in clarifying learning outcomes and teacher competencies, we are also acutely aware of the possibility that standards can become an oppressive force. This has most often been documented in regard to state standards in K–12 subject areas (see Lipman, 2006; Sleeter & Stillman, 2005), but it certainly applies to teacher educators, as well.

2. Many of these aspects of teaching are included in the ATE standards, but they are erroneously included under cultural competence and social justice, where one finds that teacher educators should "Demonstrate connecting instruction to students [lives]"; "Model how to identify and design instruction appropriate to students' stages of development, learning styles, linguistic skills, strengths and needs"; and, "Teach a variety of assessment tools that meet the needs of diverse learners." These are essential tools for teaching.

REFERENCES

Anyon, J. (2006). What should count as educational research: Notes toward a new paradigm. In G. Ladson-Billings & W. Tate (Eds.), *Education research in the public interest: Social justice, action and policy* (pp. 17–25). New York: Teachers College Press.

Banks, J. (2004). Multicultural education: Historical development, dimensions, and practice. In J. Banks & C. Banks (Eds.), *Handbook of research on multicultural education* (2nd ed., pp. 3–29). San Francisco: Jossey Bass.

Banks, J., & Banks, C. (Eds.) (2001). *Multicultural education: Issues and perspectives* (4th ed.). Boston: Allyn & Bacon.

Banks, J., & Banks, C. (Eds.) (2004). *Handbook of research on multicultural education* (2nd ed.). San Francisco: Jossey-Bass.

Banks, J., Cochran-Smith, M., Moll, L., Richert, A., Zeichner, K., LePage, P., Darling-Hammond, L., Duffy, H., & McDonald, M. (2005). Teaching diverse learners. In L. Darling-Hammond & J. Bransford (Eds.), *Preparing teachers for a changing world: What teachers should know and be able to do* (pp. 232–274). San Francisco: Jossey-Bass.

Barone, T. (2006). Making educational history: Qualitative inquiry, artistry, and the public interest. In G. Ladson-Billings & W. Tate (Eds.), *Education research in the public interest: Social justice, action and policy* (pp. 213–230). New York: Teachers College Press.

Bartolome, L. (2004). Critical pedagogy and teacher education: Radicalizing prospective teachers. *Teacher Education Quarterly*, 31(1), 97–122.

Bartolome, L. (1994). Beyond the methods fetish: Toward a humanizing pedagogy. *Harvard Educational Review*, 64(2), 173–194.

Bennett, C. (2001). Genres of research in multicultural education. *Review of Educational Research*, 71(2), 171–217.

Beyer, L. (2001). The value of critical perspectives in teacher education. *Journal of Teacher Education*, 52(2), 151–163.

Caro-Bruce, C., Flessner, R., Klehr, M., & Zeichner, K. (2007). *Creating equitable classrooms through action research*. Thousand Oaks, CA: Corwin Press.

Cochran-Smith, M. (2003). The multiple meanings of multicultural teacher education: A conceptual framework. *Teacher Education Quarterly*, 30(2), 7–26.

Cochran-Smith, M., Albert, L., Dimattia, P., Freedman, S., Jackson, R., Mooney, J., Neisler, O., Peck, A., & Zollers, N. (1999). Seeking social justice: A teacher education faculty's self-study. *International Journal of Leadership in Education: Theory and Practice*, 2(3), 229–253.

Cochran-Smith, M., Davis, D., & Fries, K. (2004). Multicultural teacher education: Research, practice, and policy. In J. Banks & C. Banks (Eds.). *Handbook of research in multicultural education* (2nd ed., pp. 931–975). San Francisco: Jossey-Bass.

Cooper, J. (2007). Strengthening the case for community-based learning in teacher education. *Journal of Teacher Education*, 58(3), 245–255.

Cornbleth, C. (2006). Curriculum and students: Diverting the public interest. In G. Ladson-Billings & W. Tate (Eds.), *Education research in the public in-*

terest: Social justice, action and policy (pp. 199–212). New York: Teachers College Press.

Darling-Hammond, L., & Bransford, J. (2005). *Preparing teachers for a changing world: What teachers should learn and be able to do*. San Francisco: Jossey-Bass.

Gay, G. (1993). Building cultural bridges: A bold proposal for teacher education. *Education and Urban Society, 25*(3), 285–299.

Gay, G. (2000). *Culturally responsive teaching: Theory, research and practice*. New York: Teachers College Press.

Gay, G. (2002). Preparing for culturally responsive teaching. *Journal of Teacher Education, 53*(2), 106–116.

Gay, G. (2004). Curriculum theory and multicultural education. In J. Banks & C. Banks (Eds.), *Handbook of research in multicultural education* (2nd ed., pp. 30–49). San Francisco: Jossey-Bass.

Gibson, M. (1976). Approaches to multicultural education in the United States: Some concepts and assumptions. *Anthropology and Education Quarterly, 7*, 7–18.

Gillborn, D. (2006). Public interest and the interests of white people are not the same: Assessment, education policy, and racism. In G. Ladson-Billings & W. Tate (Eds.), *Education research in the public interest: Social justice, action and policy* (pp. 173–195). New York: Teachers College Press.

Gollnick, D., & Chinn, P. (2006) *Multicultural education in a pluralistic society*. Needham, MA: Pearson.

Grant, C. (2006). Multiculturalism, race, and the public interest: Hanging on to great-great-granddaddy's legacy. In G. Ladson-Billings & W. Tate (Eds.), *Education research in the public interest: Social justice, action and policy* (pp. 158–172). New York: Teachers College Press.

Grant C., & Agosto, V. (2006). A multicultural learning community as a site of praxis. *Praxis, 1*(1), 17–28.

Grant, C., & Agosto, V. (2008). Teacher capacity and social justice in teacher education. In Cochran-Smith, M., Feiman-Nemser, S., McIntyre, J., & Demers, K. (Eds.), *Handbook of research in teacher education Enduring questions in changing contexts* (3rd ed., pp. 176–200). Mahwah, NJ: Taylor & Francis Publishing.

Grant, C., Agosto, V., & Jetty, R. (2007). *Achievement gaps, diversity, and power: Change/transition with teachers at the center*. Madison, WI: Wisconsin Education Association Council.

Grant, C., & Gillette. M. (2006a). *Learning to teach everyone's children: Equity, empowerment and education that is multicultural*. Belmont, CA: Thompson.

Grant, C., & Gillette M. (2006b). A candid talk to teacher educators about effectively preparing teachers who can teach everyone's children. *Journal of Teacher Education*, *57*(3), 292–299.

Grant, C., & Sleeter C. (1996). *After the school bell rings* (2nd ed.). London: Falmer Press.

Grant, C., & Sleeter C. (2007). *Turning on learning: Five approaches for multicultural teaching plans for race, class, gender and disability*. New York: Wiley.

King, J. (1991). Dysconscious racism: Identity, ideology, and the miseducation of teachers. *The Journal of Negro Education 60*(2), 133–146.

Kozol, J. (1992). *Savage inequalities: Children in America's school*. New York: Harper Collins.

Kozol, J. (2005). *The shame of the nation: The restoration of apartheid in America*. New York: Crown.

Kumashiro, K. (2002). *Troubling education: Queer activism and antioppressive pedagogy*. New York: Routledge Falmer.

Ladson-Billings, G. (1995). Toward a theory of culturally relevant pedagogy. *American Educational Research Journal*, *32*(3), 465–491.

Ladson-Billings, G. (2006). It's not the culture of poverty, it's the poverty of culture: The problem with teacher education. *Anthropology and Education Quarterly*, *37*(2), 104–109.

Ladson-Billings, G., & Tate, W. F. (2006). *Education research in the public interest: Social justice, action, and policy*. New York: Teachers College Press.

Lipman, P. (2006). This *is* America 2005: The political economy of education reform against the public interest. In G. Ladson-Billings & W. Tate (Eds.), *Education research in the public interest: Social justice, action and policy* (pp. 98–116). New York: Teachers College Press.

McDiarmid, G. W., & Clevenger-Bright, M. (2008). Rethinking teacher capacity. In Cochran-Smith, M., Feiman-Nemser, S., McIntyre, J., & Demers, K. (Eds.), *Handbook of research in teacher education: Enduring questions in changing contexts* (3rd ed., pp. 135–156). London: Taylor and Francis Publishing.

Moll, L., Amanti, C. Neff, D. & Gonalez, N. (1992). Funds of knowledge for teaching: Using a qualitative approach to connect homes and classrooms. *Theory Into Practice*, *31*(2), 132–141.

Moll, L., & Gonzalez, N. (2004). Engaging life: A funds of knowledge approach to multicultural education. In J. Banks & C. Banks (Eds.). *Handbook of research on multicultural education* (pp. 628–634). New York: Macmillan.

Mueller, J., & O'Connor, C. (2007). Telling and retelling about self and "others": How pre-service teachers (re)interpret privilege and disadvantage in one college classroom. *Teaching and Teacher Education*, *23*, 840–856.

Nieto, J. (2006). The cultural plunge: Cultural immersion as a means of promoting self-awareness and cultural sensitivity among student teachers. *Teacher Education Quarterly, 33*(1), 75–84.

Nicto, S. (2000). *Affirming diversity.* New York: Longman.

North, C. (2006). More than words? Delving into the substantive meaning(s) of "social justice" in education. *Review of Educational Research, 76*(4), 507–535.

Novak, M. (2000). Defining social justice. *First Things, 108*, 11–13.

Nussbaum, M. (2000). *Women and human development: The capabilities approach.* New York: Cambridge University Press.

Olson, C., Evans, R., & Shoenberg, R. (2007). *At home in the world: Bridging the gap between internationalization and multicultural education.* Washington, DC: American Council on Education.

Orfield, G., & Lee, C. (2005). *Why segregation matters: Poverty and educational inequality.* Cambridge, MA: Harvard Civil Rights Project.

Quartz, K., & TEP Research Group (2003). "Too angry to leave": Supporting new teachers' commitment to transform urban schools. *Journal of Teacher Education, 54*(2), 99–111.

Rios, F., Trent, A., & Castaneda, L. (2003). Social perspective taking: Advancing empathy and advocating justice. *Equity & Excellence in Education, 36*(1), 5–i4.

Sleeter, C. (1992). *Keepers of the American dream.* London: Falmer Press.

Sleeter, C. (2001). Preparing teachers for culturally diverse schools: Research and the overwhelming presence of whiteness. *Journal of Teacher Education, 52*(2), 94–106.

Sleeter, C. (2004). Critical multicultural curriculum and the standards movement. *English Teaching: Practice and Critique, 3*(2), 122–138.

Sleeter, C., & Grant, C. (1987). An analysis of multicultural education in the U. S. A. *Harvard Education Review, 57*, 421–444.

Sleeter, C., & Grant, C. (1999). *Making choices for multicultural education: Five approaches to race, class, and gender* (3rd ed.). Upper Saddle River, NJ: Merrill.

Sleeter, C., Hughes, B., Meador, E., Whang, P., Rogers, L., Blackwell, K., et al. (2005). Working an academically rigorous, multicultural program. *Equity and Excellence, 38*(4), 290–298.

Sleeter, C., & Stillman, J. (2005). Standardizing knowledge in a multicultural society. *Curriculum Inquiry, 35*(1), 27–46.

Sleeter, C., Torres, M., & Laughlin, P. (2001). Scaffolding conscientization through inquiry in teacher education. *Teacher Education Quarterly, 31*(1), 81–96.

Villegas, A., & Lucas, T. (2002). *Educating culturally responsive teachers: A coherent approach*. Albany, NY: State University of New York Press.

Vygotsky, L. (1930/1978). *Mind in society: The development of higher psychological processes*. Cambridge, MA: Harvard University Press.

Wertsch, J. (1998). *Mind as action*. New York: Oxford.

Zygmunt-Fillwalk, E., & Leitze, A. (2006). Promising practices in pre-service teacher preparation: The Ball State University Urban Semester. *Childhood Education*, *82*(5), 283–288.

CHAPTER 14

How School-Based Teacher Educators Exemplify the Standards

Mary Sowder, Utah Valley University

I have spent the better part of my life involved in discovering the art and science of teaching and learning. This rather startling (and somewhat distressing) revelation came to me as I thought about how to define my work as a teacher and as a teacher educator. I am a very "experienced" educator, which is to say I have thirty years of lived experience in the elementary classroom, combined with over two decades of mentoring novice teachers, and several years of teaching university courses in teacher education. These are overlapping, not consecutive, experiences and there is time left for me to learn a few new things.

In the twilight of my grade school career I decided that I needed to take a serious, firsthand look at the literature about knowledge of teaching. Changes in the focus and tenor of school policy formed in the wake of questionable national and local mandates for classroom practice inspired me to become more thoroughly informed about current research in teaching and learning. Because I thought that my practical experience might have something to add to the current discourse about educational policy, effective teaching practices, and teacher education, I enrolled in a doctoral program to obtain the credentials that might give my views credence with the educational community.

Through my current research with novice teachers, my experiences with university and grade school students, and my work with the Association of Teacher Educators' (ATE) Standards for Teacher Educators, my professional life has developed as overlapping and amorphous arenas. Just as puddles of watercolors on wet paper are unable to stay separate as soon as they touch, my work as a student, teacher, teacher educator, and mentor teacher blossom into one another, creating a muddle of multicolor blobs.

For me and for many other school-based mentor teachers and supervisors, our lived experiences in the classroom form a vital component of our vision of who we are as teacher educators. The line between learning about teaching and teaching about teaching becomes blurred as we constantly shift from one role to another. Any attempt to describe the concerns and challenges associated with any one area can only be considered in light of how those issues are affected by the hues of the other spheres. Our life and work in each arena contributes to the whole of our understanding about teaching and learning.

This chapter speaks to those who wonder if classroom teachers who mentor teacher candidates really meet the definition of a teacher educator as defined by the ATE Standards for Teacher Educators. Following a brief discussion of how standards are defined in this context, I present evidence from my experience as a member of a community of mentor teachers to support a definition of teacher educator that includes school-based personnel. Using my own professional narrative to represent how the work of school-based teacher educators addresses the ATE standards, I hope to illustrate "the richness and indeterminacy of our experiences as teachers and the complexity of our understandings of what teaching is and how others can be prepared to engage in this profession" (Carter, 1993, p. 5).

COMING TO TERMS WITH "STANDARDS"

In this era of standards, writers use the term in many different ways, seldom bothering to unpack the differences in meaning; standards become the answer to all questions. They are thought to provide the magic ingredient to restructuring all education (Andrews, 1997, p. 168).

The use of the term *standards* often sets off a chain reaction of excited discourse among teachers and other educators. They are often characterized as measures designed as part of a market-based perspective to create uniformity and a system of more centralized authority in teacher education (see Apple, 2001). Others view the conceptual and practice-based teaching standards, such as those promoted by the National Board for Professional Teaching Standards (NBPTS) (1989) and ATE's Standards for Teacher Educators (1996; 2008), as initiatives for teachers and teacher educators to gain control over their professional work. These standards are neither mandatory nor regulatory, but as Darling-Hammond (1999) cautions,

> Standards, like all reforms, hold their own dangers. Standard setting in all professions must be vigilant against the possibilities that practice could become constrained by the codification of knowledge that does not significantly acknowledge legitimate diversity of approaches or advances in the field; that access to practice could become overly restricted on grounds not directly related to competence; or that adequate learning opportunities for candidates to meet standards may not emerge on an equitable basis. (p. 39)

Unlike university-based teacher educators, "teachers, at least in the United States, historically have had little or no control over most of the mechanisms that determine professional standards" (Darling-Hammond, 1999, p. 11). NBPTS Certification was developed in the United States by a group of educators that included teachers who were "heavily involved in each step of the process, from writing standards, designing assessments and evaluating candidates" (NBPTS, n.d.). It is the integral participation of practitioners that gives the NBPTS creditability with teachers, just as the inclusion of teacher educators and other community leaders in the process allows National Board Certification to be generally accepted by the public as an indication of quality teaching.

The formation and subsequent revision of ATE's Standards for Teacher Educators included similar involvement. Drafts of the standards developed from a synthesis of research and experience were continually revised according to input from professionals across the United States. The revision was grounded in information gleaned from sets of pilot portfolios created by cross sections of teacher educators, including school-based teacher educators, and these individuals were involved in follow-up discussions in revising and refining the process.

The purpose of each of these documents lies not in the way they may be used to define practice, but in the way their use enables individuals to reflect on how their teaching affects their students, to examine how their efforts contribute to the larger community, and to imagine the possibilities for their future practice.

PROFESSIONAL STANDARDS AND
PROFESSIONAL IDENTITY

Because the bulk of my professional career has been centered in the elementary classroom, I begin my discussion of school-based educators as teacher educators by looking at how my teaching experiences in the context of a professional development school (PDS) influenced my understandings of standards-based practice. Two components of that experience that helped define, for me and for others, the important role of school-based mentor teachers as teacher educators: my work with teacher candidates and other mentor teachers in a professional development school, and my effort to become a National Board Certified Teacher (NBCT).

I describe how these elements facilitated reflection on my work as a teacher and mentor. I show how they influenced the ways in which I was then able to interpret and apply the ATE Standards for Teacher Educators to the work of school-based teacher educators. Finally, I explain how the process of creating a portfolio based on the ATE standards helped me form a vision for the future development of my practice as a teacher educator.

While mentor teachers are often acknowledged for their work with teacher candidates during field experiences that form part of traditional programs of preparation for the classroom, university-based teacher educators may fail to appreciate mentor teachers' professional expertise or their situated interpretations of educational theory and research. The practical orientation of mentor teachers' work with teacher candidates may be viewed as something less than, or at least fundamentally different from, the work of university faculty. But the evolving nature of mentored learning to teach as collaborative and critical reflection on experience (Schön, 1983) challenges this conception and strengthens the case for adding mentor teachers to the role of teacher educators.

The following narrative description describes how collaborative inquiry was enacted by school-based teacher educators in the context of a professional development school in order to illuminate how the fluid nature of our roles as teachers and teacher educators provide authentic, contextual motivation for discourse, research, and praxis.

SCHOOL-BASED TEACHER EDUCATORS AT WORK

While the movement for the establishment of professional development schools formed from calls for progressive reform in teacher education (Darling-Hammond, 1994; Winitzky, Stoddart, & O'Keefe, 1992), more recent changes in the focus and tenor of school policy have had a stifling effect on innovative strategies for classroom instruction and on the preparation of pre-service teachers. In the wake of questionable national and local mandates for classroom practice, our PDS community was inspired to reflect critically on the validity of administrative policies and their generating scholarship in light of how they affected the construction of knowledge by both our grade school students and the teacher candidates assigned to our school.

Groups of mentor teachers formed collaborative communities of inquiry (see Cochran-Smith & Lytle, 1999) that met to read and debate current educational research, to analyze how it connected to our classroom practice and to our work with pre-service teachers, and to devise methods to educate school district and community leaders. We met to read and discuss books and articles about the latest research on teaching and learning. We gathered in subject- and grade-level-specific groups to plan for gathering evidence about the efficacy of various methods of instruction and curricular resources. We arranged and rearranged schedules to teach and reflect collaboratively on our lessons. We met with teachers from other school sites to compare our observations.

We were teacher educators in the best sense of the term—examining our own beliefs and contributions of life experiences (ATE, Standard Four: Professional Development), engaging in inquiry to create new understandings and interpretations in the theory and practice of teaching and teacher education (Standard One: Teaching), and striving to foster learning about teaching and teacher education as we actively promoted "high quality education for all students at all levels" (Standard Seven: Public Advocacy). For school-based teacher educators there is little distinction between our professional understanding of classroom teaching and our knowledge for working with teacher candidates. Building our knowledge about teaching and learning influences our practice for teaching about teaching; reflecting on how we are educating teacher candidates affects the way we enact our classroom practice.

Our discourse often centered around the manner in which knowledge for practice, described by Cochran-Smith and Lytle (1999) as the "formal knowledge and theory generated from university-based research . . . for teachers to use to improve practice" (p. 250), is often handed down to practitioners from university faculty members, school district specialists and administrators, and governmental entities. The PDS mentor community struggled to come to terms with how to encourage novice and preservice teachers to implement innovative practices in the wake of school district policies developed from decontextualized knowledge of teaching that encouraged the implementation of instruction based on standardized, scripted lessons.

PROFESSIONAL STANDARDS AND PROFESSIONAL DEVELOPMENT

It was at this point that my work as a mentor teacher touched my experiences as university researcher and doctoral student. I was invited to participate in the Teacher Educator Standards Cohort (TESC) in which teacher educators were assembling professional portfolios based on the first draft of ATE standards. As I assembled evidence and reflected on my practice, I began to make connections between this process and the professional growth I had experienced as part of my efforts to become an NBCT.

Though initially skeptical about the possibility of concretely defining effective teaching practice outside of any specific context, the product and process of my own reflective practice during the NBPTS journey convinced me of the value of looking at specific dimensions of my own teaching in light of more universal understandings developed from others' work and from the scholarship around effective teaching practices. My PDS colleagues and I were engaged in building this collective knowledge of practice that is "generated when teachers treat their own classrooms and schools as sites for intentional investigation at the same time that they treat the knowledge and theory produced by others as generative material for interrogation and interpretation" (Cochran-Smith & Lytle, 1999, p. 250).

In contrast to traditional, bureaucratic tools for teacher evaluation, the more professional conceptions of teacher development underlying the National Teaching Standards and the Standards for Teacher Educators envision assessment not as a series of externally enforced, isolated events, but as an ongoing component of professionals' own reflective practice for development (Darling-Hammond, 1999). As I have had opportunities to interact with other teachers pursuing National Board Certification, I have often been amazed and gratified at the quality and character of the conversations about teaching generated from shared reflections on narratives drawn from classroom experiences and examples of student work.

In one particular instance, a mild conversation began with one teacher's concern about how to best facilitate and assess student learning for an interdisciplinary science unit. The discussion progressed from a brainstorming session about instructional methods, materials, and strategies into a rousing debate about how various approaches to learning theory and cognition presented in educational research were manifested in the classroom. While no clear consensus was reached about the legitimacy or usefulness of these theories (or even about what the teacher with the original question should do with her unit), these teachers were engaged in the process of examining evidence for critical connections between theory and practice drawn from their collective "wisdom of practice" (Shulman, 1986).

I realized that some of the same processes were operating as our cohort of teacher educators was putting together our professional portfolios based on the ATE standards. Online and personal conversations with other participating professionals helped me appreciate how the standards could be used to address developing practice across various educational contexts. University-based teacher educators clarified their perceptions of how the standards applied to their work, and I shared with them my efforts to evaluate and define the current nature and value of school-based mentor teachers as teacher educators.

While most of these colleagues conceded that school-based teacher educators were consistently involved in modeling teaching that demonstrates content and professional knowledge (Standard One: Teaching), they had less understanding about how these educators inquire systematically into, reflect on, and improve their own practice (Standards Three: Scholarship and Four: Professional Development; e.g., National Board Certification). I shared with them my experiences with PDS teachers and NBPTS candidates described above, and emphasized the way in which our PDS investigation provided leadership in developing, implementing, evaluating instructional experiences for our teacher candidates that were "rigorous, relevant, and grounded in theory, research, and best practice" (Standards Five: Program Development and Six: Collaboration).

I pointed to how our PDS community took seriously our roles as change agents, working to implement and model new configurations of learning for the benefit of our teacher candidates (Standard Nine: Vision). The purpose of our collective inquiry was to serve as informed, constructive advocates for high quality education for all of our university and elementary students (Standard Seven: Public Advocacy). Our shared experiences illustrated how the Standards for Teacher Educators presented avenues of possibilities for the work of the whole spectrum of teacher educators as agents of reform in teacher education, and offered direction for using these understandings to affect those reforms.

Increased awareness in the larger educational community about the importance of the work of school-based teacher educators may lead to greater opportunities for them to collaborate with universities and school districts to "provide leadership in developing, implementing, and evaluating teacher education programs" (Standard Five: Program Development). By more clearly understanding their roles as informed teacher educators, mentor teachers may help bridge the school-university gap as they advocate for policies for progressive instructional reform (Standard Seven: Public Advocacy) and contribute to establishing a vision for improving the teaching profession (Standards Eight: Teacher Education Profession and Nine: Vision).

The process of providing evidence of the NBPTS and ATE standards from my practice as a teacher and a school-based teacher educator helped me clarify and refine my individual practice. But the process of working collaboratively with other professionals involved in the same work helped me understand how a teacher, a group of teachers, or a group of teacher educators can use professional standards to become activist professionals (Sachs, 2000), empowered to define and reform the substance and scope of their work.

The potential of standards-based assessment to empower professional educators to define their work may be limited by the way in which they are understood and implemented. If ATE's Standards for Teacher Educators are offered as something more than just tools for establishing evidence of individual practice, if they are also viewed as a framework for collaborative inquiry into practice, they may help initiate the long, slow process of collecting and connecting insights from practice that can continue to contribute to the definition of *teacher educator*, and add to the common knowledge base for the reform of teacher education.

REFLECTIONS ON THE STANDARDS FOR TEACHER EDUCATORS

In the process of choosing and reflecting on evidence of standards-based practice, I began to think of professional standards less as sets of definitive knowledge for practice, and more as "generative material" for personal and contextualized inquiry into teaching. The evolution of my ideas led me to believe that the legitimacy of professional standards springs from the way in which they are formed, and that the real value of "standards" lies not in the way they seek to define exemplary practice for teachers, policy makers, and members of the public, but in the manner in which their use serves as the inspiration for the creation of bodies of inquiry into both situated and universal knowledge of practice.

In contrast to conservative controls for standardizing practice are standards that are dynamic and principled, rather than static and prescribed (Delandshire, 1996), allowing for diverse practices that respond to contextual demands. It is the enlightened implementation of more open-ended guidelines for practice formed from the synthesis of research and experience from the professional community that offers a legitimate, alternative voice for educational practice.

My experiences in developing standards-based professional portfolios also led to a curious and intriguing interplay between my personal perceptions of standards-based teaching, my work as a mentor to novice and pre-service teachers struggling to come to terms with frameworks for evaluation, and my later experiences with the development of ATE's Standards for Teacher Educators. The continuum of my work as teacher, collaborator for the development of a PDS, school and university-based teacher educator, and educational researcher has allowed me the opportunity to work with other professionals to interpret and apply three sets of professional standards—the Interstate New Teacher Support and Assessment Consortium (INTASC) standards (1992) for pre-service teachers, the NBPTS Teaching Standards, and the ATE Standards for Teacher Educators.

It would be interesting to examine how these documents might be used to inform one another in such a way as to provide a longitudinal view of teachers' and teacher educators' development. The knowledge of practice generated by a range of professionals engaging in collaborative study about how and why these different sets of standards may be connected might contribute significantly to reforming dated, hierarchical visions of the practice of teacher education. Instead of regarding the educational community as three separate entities with three separate visions of effective practice, it might be useful to any movement towards reform to regard them as elements of the whole art and science of education. Looking at how these complex, multihued, and abstract components touch, overlap, and develop in relation to the colors and forms in the rest of the image may offer a more integrated vision for teacher education reform.

REFERENCES

Andrews, M. (1997). What matters most for teacher educators. *Journal of Teacher Education, 48*(3), 167–176.

Apple, M. (2001). *Educating the "right" way: Markets, standards, God, and inequality.* New York: Routledge.

Association of Teacher Educators. (1996). *Standards for teacher educators.* Reston, VA: Author.

Association of Teacher Educators. (2008). *Standards for teacher educators (revised).* Manassas Park, VA: Author. Retrieved from www.ate1.org/pubs/uploads/tchredstds110407.pdf

Carter, K. (1993). The place of story in the study of teaching and teacher education. *Educational Researcher, 22*(1), 5–12.

Cochran-Smith, M., & Lytle, S. (1999). Relationships of knowledge and practice: Teacher learning in communities. *Review of Research in Education, 24*, 249–305.

Darling-Hammond, L. (1994). *Professional development schools: Schools for developing a profession.* New York: Teachers College.

Darling-Hammond, L. (1999). *Reshaping teaching policy, preparation, and practice*. *Influences of the National Board for Professional Teaching Standards*. Washington, DC: American Association of Colleges for Teacher Education.

Delandshire, G. (1996). From static and prescribed to dynamic and principled assessment of teaching. *The Elementary School Journal, 97*(2), 105–120.

Interstate New Teacher Support and Assessment Consortium. (1992). *Model standards for beginning teacher licensing and development: A resource for state dialogue*. Washington, DC: Council for Chief State School Officers.

National Board for Professional Teaching Standards (NBPTS). (n.d.). *Mission and history*. Retrieved December 28, 2007 from ww.nbpts.org/about_us/mission_and_history/history

National Board for Professional Teaching Standards. (1989). *Toward high and rigorous standards for the teaching profession*. Detroit, MI: Author.

Sachs, J. (2000) The activist profession. *International Journal of Educational Change, 1*(1), 77–95.

Schön, D. (1983). *Educating the reflective practitioner*. New York: Basic Books.

Shulman, L.S. (1986). Those who understand: Knowledge growth in teaching. *Educational Researcher, 15*(2), 1–22.

Winitzky, N., Stoddart, T., & O'Keefe, P. (1992). Great expectations: Emergent professional development schools. *Journal of Teacher Education, 43*(1), 3–18.

CHAPTER 15

Perspectives on Standards from a Literacy Teacher Educator

Delores Heiden, University of Wisconsin, La Crosse

She was solemn and intent as she raised her hand to ask the question. Angie was a young pre-service student in my *Reading in the Elementary School* course in the fall of 1990, the first semester of my new career as a teacher educator. Just a few moments before, I had busily described to my class certain instructional strategies that I had used with children.

"Excuse me," Angie said as I acknowledged her, "but are you a *real* teacher?" As I formulated my reply, I noticed furtive grins and heard a few muffled laughs around the room.

"Hmm," I thought. "I introduced myself to the class, detailing my prior experience. I included my recent twenty-three years in public schools as a classroom teacher, principal, and reading specialist. And, here I am, teaching a university class. What does she think I am, chopped liver?" But Angie did not appear to understand the full impact of her question. Did she imagine university instructors to be so far removed from the P–12 world that they no longer counted as "real" teachers?

Later that day, I contemplated the shift that I had made from the familiar world of elementary school to that of higher education. Had I lost something in the process?

In my new department, I was considered a junior faculty member, in spite of my prior experience. Do all those years with children not count? How was teaching at the university level so fundamentally different from teaching children that I had become a novice once again? Clearly, I had a lot to learn.

When I moved to higher education from P–12 education, my focus shifted. With a few memorable exceptions, I no longer taught children directly. My new responsibility was for the learning of the pre- and in-service teachers whom I taught, but also that of their current and future students in P–12 classrooms. In addition, the range of duties, abilities, expectations and roles demanded of a teacher educator was significantly different from those I experienced in my P–12 positions. Certainly I was expected to teach, and to do it well. But I was also required to conduct research, write, publish, present at conferences, secure grants, and so forth. My service work looked substantively different than my extracurricular work in districts where I had been employed. I was expected to take on leadership roles and to provide service to campus, community, and professional organizations. At the university, I had freedom to choose, and autonomy in decision making, but at the same time, I had to meet departmental expectations. Unfortunately, as Zeichner describes (2005), I was one of those whose doctoral program had provided very little preparation for my new role as teacher educator.

LEARNING FROM FELLOW TEACHER EDUCATORS

While it was important to hold onto what I knew about teaching children, I also had a lot to learn about teaching undergraduates. Fortunately, I had a colleague in reading/language arts teacher education who taught me a great deal. On occasion, my colleague and I team taught classes. I watched and learned from her prior experience in teaching at the university level and we engaged in many conversations including ways to stimulate student learning. Regardless, Angie's simple question came back to me repeatedly in the following years, "Excuse me, but are you a *real* teacher?" I always had considered myself to be one before, but standing in a university classroom, I came to wonder, what is real for me now? And what is my new role as a teacher educator, anyway?

Every year, as I continued to reflect on those questions, I set goals for my work and learning. I surveyed my classes, pondered their anonymous comments, and discussed teaching with interested colleagues. I read, attended conferences, and met other literacy professionals from around the country at meetings of the International Reading Association (IRA) and the Association of Teacher Educators (ATE).

Three other professors in reading/language arts became my most valued resources as we started a new ATE Special Interest Group (SIG), the Reading/Language Arts Teacher Educators (ReLATE). We built our ReLATE meetings around professional dilemmas in our work as literacy teacher educators, and continuously asked ourselves tough questions about effective instruction in teacher education (McCauley, Heiden, Azwell, & Hamilton, 2000). Those professional conversations and collegial experiences helped me consider and develop my identity as a teacher educator of reading/literacy.

STRUGGLING WITH STANDARDS

I started to think about my work in terms of my professional goals and the standards established by IRA and, eventually, ATE. At first glance, it was difficult to know where to begin with the IRA standards. The earlier version of the IRA *Standards for Reading Professionals*, published in 1998, contained sixteen standards; each of those sixteen had another two to nine subpoints for a total of ninety-three components in all (Johnson, Johnson, Farenga & Ness, 2005). How could I assist my students in addressing this extensive set of standards? How could I begin to demonstrate that I had met them? Discouraged, I set aside the IRA standards as a tool for my self-examination, although I continued to try to use them as a guide for what my students needed to know and be able to do as future teachers of literacy.

Eventually, the IRA standards were revised and streamlined down to five major standards with subpoints under each, for a total of just nineteen components (IRA, 2003b). IRA also defined the roles and expertise of the teacher educator as follows:

- Provides instruction to candidates at the graduate and undergraduate levels
- Participates in scholarly work, including researching, writing, and professional development
- Forges university-school partnerships with other educational agencies to promote the advancement of literacy
- Has a minimum of three years' teaching experience including the teaching of reading
- Has a terminal degree that focuses on reading and reading instruction

The revised standards became a regular part of my work. They appear on all syllabi for my reading/literacy courses, and course assignments and experiences are connected to them. When I supervise students in the field, my written observations include notations about evidence of specific IRA standards addressed. Graduate students in reading/literacy build their portfolios around the IRA standards and I ground the evaluation in the standards.

Addressing the IRA Standards for Reading Professionals

There are five main standards that constitute the revised *Standards for Reading Professionals* (2003b) of the International Reading Association:

1. Candidates have knowledge of the foundations of reading and writing processes and instruction.
2. Candidates use a wide range of instructional practices, approaches, methods, and curriculum materials to support reading and writing instruction.
3. Candidates use a variety of assessment tools and practices to plan and evaluate effective reading instruction.
4. Candidates create a literate environment that fosters reading and writing by integrating foundational knowledge, use of instructional practices, approaches and methods, curriculum materials, and the appropriate use of assessments.
5. Candidates view professional development as a career-long effort and responsibility.

One of the features of the IRA standards is that they are designed to address multiple roles of literacy educators across five categories, in this order: the paraprofessional, the classroom teacher, the reading specialist, the teacher educator, and the administrator (IRA, 2004). For each of the five categories, individuals are accountable to the standards and the subpoints under each standard, at increasingly complex levels. Criteria for each category are cumulative; individuals are to meet criteria at their own level, in addition to all the criteria at each of the preceding category levels. For example, teacher educator candidates in category IV must meet the criteria in their category in addition to all of those for the three previous levels including those for paraprofessionals, classroom teachers, and reading specialist candidates. I have worked with the IRA standards on a regular basis and followed their dictum for teacher educators to "prepare and coach" students as teachers of literacy. However, I have not really used the revised IRA standards to reflect on my own work, preferring instead to utilize the ATE standards. A comparison of the two sets of standards illustrates the reasons for my decision.

Reconciling IRA and ATE Standards

In this section, I have mapped the five IRA *Standards for Reading Professionals* onto the nine ATE standards (Association of Teacher Educators, 2008). Where there was not a strong match between the standards, I found a subpoint under the IRA standard that would partially address the ATE standard.

At times, only a portion of the subpoints under an IRA standard is applicable to an ATE standard, as is the case with ATE Standard Two:

Table 15.1

ATE Standards for Teacher Educators	IRA: Standards for reading professionals
ATE 1 Teaching	IRA 1: Foundational knowledge
	IRA 2: Instructional strategies and curriculum materials
	RA 3: Assessment, diagnosis and evaluation
	IRA 4: Creating a literate environment
ATE 2 Cultural Competence	IRA 2.2 and 2.3:
	(Use of instructional practices and materials . . . for learners at differing stages . . . and from differing cultural and linguistic backgrounds.)
ATE 3 Scholarship	IRA 1.1: . . . Conduct and publish research
	IRA 5.2: Continue to pursue the development of professional knowledge and dispositions.
ATE 4 Professional Development	IRA 5: Professional development
ATE 5 Program Development	—
ATE 6 Collaboration	—
ATE 7 Public Advocacy	—
ATE 8 Teacher Education Profession	IRA 5.4: Participate in, initiate, implement, and evaluate professional development programs
ATE 9 Vision	—

Cultural Competence; the corresponding IRA standards are not a direct match, but subpoints under IRA standards two and three do address issues of cultural and linguistic diversity. Although IRA standards certainly address program development in literacy education, ATE standard five is specific to program development in teacher education, so there is no match between the two.

The IRA standards do not address the wider spectrum of teacher educator responsibilities and roles, even though there is specific language for teacher educators under each standard. The four criteria for IRA standard one are about knowing theories and articulating and synthesizing knowledge. The eleven subpoints under IRA standards two, three, and four are about preparing and coaching pre-service and in-service teachers in instructional strategies, assessment, and creating a literate environment. The primary and pervasive emphasis is on preparing and coaching others.

Having been a classroom teacher of reading, a reading teacher, a reading specialist, a building principal, and a teacher educator in reading/ literacy, I have held all the positions addressed by the full set of IRA standards (save for paraprofessional). All of the criteria for each of those categories made sense to me, except for one. When I came to the teacher educator category, something was missing. For almost every component under a standard, the criteria for the teacher educator begins with the words, "Prepare and coach pre-service candidates and in-service teachers to. . . ." For example, "prepare and coach" them to "use a wide range of instructional practices, approaches, and methods . . ." or "prepare and coach" them to "use a wide range of assessment tools" and so on. The focus is clearly on the work of educators in the preceding roles or categories; there is no explication of the knowledge, skills, and dispositions required of teacher educators when they "prepare and coach."

The IRA standards do not address leadership in teacher education, nor do they address advocacy directly, in spite of the fact that advocacy is purportedly encouraged and valued by the International Reading Association. In most cases, the category of reading specialist appears to be described as far more proactive than that of the teacher educator. Conversely, I found that the ATE standards captured the array of teacher educator responsibilities and roles as I apprehend them.

The ATE standards have been the primary standards informing my goal setting and reflection. I referenced them in my promotion file and used them as the basis for my goal setting for posttenure review. Although I am now semiretired, the ATE standards continue to mirror my professional life. I continue to serve as director of the Graduate Reading Program and teach graduate courses in reading/literacy. Because it is almost impossible for me to introduce myself as a teacher educator without specifying that I am a reading/literacy teacher educator, I cross-listed the IRA standards for reading professionals with the original seven ATE standards to address my subject area specialty within my own professional portfolio.

Creating a Standards-Based Portfolio

Our teacher education students began building portfolios around the Interstate New Teacher Assessment and Support Consortium (INTASC) Standards in the mid-1990s. I discovered that I could not relate to their struggles in addressing the standards through creating portfolios because I had not created one of my own. I did not fully understand what they experienced, what questions they had, and the effect of the work upon their own abilities to reflect, self-assess, and set new goals for themselves. I also did not know what meaning, if any, they attached to the standards that they addressed or if they were merely jumping through the proverbial hoop.

It became increasingly evident to me that I had no right to ask my students to engage in the creation of a standards-based portfolio unless I was willing to do the same. How could it be important for them, but not for me? Like Robbins and her colleagues (1991), I realized that I could not ask my students to reflect on their work unless I, too, reflected on my own practice in ways that made my thinking public. Similarly, if I believed a standards-based portfolio to be an important vehicle by which students would reflect upon and demonstrate their learning, then it ought to be important for me to create my own standards-based portfolio.

When the first iteration of the ATE standards was presented, I decided to use them as a guide for my own work and model for my students. I took the standards to my class, explained that I was engaging in a process similar to their own, and that I planned to regularly describe and share my ongoing work in relation to the ATE standards (Heiden,

2005). Across the semester, I pointed out the parallels between their progress toward the standards and my own.

I videotaped and analyzed my teaching as part of the introspective process. I wrote a journal about my work and shared excerpts with the class. My students' responses were overwhelmingly positive. Portions of their comments directly related to my modeling reflection in regard to the standards:

- "What helped me the most was Dr. Heiden modeled what she was teaching."
- "Throughout the whole semester she learned right along with us and was reflective in her teaching as we were in ours."
- "I like that you tried new things. . . ."

Perhaps all of us in teacher education should have started by examining our own teaching in the light of standards before expecting it of our students, particularly because most standards are written in the "obscure style" (Raths, 1999). Experienced teacher educators have the background and perspective to grasp the full import of professional standards and can interpret them in ways that the novice is not yet ready to do.

Teacher Educator Standards Cohort

In 2004, ATE announced the formation of the Teacher Educator Standards Cohort (TESC), a group of teacher educators who would apply the original ATE standards to the creation of their own professional portfolios. In so doing they would provide insights into the process and the relevance of the ATE standards to the work of teacher educators that would inform the revision of the standards. I applied and was accepted into TESC and spent the ensuing year developing a standards-based electronic portfolio (Heiden, 2006).

The process of creating my professional portfolio caused me to take a focused, introspective look into all facets of my work, and to determine how aspects addressed the ATE standards. TESC met at intervals to discuss our observations and struggles during the process. Smaller subgroups of TESC members served as a type of support system as we wrote and shared portions of our reflections on the standards. Ultimately, we made numerous individual decisions about places where documents from our work would best address specific standards. At the same time, we were encouraged to consider important questions such as these: "Is this standard an important indicator of a professional teacher? Can it be observed? What kinds of evidence will help you to document competency of this standard?" (C. Klecka, personal communication, July 31, 2005).

In some regard, creating the portfolio within the span of a single year was not unlike preparing a promotion file; it was summative, rather than formative, in nature. We drew from documentation we already possessed, teaching that was already evaluated, writing that was already published. Of course, our TESC portfolios were designed to provide feedback to ATE on the first set of standards. I had little difficulty documenting my work relative to any of the original seven standards, but building the rationale for each was challenging. By its very nature, a standards-based portfolio always remains a fluid work in progress.

EXAMINATION OF STANDARDS

The new version of the ATE standards captures a wider realm of teacher educator responsibilities, specifically expanding to include cultural competence, program development, and vision. In addition, the revised standards document includes a worthy attempt to anchor the standards in research on teacher education. ATE has included a statement of rationale for each standard, and reference citations for supporting documents, many of which are theoretical or philosophical in nature. As ATE further refines and develops its standards, no doubt we can look forward to a strengthened research base that includes more studies conducted within teacher education. The same can be said of the research base for the IRA standards.

Much like ATE's Commission on Standards in Teacher Education, the National Commission on Excellence in Elementary Teacher Preparation for Reading Instruction was convened in 1999 and charged with the task of studying teacher preparation and providing leadership for change. In the IRA publication *Prepared to Make a Difference: An Executive Summary of the National Commission on Excellence in Elementary Teacher Preparation for Reading Instruction* (2003a), eight critical features of excellence in reading teacher preparation programs were presented: content, apprenticeship, vision, resources and mission, personalized teaching, autonomy, community, and assessment.

In addition to a national survey of reading teacher educators, the commission gathered data about eight programs at universities around the country across a three-year period in order to identify the common characteristics of excellent reading teacher preparation programs. It was reported that all eight sites "believe the eight features are critical standards of excellence" (p. 12). In considering next steps for teacher educators, the commission made this observation:

> The Commission's research findings bolster the credibility of the IRA and NCATE standards. The Commission did not set out to support the professional standards. The findings of critical features reported here spring directly from the research, not from any preconceived notions about professional excellence. Still, educators seeking to improve their programs can work toward the same goal whether they use IRA and NCATE standards or Commission research findings. Both represent valid paths toward self-study, reflection, and improvement (p. 12).

In contrast, other authorities in literacy believe there is a paucity of research related to the connection between standards and reading instruction (NICHD, 2000; Johnson, Johnson, Farenga, & Ness, 2005). The *Report of the National Reading Panel* (NRP) (2000) found no experimental studies in the sample reviewed by the subgroup on teacher education and reading instruction that addressed the use of standards in either pre-service or in-service teacher education. No mention was made of staff development for teacher educators or of the work of teacher educators, much less in relation to any set of standards.

In her minority view of the NRP report, Joanne Yatvin pointed out that eight of the topics on the International Reading Association's annual list of "Hot Topics" in literacy were not investigated by the NRP; "Standards" was one of the eight. Johnson, Johnson, Farenga, and Ness (2005) state that NCATE standards and standards of specialized professional associations (SPAs) such as those of the International Reading Association are not "undergirded by empirical research findings, nor have they been field tested and shown to make a difference in program graduates' teaching abilities" (p. 2). At best, these authors claim, most sets of standards have been arrived at by consensus rather than through avenues of research.

IRA does draw on a research base in support of its standards, but in very broad strokes, at times listing entire handbooks of reading research as the basis for particular standards. I have no doubt that the research base is there; the links to the standards just need to be made more explicit.

To build on the strong foundations that have been laid, it appears that next steps for both IRA and ATE would include additional work such as the following: a) building a stronger research base to support each and every standard and subpoint; b) further clarifying the ways in which criteria for the standards can be addressed; and c) developing mechanisms to ascertain the degree to which standards are being met.

EXPERIENCE AND EXPERTISE: EXPLORING POSSIBILITIES

When educators speak of standards, they often refer to "meeting," or "addressing," or "mastering" them. What is often ignored is the question of how well standards are met. How much evidence is enough? We might also ask who decides, and for what purpose? Is it enough to say one has met a set of standards? Surely there are degrees of competency and expertise.

Edelfelt and Raths (1998) make the critical distinction between criteria and standards, noting, "A pervasive problem in the professions is people operating with criteria and no standards" (p. 3). Raths (1999) suggests that standards ought to be viewed as "hypotheses worthy of testing" until there are rubrics associated with them.

In describing his research on expert teachers, David Berliner noted, "We don't know yet how to carve out experience from expertise. We're quite sure that a person with many years experience is not necessarily an expert, but all our experts have ten years or so experience. In other words, experience is a necessary but not a sufficient condition for being an expert" (as cited in Brandt, 1986, p. 7). Berliner was speaking of P–12 teachers, but it begs the question: what about the experience and expertise of teacher educators?

A review of current position descriptions on *The Chronicle* Web site shows that many positions, including that of an assistant professor of reading, require just "three or more years elementary public school teaching experience." Is that sufficient? Can any teacher educator develop enough expertise in the P–12 setting within three years to be qualified to teach future educators? One ad for an instructor in secondary English considered prior experience in teaching high school English to be "highly desirable," and yet the duties of the position required someone who would "participate in curriculum development and supervise student teachers." Several descriptions, including one for an assistant professor of reading/language arts, merely asked for "prior K–12 teaching experience" without specifying a minimum number of years of experience.

In its description of category IV teacher educator, the International Reading Association specifies a "minimum of three years' teaching experience including the teaching of reading." If one considers the full range of competencies delineated in the categories of the IRA Standards for Reading Professionals for a classroom teacher and reading specialist/literacy coach, it is doubtful that anyone could acquire such capabilities within a scant three years, much less begin to address any of the IRA standards at the teacher educator level. And yet, it is not unusual for entry-level university faculty to be hired with just three years' experience in P–12 settings.

In most school districts, a teacher with three years of experience is considered probationary. Can any teacher educator with only three years of teaching in P–12 claim to be highly qualified? It takes an experienced teacher educator to model best practices for his or her students. Do we want probationary-level educators preparing future teachers? It is incongruous to sidestep this question in our teacher education programs while we tout rigorous standards for teacher educators.

Linda Darling-Hammond (2006) deplores the notion commonly held by "many laypeople and a large share of policy makers" that almost anyone who knows something about a subject can teach it, and that the ins and outs of teaching can be learned on the job. But how is that different from the view of most disciplines in the academy that simply having achieved a terminal degree is enough to qualify an individual to teach a particular subject? Clearly, there is no magic number for years of experience that qualifies a person as a literacy teacher educator. It is safe to assume that a teacher educator ought to have moved beyond the novice stage as a P–12 educator to be able to prepare future educators to teach children to read and write and to implement effective interventions for struggling readers and writers. We need some way to know if the candidate possesses expertise, and this is where the standards could prove to be invaluable.

Even as we have moved beyond seat time in courses as an indicator of learning, perhaps we should move beyond counting years of experience and institute a requirement for evidence of a candidate's knowledge, skills, and dispositions as a teacher educator. Rather than merely suggesting prior P–12 experience to be "highly desirable," a standards-based approach to the search and screen process would call for highly qualified teacher educators who are ready and able to prepare future teachers. We need evidence that candidates have met the standards, and we also need to know how well they have met them. In the pursuit of excellence, and the highest standards, it may be that both the ATE and IRA standards for teacher educators hold great potential to inform and reform hiring practices at the university level.

DEVELOPING HIGHLY QUALIFIED TEACHER EDUCATORS

In 1996, the National Commission on Teaching & America's Future presented its self-described "audacious" goal for America's future: that within ten years every student in the country would be provided "access to competent, caring, qualified teaching in schools organized for success" (p. 10). To accomplish this goal, the commission emphasized the need, among other things, to "get serious about standards, for both students and teachers," and to "organize teacher education and professional development programs around standards for students and teachers" (p. 11). During the past ten years, we certainly have witnessed significant changes in teacher education, including the implementation of standards-based programs that review candidates on the basis of what they know and are able to do, instead of the number of credit hours they have completed. The commission also noted,

> For new teachers, improving standards begins with teacher preparation. Prospective teachers learn just as other students do: by studying, practicing, and reflecting; by collaborating with others; by looking closely at students and their work; and by sharing what they see. For prospective teachers, this kind of learning cannot occur in college classrooms divorced from schools or in schools divorced from current research (p. 31).

Can this recommendation be any different for early-career teacher educators who are committed to ongoing learning and growth? Using standards to set goals for professional development may be particularly helpful for early-career teacher educators who, like myself, enter an institution of higher education with no real preparation for the role of teacher educator. Standards set a strong focus in the face of sometimes conflicting demands of teaching, scholarship, and service that can pull the newer faculty member in many different directions. Using the standards to keep a focus on professional self-improvement also sends a clear message to a promotion and tenure committee that the teacher educator is capable of setting important goals and is committed to continuous improvement.

As a literacy teacher educator, I believe that the best uses of the ATE standards have included fostering reflection and goal setting, stimulating shared conversations with my colleagues, and modeling those habits of mind for my students. I believe that the ATE standards hold particular potential for informing the recruitment, screening, and hiring of highly qualified teacher educators and for guiding the work and development of early-career teacher educators.

ASPIRATIONS

Perhaps the ultimate question for a teacher educator is whether or not she accepts the standards as important, meaningful, and representative of her own philosophical orientation. That is to say, it is up to the individual to decide whether or not she would consider herself to be a participant in the consensus that established the standards. While I might quibble about wording here or there, I do ascribe to the standards of both ATE and IRA. I need to know and understand the IRA standards because they focus on the knowledge, skills, and dispositions of the future reading teachers, reading specialists, and classroom teachers of reading whom I help prepare. The ATE standards are important to me because they focus on my own knowledge, skills, and dispositions as a teacher educator.

The best result of examining myself according to a set of standards is the opportunity it provides to reflect upon my own work, to identify areas in need of improvement, and to consider seriously the ways in which I might seek to become a better, more effective educator. In other words, working toward standards means pursuing a path "toward self-study, reflection, and improvement" (International Reading Association, 2003a). In his treatise on faculty professionalism and ethics in higher education, Neal Hamilton observed, "Each professor should strive, over a career, to realize the ethics of aspiration—the ideals and core values of the academic profession, the professor's discipline and the professor's institution including internalizing the highest standards for professional skills" (2006, pp. 15–16).

As for me, I aspire to be a *real* teacher educator. Thanks, Angie.

REFERENCES

Association of Teacher Educators (2008). *Standards for teacher educators (revised)*. Retrieved July 1, 2008 from www.ate1.org/pubs/uploads/tchredstds 110407.pdf

Brandt, R. S. (1986). On the expert teacher: A conversation with David Berliner. *Educational Leadership, 44*(2), 4–9.

Darling-Hammond, L. (2006). Constructing 21st-century teacher education. *Journal of Teacher Education, 57*(3), 300–314.

Edelfelt, R. A., & Raths, J. D. (1998). *A brief history of standards in teacher education*. Reston, VA: Association of Teacher Educators.

Hamilton, N. (2006). Faculty professionalism: Failures of socialization and the road to loss of professional autonomy. *Liberal Education, 92*(4), 14–21.

Heiden, D.E. (2005). How do I measure up? A teacher educator examines her own work in relation to professional standards. *ReLATE: The Online Journal of Reading and Language Arts Teacher Educators*. Retrieved from www.readinglanguagearts.org/articles/heiden01.html

Heiden, D.E. (2006) *Professional Portfolio*. Retrieved from www.taskstream.com/main/?/heiden/portfolio.html

International Reading Association (2003a). *Prepared to make a difference: An executive summary of the National Commission on Excellence in Elementary Teacher Preparation for Reading Instruction*. Newark, DE: Author.

International Reading Association (2003b). *Standards for reading professionals (revised)*. Newark, DE: Author. Retrieved from www.reading.org/resources/issues/reports/professional_standards.html

Johnson, D. D., Johnson, B., Farenga, S. J., & Ness, D. (2005). *Trivializing teacher education: The accreditation squeeze*. Lanham, MD: Rowman & Littlefield.

McCauley, J. K., Heiden, D. E., Azwell, T. A., & Hamilton, A. C. (2000). Dilemmas in teacher education. *Reading Online*. Retrieved from www.reading online.org/past/past_index.asp?HREF=../critical/dilemmas/index.html

National Commission on Teaching & America's Future. (1996). *What matters most: Teaching for America's future*. New York, NY: Author.

National Institute of Child Health and Human Development. (2000). *Report of the National Reading Panel. Teaching children to read: An evidence-based assessment of the scientific research literature on reading and its implications for reading instruction: Reports of the subgroups* (NIH Publication No. 00-4754). Washington, DC: U.S. Government Printing Office.

Raths, J. (1999). A consumer's guide to teacher standards. *Phi Delta Kappan*, *81*(1), 136–42.

Robbins, M. E., Brown, G., Osburn, E. B., Patterson, L., Prouty, J. L., & Swicegood, P. (1991). *Transforming teaching and learning through collaboration*. Paper presented at the Annual Meeting of the College Reading Association. Crystal City, VA.

Zeichner, K. (2005). Becoming a teacher educator: A personal perspective. *Teaching and Teacher Education*, *21*(2), 117–124.

CHAPTER 16

Teacher Educator Standards through the Educational Technology Lens

Loretta Donovan

California State University, Fullerton

In 2005, the computer to student ratio in schools was 3.8:1 (compared to 12:1 in 1994 and 4.1:1 in 2003), and 94 percent of schools had class-room Internet access (National Center for Education Statistics, 2006). The American Digital Schools Survey (2006) suggests that by 2011, over 50 percent of schools will have one-to-one laptop programs in which each student has a personal laptop. Despite this increased access, the most common K–12 student use of classroom computers is for re-search and word processing, particularly the writing process (Becker, 2001; Donovan, 2006). Classroom teachers are concerned with the impact that greater access to technology in the classroom has on them-selves as teachers in addition to their ability to teach effectively (Dono-van, Hartley, & Strudler, 2007).

The abovementioned conditions inform my role as educational technology faculty, which is to promote meaningful integration of tech-nology into teaching and learning. In the Department of Elementary and Bilingual Education at California State University, Fullerton, my primary responsibility is to teach courses in the educational technology masters programs. In this capacity, I develop and implement a variety of educational technology courses for K–12 teachers. Additionally I serve as the cohort leader for students in a K–8 initial licensure pro-gram. These roles in combination with my research centered on tech-nology integration in teaching and learning contexts define me as an educational technology faculty member.

Prior to my introduction to the Association of Teacher Educators (ATE) and the Teacher Educator Standards, the International Society for Technology in Education (ISTE) standards were most familiar to me. The ISTE National Educational Technology Standards (NETS) are available for students, teachers, administrators, and technology leaders and facilitators (see http://www.iste.org/ for a link to the specific NETS). These standards define what students, teachers, administrators, technology leaders, and facilitators need to know and be able to do. They also provide guidelines for essential conditions for effective technology integration in schools.

The standards for technology leaders and facilitators were developed jointly between ISTE and the National Council for Accreditation of Teacher Education (NCATE). These focus primarily on the knowledge, skills, and dispositions that graduating teacher candidates should have at the conclusion of their teacher education programs. These standards further indicate what we, as teacher educators, should do to facilitate teacher candidates' learning in relation to technology.

In this chapter, I share my initial reactions to the ATE Teacher Educator Standards as a whole. Following this, I delve further into individual standards and how each connects to educational technology. In doing so I primarily reflect on how, as an educational technologist, I am able (or not) to address standards and indicators. This is not intended as a means to provide evidence of being an accomplished teacher educator but rather as a way to identify the place of technology in the ATE Teacher Educator Standards. I end this chapter with a brief discussion of the relationship between the ATE Teacher Educator Standards, my current retention and promotion standards at California State University, Fullerton, and the ISTE NETS. I conclude with a reflection on how this examination has impacted me in my role as an educational technologist.

EDUCATIONAL TECHNOLOGIST OR TEACHER EDUCATOR?

I have always viewed myself as an educational technologist, rather than a teacher educator. My focus has always been on how to best integrate technology to meet the needs of the K–12 students. This is central to my roles as a cohort leader for teacher candidates seeking initial licensure as elementary school teachers and as part of a small team of faculty who work with students earning masters degrees in educational technology.

The educational shift from teaching about computers to teaching with them began with the Apple Classrooms of Tomorrow (one computer per student) initiative (Sandholtz, Ringstaff, & Dwyer, 1997). This research coupled with more current research on the disconnect between students today and what is often occurring in classrooms (Apple, 2008) led me to view technology as a virtual net that covers all areas of education and not a subject itself. This perspective is that which the ISTE NETS promote, which is the ultimate direction of teacher education, and the reason that I view myself as an educational technologist.

Teacher candidates need varied and frequent opportunities to engage in technology-rich learning experiences (Duran, Fossum, & Leura, 2006). I apply my expertise as I merge technology with learning to teach for my cohort of teacher candidates by facilitating a one-to-one cohort. In this, all teacher candidates have laptops whose use is infused into coursework. Candidates are encouraged to engage in technology-rich teaching in their field experiences and in student teaching.

For example, teacher candidates watch digitally streamed videos that are paused at specific places so students and the instructor have an opportunity to discuss the issues being raised. Students use their personal Weblogs (blogs) to write reflections on what they learned. In the K–12 classroom, students blog about content and teachers use them as a method for assessment. In a teaching methods course, candidates blog about content but also about using technology as a tool for teaching and learning while the instructor uses it to evaluate understanding content and pedagogy.

When working with students who have elected a masters degree with a technology focus, I view technology as having a similar virtual net purpose. In these courses we are able to focus on specific ways to integrate technology with the ultimate goal of expanding and extending the seamless use of technology available in the teacher's individual classroom. For example, teachers complete course assignments in which they create WebQuests, which are instructional Web pages based on content standards that promote higher order thinking skills for use in their classroom (see http://webquest.org/index.php for more information on WebQuests). In this and other educational technology courses, I introduce students to new technology but do not make it the focus of our instruction, but rather a method for it.

While this model of teaching is part of my everyday practice, I recognize that this is not the case for most teacher educators. Teacher education faculty voice concerns about being able to integrate technology into their courses in such a way that it would transfer to the K–12 environment (Gunter, 2001). Introducing additional technology to a teacher education program may cause high level concerns about one's personal role as a teacher educator. Many times this is representative of teacher educators who are nonusers of technology themselves (Donovan & Green 2008a; Donovan, & Green, under review).

THE ATE STANDARDS THROUGH THE TECHNOLOGY LENS

Given the context of my work, my initial reaction to the ATE standards was "where is the technology standard?" Surely, I thought, these standards would include technology as pivotal in determining qualities of an accomplished teacher educator. If not, according to me, these standards would not be realistic or current. Upon closer examination, even without a specific standard exclusively dedicated to technology, I detect traces of consideration of the importance of technology.

Standard One: Teaching suggests that an accomplished teacher educator models teaching that includes "proficiency with technology and assessment" and indicates that they further "[d]emonstrate a variety of instructional and assessment methods including use of technology." As educational technology faculty, this is the foundation of my courses. As the cohort leader and math methods instructor for the initial licensure program, I naturally model using technology as a teaching and learning tool.

As an example, I model lessons using a variety of technology such as digital cameras, spreadsheets, virtual manipulatives, and interactive whiteboards. It is our responsibility as teachers and teacher educators to meet the needs of all learners in our classes. These students include those digital kids who grew up with technology and are multitaskers, goal planners, and active learners (Apple, 2008). Without sharing technology as a teaching and learning tool, I believe that we would not be doing our job of meeting their needs.

Through my technology lens, I consider several of the other indicators for this standard. It is clear to me that I address many of them through my use of technology in teaching and learning. For example,

I implement technology to promote problem solving and critical thinking in all my students by having them examine WebQuests (http://webquest.org/index.php) and create student-centered, nonlinear PowerPoint presentations. I revise courses to reflect best practices in educational technology such as the digital copyright awareness and Web 2.0 including Google docs, blogs, and wikis. Outside of my courses, I facilitate professional development experiences related to effective teaching with technology as part of my responsibilities on the college technology committee.

Standard Two: Cultural Competence suggests that an accomplished teacher educator "applies cultural competence and promotes social justice in teacher education." I admit that my initial reaction to the lack of specific reference to technology disheartened me. However, through the educational technology lens, multicultural education, which calls for examining, critiquing, and transforming education to promote equity and social justice, without question includes technology.

The increased prevalence of technology in education is unfortunately paralleled by increased inequity in availability of resources (e.g., hardware and software, projectors, interactive whiteboards) and access across socioeconomic status, race, and gender to such technology. Issues such as teacher training and teacher comfort level with using technology for learning contribute to the inequitable student use of technology for authentic learning. Further, it is evident in evaluations of one-to-one laptop programs in K–8 schools (e.g., Donovan & Green, 2008b) that this inequity of appropriate and adequate use is dependent on the support teachers receive from administration.

Addressing the digital divide, the gap between those who do and do not have adequate and appropriate access to and use of technology is one way that I promote social justice in my courses. I accomplish this by integrating the use of technology into coursework, but more importantly, by modeling the way technology can be used to break down cultural barriers, extend classroom walls, communicate with the community, and meet the individual needs of students. In addition, the topic of the digital divide and how to bridge it through grant writing, effective teaching practice, and social awareness is a critical discussion in all my courses. These interpretations of the ATE standards lead me to believe than technology is more prevalent than I originally surmised.

Standards three and four relate to scholarship and professional development respectively. Neither of these standards makes any explicit reference to technology. Indicators for standard three include investigating theoretical and practical problems in teaching, learning, and/or teacher education, conducting program evaluation, acquiring research-based and service-based grants, and disseminating research findings. As educational technologists, we engage in these activities with a specific eye toward the technology lens.

My research focuses on both K–12 schools, including evaluations of technology programs and effective use of technology, and teacher education environments involving faculty concerns about technology for teaching and relationship between technology in schools and in teacher education. I strive to balance publications among educational technology journals such as *Journal of Research on Technology in Education*, journals that blend technology and teacher education such as *Journal of Computing in Teacher Education*, and more specific teacher education journals such as *Action in Teacher Education*. This balance allows me to be true to the educational technologist with whom I identify, in addition to the teacher educator that I am learning I am.

Standard four stresses the importance of continuous professional development to improve one's own practice. In educational technology, there is something new to be learned every day. Enrollment in technology-based distance education K–12 courses increased from approximately 317,000 in 2002 to 517,000 students in 2004 (National Center for Education Statistics, 2008). The number continues to grow with policies such as that of Michigan's Department of Education requiring all students to complete at least one online distance education course (see www.michigan.gov/mde).

Similarly, Weblogs (web-based journals) were only just starting to become popular in the late 1990s. Now, sites such as Edublogs (http://edublogs.org/) that are dedicated specifically for teacher and student blogging each host nearly 200,000 individual blogs. Participation in these new contexts for teaching and learning requires that I learn the new technologies along with the ways in which they can enhance teaching and learning in both teacher education programs and in K–12 schools.

With these incredible advances in the uses of technology in education, it would be impossible for me to ignore these technological advances and not pursue professional development opportunities and be effective as a teacher educator. I am surprised that the ATE standards imply that accomplished teacher educators are not expected to engage in specifically technology-related professional growth and development.

Standard Five: Program Development suggests that an accomplished teacher educator "contributes to development, refinement, and revision of programs and portions of programs." The development and evaluation of programs to meet the needs of a technologically experienced society extends across pre-service and in-service teacher education programs yet it is not articulated as such in this standard. As teacher educators, we should prepare teachers to teach children in a technological society. We need to educate teachers to work with diverse students who will be employed in careers that currently do not exist. In many cases this emphasis will result in change at the program level.

With the increasing demand of technology use in society and in education, this is one standard that should explicitly mention educational technology. As educational technology faculty, I am in support of and involved in enhancing technology such as interactive whiteboards, student laptops, and online courses in the various teacher education programs in the college. I expect that all teacher educators who are teaching in these programs would also be involved to a certain extent.

Standards Six: Collaboration, Seven: Public Advocacy, and Eight: Teacher Education Profession stress that accomplished teacher educators collaborate with the greater community (relevant stakeholders) and serve as advocates for and contributors to quality education. These three standards go hand in hand as they take teacher education outside the realm of formal education. Although technology is not specifically mentioned, evidencing these standards would be made easier with technology and in some cases, practices require technology to be most effective.

Standard Six: Collaboration does not necessitate technology but it enhances opportunity to do so. As one example, in a partnership with California State Universities, Boeing, and several informal science institutions such as children's museums and aquariums, we collaborate to construct a Web page (www.socalcrest.org/) that focuses specifically on preparing teachers to work with informal science learning institutions. This collaboration provides teachers and teacher candidates opportunity to access information that might otherwise be limited to only one institution, and possibly one instructor's course. Thus, the technology focus of this collaboration ultimately improves teaching and student learning.

Standard Seven: Public Advocacy does not particularly require technology as being essential to being an accomplished teacher educator. Yet like standard six, it is facilitated by the use of technology. Standard seven prompts teacher educators to, for example, "actively address policy issues which affect the education profession." Without the use of technology, teacher educators are limited in their availability of resources and communication with policy makers.

Glennan and Melmed (1995) wrote: "Technology without reform is likely to have little value: widespread reform without technology is probably impossible" (pp. xix–xx). This statement, coupled with the understanding that we are in fact a digital society, illustrates the relevance of technology to public advocacy. As teacher educators, we need to prepare teachers to educate students for a digital society, but how can we do that without technology? Through the educational technologist lens, standard seven should specifically include technology, even if only within the indicators themselves. In this instance, the importance of technology should not be specific to educational technologists but rather significant to all teacher educators.

Standard Eight: Teacher Education Profession points again to preparing teachers to teach in a digital environment and how technology can, and should, be used to do so. Indicators point to work such as reviewing manuscripts and recruitment that would be more easily accomplished with the use of technology, despite it not being a requirement. For example, I retrieve and review manuscripts through electronic media and I develop Web sites and list serves to recruit pre-service teachers and future teacher educators. As an educational technologist, my medium of choice for addressing many if not all the indicators for this standard would be through technology. However, the specific mention of development of multimedia resources shows the relevance of educational technology for all teacher educators.

Standard Nine: Vision returns me to my roots with its emphasis on technology use in teacher education. I feel a natural connection to this standard as I did with Standard One: Teaching. Much of this standard describes what educational technologists do on a daily basis. In particular, I am an early adopter of technology, which is exemplified in my facilitation of the one-to-one laptop cohort. As a change agent, I introduce to and model for my colleagues new practices incorporating technology such as utilizing interactive whiteboards and developing online or hybrid courses. Similarly, I support innovation adoption with research. I examine concerns of teacher educators when introducing technology innovations, which can help to plan meaningful collaboration and professional development to ensure sustainability of the innovation (Donovan & Green, under review).

REFLECTING ON MULTIPLE SETS OF STANDARDS

Upon reflection, the ATE Teacher Educator Standards are in fact very relevant to me as an educational technologist. In addition, I believe that they share many commonalities to my own tenure and promotion personnel standards and the ISTE NETS for technology leaders and facilitators. The ISTE NETS for technology facilitators include standards for learning environments and experiences, teaching, professional practice, social, ethical, legal and human issues, planning, and vision. From these simple headings, it is clear there are parallels between what is expected of me as an accomplished educational technology facilitator and as an accomplished teacher educator. Although each standard is organized differently, the underlying themes of the standards as a whole are similar. For example, both the NETS and the ATE Teacher Educator Standards prompt me to evaluate and reflect on my practice to promote enhanced student learning, communicate and collaborate with peers, parents, and the community, and use learner-centered strategies to support the needs of diverse learners. However, where the ATE standards lacked specific references to technology for each standard and/or indicator, the NETS address the use of technology for each and every one.

This brief discussion of how the standards relate to me as an educational technologist has highlighted the similarities between my department personnel standards and the teacher educator standards, which include high quality teaching, service at many levels, and collaborating with colleagues for scholarship and contribution to the profession. Where the similarities with the NETS were more specific instances, the most striking resemblance between personnel standards and the teacher educator standards is in the way they are written. It is not the format of the standards documents per se, but rather the sense that the standards provide solid guidelines for defining an accomplished teacher educator while they also allow for individual interpretation.

As I considered the standards separately, I was able to interpret them through an educational technology lens. I go through the same process when creating my portfolio for tenure and promotion. It is my responsibility to make my case that my experiences and expertise in technology demonstrate that I meet the standards developed in my department.

LOOKING FORWARD

Where I may have had some doubts about the prominence of technology within the Association of Teacher Educators Standards for Teacher Educators, I now feel that these standards are what each individual makes of them. Where I want them to have a greater technology emphasis, others may want them to have a greater multicultural emphasis. I feel that the standards can be viewed as being very personally relevant depending on an individual's interpretation. This exploration of the ATE Teacher Educator Standards has impacted me as a professional in that I continue to see myself as an educational technologist, but I now view myself as a teacher educator as well.

REFERENCES

American Digital Schools. (2006). American digital schools 2006: A five-year survey. Retrieved July 4, 2008, from http://21centuryconnections.com/node/117

Apple. (2008). *Digital tools for digital kids*. Retrieved July 10, 2008 from www.apple.com/ca/education/digitalkids/

Association of Teacher Educators (2008). *National standards for teacher educators (revised)*. Retrieved July 1, 2008 from www.ate1.org/pubs/Home.cfm

Becker, H. J. (2001). *How are teachers using computers in instruction?* Retrieved July 7, 2008 from www.crito.uci.edu/tlc/findings/conferences pdf/how_are_teachers_using.pdf

Donovan, L. (2006). *Laptops for learning: Year 2 evaluation. Fullerton School District one-to-one laptop initiative evaluation.* Retrieved July 6, 2008 from www.fsd.k12.ca.us/menus/1to1/evaluation/index.html

Donovan, L., Hartley, K., & Strudler, N. (2007). Teacher concerns during initial implementation of a one-to-one laptop initiative at the middle school level. *Journal of Research on Technology in Education*, *39*(3), 269–283.

Donovan, L., & Green, T. (under review). One-to-one computing in teacher education: Faculty concerns and implications for teacher educators.

Donovan, L., & Green, T. (2008a). Technology-rich teacher education: Faculty concerns during involvement in a technology-rich cohort of teacher candidates. In C. Crawford et al. (Eds.), *Proceedings of Society for Information Technology and Teacher Education International Conference 2008* (pp. 4084–4089). Chesapeake, VA: AACE.

Donovan, L., & Green, T. (2008b). *Laptops for learning: Year 4 evaluation. Preliminary report. Fullerton School District one-to-one laptop initiative program evaluation.* Retrieved July 7, 2008 from www.fsd.k12.ca.us/menus/1to1/evaluation/index.html

Duran, M., Fossum, P. R., & Luera, G. R. (2006). Technology and pedagogical renewal: Conceptualizing technology integration into teacher preparation. *Computers in the Schools*, *23*(3), 31–54.

Glennan, T. K., & Melmed, A. (1995). *Fostering the use of educational technology: Elements of a national strategy.* Washington, DC: RAND. Retrieved July 8, 2008, from www.rand.org/publications/MR/MR682/

Gunter, G. A. (2001). Making a difference: Using emerging technologies and teaching strategies to restructure an undergraduate technology course for pre-service teachers. *Educational Media International*, *38*(1), 13–20.

National Center for Education Statistics (2006*). Internet access in U.S. public schools and classrooms: 1994–2005.*Retrieved July 1, 2008 from http://nces.ed.gov/.

National Center for Education Statistics (2008). *Technology-based distance education courses for public elementary and secondary school students: 2002–03 and 2004–05.* Retrieved July 2, 2008 from http://nces.ed.gov/pubsearch/pubsinfo.asp?pubid=2008008

Sandholtz, J. H., Ringstaff, C., & Dwyer, D. C. (1997). *Teaching with technology: Creating student-centered classrooms.* New York: Teachers College Press.

CHAPTER 17

Voices: Alternative Routes to Licensure

Karen Peterson, Governors State University

INTRODUCTION

Standards? Yes, we have standards. The Governors State University Alternative Certification Partnership was developed nine years ago when the professional education unit at the university was preparing for initial National Council for Accreditation of Teacher Education (NCATE) accreditation. This provided the opportunity for utilizing standards driven, performance-based practice in initial program development rather than transitioning from a content driven model, as many other programs have evolved.

As one of the developers and as the director of a standards-based program, I have had experiences and challenges in working with standards in our program and in other arenas. Currently, I am a member of the Illinois Induction Policy Team Standards Committee, which is developing the first induction and mentoring standards for the state of Illinois. I also serve on the newly formed National Association of Alternative Certification Quality Indicators Panel, which is developing a model of best practice for nontraditional routes to teacher certification.

This chapter provides background on alternative certification and the voice of an experienced standards-based educator from one higher education institution. I provide my perspective on the potential for the Association of Teacher Educators (ATE) Standards for Teacher Educators' application to alternative certification programs in general, with specific focus on the role of high quality teacher educators providing teacher preparation for those gaining certification through alternative routes.

BACKGROUND ON ALTERNATIVE CERTIFICATION AND THE DEVELOPMENT OF QUALITY INDICATORS

Although some programs have been in operation since the 1980s, alternative certification of teachers is still controversial in the educational community. These programs may be referred to as alternative certification programs, alternative or alternate route programs, or nontraditional programs. There is a wide range of providers such as institutions of higher education, state or district entities, regional offices of education, and online, which may be offered by any of the aforementioned. The variety of programs has a wide range of rigor and accountability (Berry, 2001; Feistritzer, 2008; Walsh & Jacobs, 2007). There is also tremendous latitude in state guidelines of what comprises and what is required in alternative route programs.

Chester Finn and David Petrilli voiced one perspective of alternative certification in the foreword to the recent Thomas B. Fordham Foundation report *Alternative Certification Isn't Alternative* (Walsh & Jacobs, 2007). They indicated that alternative certification programs are too similar to traditional higher education programs. "So alternative certification has been co-opted, compromised, and diluted. Education schools—brilliantly turning a threat into an opportunity—have themselves come to dominate this enterprise, blurring the distinctions that once made it alternative" (p. 9).

The Fordham study researchers interviewed program directors from forty-nine randomly selected programs in eleven states. They note that the programs are truly diverse, but that now colleges of education operate most of the alternative certification programs in the nation, which, from their perspective, compromises the original intent of such programs. In fact, the data from 2006 indicate that institutions of higher education house nearly half (46 percent) of the alternative certification programs in the country (Feistritzer, 2008). There is still a great deal of controversy over intent and form, but there is an increasing emphasis on research related to alternative route teacher certification to determine what constitutes quality. The National Association for Alternative Certification has recently convened a Quality Indicators Task Force to establish research-based guidelines for alternative route programs.

Stoddart and Floden (1995) highlight the potentially positive impact of alternative certification, noting that "alternative route programs give school districts a choice between hiring teachers with two kinds of qualifications: those with academic and professional credentials and those with academic credentials alone" (p. 1). With added institutional and professional experience, alternative certification teachers also bring experience, which, they add, can "challenge the status quo or conceive of different ways of organizing schools" (p. 1).

While many institutions and individuals have strong views about alternative routes to certification, there has been tremendous growth in the number of programs over a very short time period. The National Center for Alternative Certification's data indicate that 60,000 teachers received certification through alternative routes in 2007, nearly one third of new teachers. Every state has at least one program with approximately 500 programs nationwide (Feistritzer, 2008). The Department of Education, through its Transition to Teaching grant program, has provided resources to support the development and operation of programs throughout the country. Since 2001, 237 programs have received funding from the Office of Innovation and Improvement (U.S. Department of Education, 2008).

There is agreement that this is a burgeoning area on the educational landscape with most programs having been established in the last fifteen years (Powers, 2007). Another area of consensus is that there is conflicting research in the growing field with both proponents and opponents putting forth varied findings (Zhao, 2005). To a great extent, this is based on the reality that alternative certification is a "complicated research topic" (Shen, 1998).

There is a developing, although conflicting, research base that merits further exploration of the positive impact of alternate routes, particularly those serving high need schools. There are three key findings that warrant the continued research and development on the potential of the alternative certification movement:

- the increase in minority teacher candidates (Feistritzer, 2008; Peterson, 2007; Shen & Palmer, 2005)
- the increased rate of retention of alternative route candidates in high needs schools (Consortium on Chicago School Research, 2007; Peterson, 2007)
- the relationship of improved student achievement to more rigorous selection of high quality candidates (Boyd, Lankford, Loeb, Rockoff, & Wyckoff, 2008)

As the director of an alternative route program that was one of six national finalists for the prestigious Christa McAuliffe Award for Excellence in Teacher Education in 2006 (American Association of State Colleges and Universities), I believe that high quality standards-based programs can perform at the same level as traditional teacher preparation programs. I am proud to be a member of the newly formed national Alternative Certification Quality Indicators Task Force, a part of the National Association of Alternative Certification (NAAC). The task force adopted its vision statement in December, 2007.

> Through a review of current literature and the combined expertise of its members, the Task Force will delineate the important components of high quality nontraditional teacher preparation programs and describe the indicators for those components. The result will be a report that is adopted by the NAAC membership as a framework for program self-evaluation and for providing [quality indicators] to help programs improve their preparation of teachers.

The operating premise of the NAAC Teacher Quality Committee is that, in order for quality indicators to be meaningful, the indicators must:

- be based on a thorough review of current research
- be flexible enough to honor the diversity inherent in alternative routes to certification
- recognize the unique strengths of alternative routes to certification as they respond to the need for streamlined pathways that bring diverse, talented new teachers into the classroom
- focus on teacher and student outcomes, and on an ability to document effective results
- promote high expectations, not minimal levels of achievement or entry standards, for alternative certification programs
- be developed and driven by stakeholders in the field

The NAAC plans to share the results of its national quality-indicators project as a contribution to the ongoing dialogue on the improvement of teacher preparation programs.

The current debate about alternative certification and the beginning of a standards movement within the field both suggest that the timing might be right to bring the ATE Standards for Teacher Educators into the alternative certification standards discussion.

ALTERNATIVE CERTIFICATION PARTNERSHIP'S UTILIZATION OF STANDARDS

The Governors State University (GSU) Alternative Certification Partnership is now in its ninth year. A team of GSU educators spent a full year planning the program. The team utilized multiple sets of standards in the planning, implementation, and evaluation of the program: NCATE (National Council for the Accreditation of Teacher Education), ACEI (Association for Childhood Education International), IPTS (Illinois Professional Teaching Standards); Illinois Elementary Education Content Area Standards, Illinois Technology Standards for all Teachers, Illinois Reading and Language Arts Standards for all Teachers, Illinois Learning Standards, and Illinois Social and Emotional Standards.

It is apparent in the current standards era: educators have the overwhelming task of designing and/or refining programs linked to numerous sets of required standards. At the same time, it presents important resources, as the state and national standards were developed by multiple stakeholders and are research-based compilations of best practices in the field. This is particularly important for alternative route programs, due to the widespread controversy over alternative program design and operation.

As indicated earlier, standards-based programs, depending on their context, have numerous sets of standards that are required as part of program approval and accreditation. Optional sets of standards such as the ATE standards, while very worthwhile, may be more useful for program refinement once the programs have been in operation. On the other hand, one area in which the ATE standards could be very valuable is in facilitating initial alternative route program design and training of faculty.

At GSU, we have been working with our required standards over time and are now at a place to explore optional sets of standards to further facilitate program improvements.

We anticipate working on program refinement with the frameworks of best practice provided by the ATE standards, the new Alternative Certification Quality Indicators, as well as the Illinois Standards for

High Quality Induction and Mentoring, which are currently in the final stages of development. What follows is an analysis of the how the ATE standards could be used in programs such as ours.

THE ATE STANDARDS FOR TEACHER EDUCATORS AND ALTERNATIVE CERTIFICATION PROGRAMS

My experience with the variety of standards implemented within our alternative certification program confirms the value of a structured program analysis that standards facilitate. In a December 2007 informal survey of the members of the national Alternative Certification Quality Indicators Task Force, all respondents indicated that they utilized standards in the development and operation of their programs. None had, at that point, utilized the ATE Standards for Teacher Educators. Because alternative certification programs are varied in form and substance, both the NAAC-sponsored Quality Indicators for Alternative Programs and the ATE Standards for Teacher Educators potentially provide valuable frameworks for both program development and enhancement.

APPLICATION OF ATE STANDARDS TO ALTERNATIVE CERTIFICATION

Individuals in school districts, regional offices of education, and institutions of higher education are among those who develop alternative certification programs. The teacher educators within these diverse institutions involved in alternative certification may not be familiar with the ATE Standards for Teacher Educators despite their potential use. It would be valuable for the Association of Teacher Educators to make a concerted effort to bring these standards to the alternative certification community.

To introduce the standards to program administrators and to discuss the utility of these standards, presentations at the two national alternative certification conferences, National Association for Alternative Certification (NAAC) and National Center for Alternative Certification (NCAC), would enhance the standards' visibility. Below I briefly explain the relevance of each of the ATE standards to the field of alternative certification with a specific focus on Standard Six: collaboration.

Standard One: Teaching

Standard one provides a standard of excellence in an area of alternative certification where there exists a tremendous range in program design and operation, in addition to the background of those providing instruction to teacher candidates. Teachers still in preparation are regarded as highly qualified according to *No Child Left Behind* guidelines (Ludwig, Bacevich, Wayne, Hale, & Lickawa, 2007). To have such responsibility and accountability as novice teachers in an internship, it is critical that their teacher preparation includes instructors who "use research-based, proven best-practices in order for those behaviors to be appropriately applied."

The importance of teacher quality (Bennet, 2001; Darling-Hammond & Baratz-Snowden, 2007; National Commission on Teaching and America's Future, 2003) and the critical role of teacher educators cannot be emphasized enough. This is particularly important for teacher candidates who are often the teacher of record while still in their preparation programs. In this era of accountability, it is also important that no teacher be left behind (Gray & Smith, 2005).

Standard Two: Cultural Competence

A high percentage of alternative route programs have been developed to meet staffing demands in high needs schools. This makes it essential for alternative certification teacher educators to align their practice with this standard. This standard highlights the importance of a strong theoretical foundation in cultural competence, but also emphasizes the successful application of these theories in classrooms. In most programs, candidates are actively working under guidance during the implementation phase and in internships to develop strategies for working with diverse populations. Using the indicators as a framework for this work could prove useful in developing candidates' ability to teach minority and low-income students.

Standard Three: Scholarship

Scholarship is essential for the field of alternative certification because it is a relatively new, yet burgeoning field, still clouded with controversy in some circles. "In the course of nearly twenty years of implementation of alternative certification, the policy landscape has been dominated by a myriad of definitions and programs, intense debate about the professional legitimacy of the solution, and mixed, inconclusive, and even contradictory research in terms of the effectiveness of such programs" (Zhao, 2005, p. 1). Since alternative certification teacher educators are often working with candidates in high need areas, it is essential that we work to identify best practices for working with children of promise. High quality programs need to publish their findings for the larger educational community to illustrate that this model is having impact and to more clearly define what works and what does not.

Standard Four: Professional Development

High quality professional development for teacher educators in alternative certification is essential. According to the standards, teacher educators should "maintain a philosophy of teaching and learning that is continuously reviewed based on a deepening understanding of research and practice." Alternative route teacher educators, however, are still establishing the validity of the format. It is important to substantiate the rigor of the programs by providing systems to update and refine them continuously. Alternative certification teacher educators have two national professional organizations (NAAC and NCAC) to "engage in purposeful professional development focused on professional learning goals." The use of the ATE Standards for Teacher Educators can introduce some of the programs, which are not housed in institutions of higher education, to ATE. Many programs may not be familiar with the association and the fine resources and professional development opportunities ATE can provide.

Standard Five: Program Development

As most alternative route programs are relatively new, many teacher educators in these programs are accustomed to being "leaders in the development, refinement, and revision of programs and portions of programs focused on initial teacher preparation. . . ." The indicators may set a higher standard for goal setting such as "providing leadership" and "contribut[ing] to research."

Standard Six: Collaboration

Although all of the ATE standards would contribute research-based insight to the process of preparing high quality teacher educators to work with alternative certification candidates, the standard that I would like to focus on is collaboration. There are several specific indicators, which are critical to the success of candidates. This standard notes the work of Fullan and Hargreaves (1992) in highlighting the importance of collaboration in educational change. This standard perhaps most strongly lends itself to circumventing the divide between traditional and alternative route proponents as well. The particularly noteworthy areas for high quality collaboration to have positive impact on alternative routes are *cross-institutional collaboration* and the *support* indicator, which I break down into two areas, *induction and mentoring* and the importance of *school culture*.

Two specific indicators highlight the importance of collaboration: *reciprocal relationships and cross-institutional collaboration*. Since most alternative certification programs place candidates in schools during internships and most often as teacher of record, it is essential that partnerships are forged between programs and placement sites. Placement is critical to success and retention of alternative certification candidates (Humphrey, Wechsler, & Hough, 2005). In these programs, strong reciprocal relationships need to be established with the district(s) and schools to optimize the internship experience. Just as the early policy transformation that strengthened the field experience component of traditional teacher education linking theory to practice (Holmes Group, 1986), this even more intensive practicum experience necessitates strong collaborative ties between the preparation entity and the placement site.

The case can also be made for linking practice to theory for programs that are not connected to institutions of higher education. An example of strong collaboration linking practice to theory is the Texas Region XIII's professional development initiative with the American Association for Colleges of Teacher Education, Alverno College, and the Council of Chief State School Officials (Washington, 2008). Regional XIII's program was one of six programs highlighted in the Department of Education's publication *Alternative Routes to Teacher Certification* (2004). When refining their program, the regional office leadership sought out the expertise and the theoretical perspectives from the higher education community. This highlights that alternative routes are an outstanding opportunity for developing partnerships along both directions of the theory to practice continuum.

Collaboration in the P–12 Context

Another essential collaborative venture necessary for alternative program success is linked to the indicator *"support teacher education in the p–12 school environment."* I discuss two avenues that are particularly important in the alternative certification realm related to this indicator: high quality induction/mentoring and assisting alternative certification candidates in making the transition to school settings.

There is increasing emphasis and strong research on the importance of high quality induction and mentoring and the impact on retention and teacher performance (Consortium on Chicago School Research, 2007; Strong & Villar, 2007). Since most alternative certification candidates have had neither extensive coursework nor long-term field experiences before their internships, the support component is even more essential. The ATE standard on collaboration provides a framework to articulate the importance of teacher educators being directly linked to the support initiatives.

The Consortium on Chicago School Research (2007) study on influences of induction in the Chicago Public Schools highlights both the importance of high quality induction, including intensive mentoring in the school system overall, and its particular influence on alternative certification candidates. In this study, new elementary teachers receiving the high quality intensive model of induction were twice as likely to report a good experience than those with weak mentoring experiences. Novice high school teachers were more than four times more likely to report positive experiences from the model. The study also found that teachers with prior work experience, many of them alternative certification teachers, were more likely to report a good teaching experience and intended to stay in the profession.

Contextual factors are another important consideration related to teacher retention and success (Consortium on Chicago School Research, 2007; Costigan, 2005; Dickar, 2005; Wolfe, Bartell, & DeBolt, 2000). The issue reflects the ATE Standard Six: Collaboration, indicator "*support teacher education in the P–12 school environment.*" In the Consortium on Chicago School Research Study (2007), it is reported that new teachers are "influenced by the strength of school leadership and the extent to which they are welcomed into the school community and helped by other teachers" (p. 38). The administrator role is important in supporting new teachers (Brock & Grady, 1997; Moir, 2008; Saphier, 2001). This is particularly important for alternative certification candidates, who often experience a disconnect from their prior work experience while acclimating to the new school's culture.

The Interim Report of 2002 Transition to Teaching programs (Ludwig et al., 2007) reported school administration and school working conditions as the top two reasons cited for alternative certification candidates not completing their internships. In a recent study, this author (Peterson, 2007) examined alternative certification candidates' views on different dispositional expectations in various work settings. This may necessitate different behaviors in school settings than in their previous career settings. It is important that teacher educators not only be aware of these challenges, but actively address issues and develop programming to help facilitate the transition.

Facilitating the transition in alternative certification includes teacher educators working closely with the administrators and the schools where the candidates are placed. Too often alternative route programs provide coursework while operating independently from the placement sites. To address this at GSU we recently added the requirement that all administrators in partner districts attend a workshop on the role of the administrator in supporting novice teachers. This training includes research on new teacher development, alternative certification, and the importance of the administrator in supporting new teachers, particularly alternative certification interns who are still in the final phase of their teacher preparation program.

The ATE standard on collaboration can serve as a vehicle for teacher educators to explore possibilities for the critical link of theory to practice, support through comprehensive induction with intensive mentoring, and a supportive administration and school culture. All of these elements are important for all teachers, but particularly for alternative route teachers. Alternate routes to education provide a vehicle for strong collaboration among stakeholders, as a large percentage of teacher preparation is taking place while candidates are in the field. These indicators highlight important areas of collaboration, which many nontraditional programs already provide. It is not, however, a standard of practice in all alternative certification programs. Successful programs focus on the importance of collaboration, particularly ongoing mentor support and university-school district partnerships (Hayes, 2005).

Standard Seven: Public Advocacy

Those who operate high quality alternative route programs are called to "serve as informed, constructive advocates for high quality education for all students" as cited in one indicator for this standard. The Quality Indicators panel of the NAAC serves as an exemplary vehicle to set standards for high quality alternative certification programs. It is the reason that the panel is committed to "acquiring research-based background information . . . as the basis for advocacy at all levels" as noted in this standard and in the panel's mission statement.

Standard Eight: Teacher Education Profession

Alternative route programs have expanded the view of teacher preparation beyond traditional programs in institutions of higher education to a variety of educational entities and formats. This standard, considered from the perspective of alternative route programs, provides a means to extend our thinking. As we contemplate this standard's focus to "contribute to improving the teacher education profession" this is foundational to the teacher quality research (The National Commission on Teaching and America's Future, 2003; Angrist & Guryan, 2004).

Standard Nine: Vision

This standard is a strong fit for alternative route teacher educators. Many have worked to develop programs with limited resources based on a strong need to provide high quality teachers in high need settings. Teacher educators within alternative route programs have established themselves "firmly in the forefront of educational change" as indicated by this standard.

CONCLUSION

The growth of alternative certification programs over the past fifteen years indicates that these programs are meeting a need. It is unsettling, however, that there is such a tremendous range in the quality of programs. The NAAC initiative to develop high quality indicators for program development and refinement is one initiative designed to strengthen programs. The ATE Teacher Educator Standards are also an excellent resource, emphasizing the importance of the role of the teacher educator in high quality teacher preparation. The challenge to ATE is to explore strategies to collaborate and build partnerships with both the National Center for Alternative Certification and the National Association of Alternative Certification to facilitate this process.

Alternative route programs are grounded in vision, which is aligned with Rogers' (2003) work cited in the rationale for standard nine. "Accomplished teacher educators embrace their role as change agents, understand the impact teacher education has on classroom practices, and are early adopters of new configurations of learning." As the NAAC Quality Indicators panel demonstrates, there is a strong movement to strengthen program quality. A collaborative working partnership with the NCAC and the NAAC, utilizing the ATE Standards for Teacher Educators, could move us closer to Zeichner's (2006) goal:

> We need to support teacher education programs of all kinds that have. . . characteristics that are shown by research to enable the achievement of desired outcomes, whether they are traditional or alternative, and criticize and/or close down those that do not have them (p. 332).

As an educator who has been working closely within the standards movement for quite some time, I believe that the ATE Standards for Teacher Educators have the potential to benefit the alternative certification community. It involves, however, making the standards more accessible and, perhaps, bridging some divides. With the overarching vision of facilitating excellence, it is worth the challenge.

REFERENCES

Angrist, J., & Guryan, J. (2004). Teacher testing, teacher education, and teacher characteristics. *American Economic Review, 94*(2), 241–246.

Berry, B. (2001). No shortcuts to preparing good teachers. *Educational Leadership*, *58*(8), 32–36.

Boyd, D., Lankford, H., Loeb, S., Rockoff, J., & Wyckoff, J. (2008). The narrowing gap in New York City teacher qualification and its implications for student achievement in high-poverty schools. *Journal of Policy Analysis and Management*.

Brock, B. L., & Grady, M. L. (1997). *From first-year to first-rate: Principals guiding beginning teachers*. Thousand Oaks, CA: Corwin Press.

Consortium on Chicago School Research. (2007). *Keeping new teachers: A first look at the influences of induction in the Chicago Public Schools*. University of Chicago.

Costigan, A. (2005). A "traditional" alternative route to certification: Narrative research and implications for teacher education and teacher retention. In J. Rainer Dangel & E. Guyton (Eds.), *Research on alternative and non-traditional education* (pp. 27–38). Lanham, MD: Association of Teacher Educators.

Darling-Hammond, L., & Baratz-Snowden, J. (2007). A good teacher in every classroom: Preparing the highly qualified teachers our children deserve. *Educational Horizons*, *85*(2), 111–131.

Dickar, M. (2005). When they are good. . . . A comparison of career changers and recent college graduates in an alternative certification program. In J. Rainer Danger & E. Guyton (Eds.), *Research on alternative and non-traditional education* (pp. 91–104). Lanham, MD: Association of Teacher Educators.

Feistritzer, E. (Ed.). (2008). *Building a quality teaching force: Lessons learned from alternate routes*. Upper Saddle River, NJ: Pearson/Merrill Prentice Hall.

Fullan, M., & Hargreaves, A. (Eds). (1992). *Teacher development and educational change*. New York: The Falmer Press.

Gray, D. L., & Smith, A. E. (2005). No teacher left behind. *Kappa Delta Pi Record*, *42*(1), 7–9.

Hayes, J. H. (2005). Summary and conclusion: Alternative certification programs: Effects of program models on teacher performance. In J. Rainer Danger & E. Guyton (Eds.), *Research on alternative and non-traditional education* (pp. 159–165). Lanham, MD: Association of Teacher Educators.

Holmes Group. (1986). *Tomorrow's teachers: A report of the Holmes Group*. East Lansing, MI: Author.

Humphrey, D., Wechsler, M., & Hough, H. (2005). *Characteristics of effective alternative certification programs*. Menlo Park, CA: SRI International.

Ludwig, M., Bacevich, A., Wayne, A., Hale, M., & Lickawa, K. (2007). *Transition to teaching program evaluation: An interim report on the 2002 grantees*. Washington, DC: American Institute for Research.

Moir, E. (2008). Quality induction: Mentoring and support. In C. E. Feistritzer (Ed.), *Building a quality teaching force: Lessons learned from alternate routes* (pp. 36–59). Upper Saddle River, NJ: Pearson, Merrill Prentice Hall.

The National Commission on Teaching and America's Future (2003). *No dream denied: Report of the national commission on teaching and America's future*. Washington, DC: Author.

Peterson, K. (2007). Alternatively certified teachers' perceptions of dispositions. In. M. Diez & J. Raths (Eds.), *Dispositions in teacher education*. Charlotte, NC: Information Age Publishing.

Powers, E. (2007). The state of alternative teacher certification. *Inside Higher Education*. Retrieved January 28, 2008, from www.insidehighered.com/news/2007/09/18/teacher

Rogers, E. M. (2003). *Diffusion of innovations* (5th ed.). New York: Free Press.

Saphier, J. (2001). *Beyond mentoring: Comprehensive induction programs: How to attract, support, and retain new teachers*. Newton, MA: Teacher 21.

Shen, J. (1998). Alternative certification: A complicated research topic. *Educational Evaluation and Policy Analysis, 20*(4), 316–319.

Shen, J., & Palmer, L. B. (2005). Attrition patterns of inadequately prepared teachers. In J. Rainer Danger & E. Guyton (Eds.), *Research on alternative and non-traditional education* (pp. 143–157). Lanham, MD: Association of Teacher Educators.

Stoddart, T., & Flosen, R. E. (1995). *Traditional and alternative routes to teacher certification: Issues, assumptions, and misconceptions*. East Lansing, MI: National Center for Research on Teacher Learning.

Strong, M., & Villar, A. (2007). *Research brief: The costs and benefits of a comprehensive induction program*. Santa Cruz, CA: The New Teacher Center.

U.S. Department of Education Office of Innovation and Improvement (2004). *Alternative routes to teacher certification*. Washington, DC: Author.

U.S. Department of Education Office of Innovation and Improvement (2008). *Awards—TTT programs*. Retrieved August 4, 2008 from www.ed.gov/programs/transitionteach/awards.html

Walsh, K., & Jacobs, S. (2007). *Alternative certification isn't alternative*. Washington DC: The Thomas B. Fordham Institute. Retrieved January 20, 2008, from www.edexcellence.net/foundation/publication/publication.cfm?id=375

Washington, B. (2008). Standards-based curriculum development: One program's journey. In C. E. Feistritzer (Ed.), *Building a quality teaching force: Lessons learned from alternate routes* (pp. 60–87). Upper Saddle River, New Jersey: Pearson Merrill Prentice Hall.

Wolfe, M. P., Bartell, C. A., & DeBolt, G. P., (2000). School, district, and university cultures and responsibilities (Mentoring framework: Dimension II).

In S. J. Odell & L. Huling (Eds.), *Quality mentoring for novice teachers* (pp. 47–56). Indianapolis: Kappa Delta Pi.

Zeichner, K. (2006). Reflections of a university-based teacher educator on the future of college and university based teacher education. *Journal of Teacher Education, 57*(3), 326–340.

Zhao, Y. (2005). *Alternative certification for science teachers: Policy and context.* Paper presented at the National Association for Research in Science Teaching annual conference, Dallas, TX.

CHAPTER 18

Diversity Perspective

Diane Rodriguez, East Carolina University

No one should claim of being educated until he or she has learned
to live in harmony with people who are different. — A.H. Wilson

MY PERSONAL PERSPECTIVE ON DIVERSITY

Diversity defines the professional life that I lead. As an American educator from a minority background, I see educational diversity through
a different lens than the majority of the population of East Carolina
University. Through my lens I see cordial colleagues and students doing their best to make me feel as comfortable as possible. I often find
that we share common perceptions and behaviors, but at times I find
theirs to be intriguing or on some occasions disheartening. For instance, recently a well-meaning student asked me, in her deep southern
drawl: "Are you aware that you speak with an accent?" Of course, from
my perspective, the student is the one with the accent, since she is the
one who sounds different than I do. Numerous miscommunications and
awkward interactions with students and colleagues have shaped my
teaching and research endeavors.

Teaching

A major goal of my teaching efforts in diversity is to increase my students' understanding of the academic, social, and emotional needs of
school-aged children and youth from diverse backgrounds. I focus on
the special needs of those who are English language learners. My work

with pre-service and in-service teachers who educate students from culturally and linguistically diverse backgrounds informs my course objectives that address both awareness and competence. To assess how my students are increasing their awareness of culturally and linguistically diverse populations, I give assignments for them to create various artifacts. In this section, I first describe the course objectives and my approaches to helping students achieve them. Second, I discuss the artifacts that I require students to create.

For a diversity course, students are expected to develop awareness and understanding of the cultures represented by the different culturally and linguistically diverse populations within the United States. In my teaching, I emphasize the following points to understand the influences of one's own cultural heritage: 1) understand and appreciate different cultural influences within society and how various media may influence us; 2) examine instructional approaches, strategies, and materials that result in meaningful cross-cultural communication and understanding among students; and (3) write reflections about their assumptions, beliefs, and teaching practices.

I also draw on research to guide in-service and pre-service teachers in planning instruction and assessment activities that meet the needs of diverse students. Further, I feel it is important for teacher educators to examine their own cultural bias and attitudes as they relate to culturally and linguistically diverse students.

Association of Teacher Educators' Standards

Educators have the responsibility to provide and to facilitate instruction that is meaningful to all students, including students from diverse backgrounds. The Association of Teacher Educators has published a document entitled *Standards for Teacher Educators* (2008). Its overall goal is "To help all teacher candidates and other school personnel impact student learning." My teaching is aligned with the standards that relate to educational diversity. They are covered in this section.

The first three of the ATE standards address diversity education: 1) teaching, 2) cultural competence, and 3) scholarship. Under the first standard, teaching, the point most specific to my area of teaching is indicator one: "Model effective instruction to meet the needs of diverse learners." This standard is evident in my work when I model appropriate and accepted behavior to use with diverse groups of individuals.

The second ATE standard, cultural competence, reads: "Apply cultural competence and promote social justice in teacher education." This standard serves as the basis for teacher educators to teach their students about the pedagogical needs of culturally and linguistically diversity populations.

Each standard includes a narrative description, which follows the main goal. In standard number two, the narrative defines cultural competence by using excerpts from educational research. Below are highlights from the narrative:

- "Prepare teachers to connect and communicate with diverse learners"
- "Know [your] own culture"
- "Have high expectations for all students"
- "Understand developmental levels and what is common and unique among different groups"
- "Reach out to families and communities to learn about their cultures"
- "Select curriculum materials that are inclusive"
- "Use a range of assessment method"
- "Be proficient in a variety of pedagogical methods that facilitate the acquisition of content knowledge for all learners"

As suggested in the artifacts section of the ATE cultural competence standard, teacher educators can demonstrate their knowledge of diversity issues by: 1) creating course syllabi with explicit objectives concerning culturally and linguistically diverse populations; 2) incorporating diverse and culturally appropriate instructional materials; and 3) using culturally appropriate video and/or audiotapes of teaching. Teachers are asked to provide appropriate student work samples; to include a "philosophical statement that reflects attention to diversity"; and to choose "assessment tools appropriate for use with diverse learners" (ATE, 2005).

In my course, I apply the cultural competence standard when I ask the students to reflect, document, apply, and internalize scholarly readings and class discussions concerning diverse individuals and groups. Although the Association of Teacher Educator (ATE) standards encourage multifaceted approaches to teacher preparation, which is an important component of effective teacher preparation programs, I feel the standards are not providing the necessary guidance for teacher educators to examine their own cultural biases and attitudes.

To meet course objectives, the students create the following artifacts: (a) a reflective essay, called a *Diverse Self-Portrait*, to promote each learner's recognition as a diverse human being and educator; (b) a list, log, or diary of reflections to address differences on cultural influences; and (c) an interdisciplinary unit of study with a diversity focus. For the interdisciplinary unit, my students choose a cultural group that is well represented in schools across the United States. Then they choose a grade level and educate the students in this grade level about the chosen cultural group. Anecdotal evidence shows that these artifacts improve at least short-term awareness and understanding of culturally and linguistically different groups, but I have little empirical evidence on the effect of all these activities related to long-term effects.

Over the years my teaching efforts have been enhanced by federal grants for personnel preparation projects, which provide funds for inservice teachers to take multiple courses related to diversity issues. I find that multicourse programs are more favorable for diversity education than single courses and workshops. There is nothing wrong with a single diversity workshop as many benefits may accrue from them, but courses over multiple months are better.

Research

My research interests include diversity training within teacher preparation programs, particularly ones that include bilingual education, English language learners, and disabilities. With respect to results generated by many researchers in this field, I suggest that educators take note of performance indicators that influence academic performance of culturally and linguistically diverse students. For example, research suggests that when teachers participate in multicultural teacher education preparation, they are less likely to embrace cultural deficit views (Irvine, 2003). In addition, Morrier, Irving, Dandy, Dmitriyev, and Ukeje (2007) advise that "quality teachers take the time and effort to differentiate instruction on several variables related to the child, with one of those variables being the child's culture" (p. 33).

Researchers in this field have examined the need to address diversity from multidisciplinary perspectives. In particular, teachers lack the skills to provide diverse instructional methodologies that match the learning styles of culturally and linguistically diverse students, which would make their learning more effective. Instead of putting a Band-aid on a superficial wound of differences, educators need to be open to the wealth of knowledge students from culturally and linguistically diverse backgrounds bring. If teachers recognize the unique qualities of these students as assets, teachers can help build upon them to enrich academic and social knowledge for all students.

As stated by Gollnick and Chinn (2002), today's classroom teachers educate and instruct students from culturally and linguistically diverse backgrounds. To face this complex challenge, it is helpful for educators to understand the theoretical framework known as *culturally responsive pedagogy*. The framework includes politics, poverty, linguistics, culture, and education. Accordingly to Kea, Campbell-Whatley, and Richards (2004), teachers who implement a culturally responsive pedagogy create curricula and field experiences that are committed to diversity, which "enable future practitioners to engage in pedagogy with insight and view all communities as resources for learning and social justice" (p. 11).

We, in teacher preparation, need to ensure that issues concerning cultural and linguistic diversity continue to be studied within our educational system. When the complexities surrounding diversity are not recognized and addressed by an institution and its teacher preparation programs, the faculty and the students who succeed will come from the same monocultural and monolingual culture. The result will be that teachers will not be prepared to teach students from backgrounds different than their own.

Institutions of higher education and teacher preparation programs ignoring the increasingly diverse population, or paying only superficial attention to issues concerning diverse communities, will continue to fail their constituents. Although the standards provide benchmarks of competencies for teacher preparation programs, professional development in cultural diversity in education must be offered to faculty in teacher preparation programs who lack the necessary knowledge needed to attain the competencies.

Awareness of our Growing Diversity

Teacher education and diversity are of such importance within our society that legislators and state representatives have introduced the "Improving Teacher Diversity Act." If passed, the Improving Teacher Diversity Act would award grants to minority institutions in order to establish centers of excellence for teacher education. In other words, this piece of legislation demonstrates an awareness that schools, like other social institutions, are shaped by cultural values and practices (Hollins, 1996). Therefore, there is support for teacher education programs to promote research-based effective practices for disseminating knowledge on educational diversity issues.

ATE Standards for Teacher Educators also bring attention to the need for educators to become knowledgeable about diversity. Further, the ATE Standards for Teacher Educators provide educators with a starting place for reflecting on their professional practices. To begin, each educator does well to ask herself/himself: What does diversity mean to me? Does the push for assimilation imply that children and youth in public schools have to deny their diverse backgrounds in order to acculturate, to participate in society in the United States? One key advantage of the ATE Standards for Teacher Educators is that they help to keep us focused on vitally important goals, such as the need to respect diverse people, to understand their unique approaches to learning, and to improve communication among all of us with a stake in the field of teacher preparation.

The ATE standards also provide leadership for teacher educators by describing a host of issues to reflect upon. As teacher educators, how can we teach our pre-service and in-service teachers the realities of diversity in the United States? Strasser and Sesphocha (2005) expressed that exploring diversity and multiculturalism is an exciting and often frightening challenge for institutions of higher education. The ATE standards, working to implement an educational agenda that includes diversity, must consider the cultural contexts in which everyone learns. The ATE standards should also recognize the rich contributions to be made by students from diverse backgrounds, all of whom have many different ways of knowing. The ATE standards must bring a more rigorous set of competencies that lead to rich cultural environments for all students, which will contribute to intellectual, social, and personal development in the lives of everyone.

Diversity training promotes learning and understanding of different views of culture, language, traditions, religions, and many more characteristics. As teacher educators, we must become innovators of diversity programs to attract prospective teachers who are willing to address diversity within their school and community. I agree with Ladson-Billings (1995) that institutions of higher education are obligated to re-educate teacher educators who teach pre-service and in-service teachers. Each teacher should become aware of his or her own cultural identity and biases; gain a worldview which encompasses learning about groups who are culturally different from himself or herself; and develop culturally responsive teaching strategies that are inclusive of the cultural norms of all student groups (Gay & Kirkland, 2003).

We as teacher educators must inform teachers educating students from diverse backgrounds that they need to have high performance expectations for all students. Once teachers understand the importance of respecting diversity, students from diverse backgrounds will perform better academically, personally, and socially. The National Collaborative on Diversity in the Teaching Force (2004) released a report on diversity of America's teaching force and stated, "The challenge of ensuring excellence and diversity are not new" (p. 5). In addition, "States across the country are recognizing the urgent need to recruit and retain teachers of diverse backgrounds and are implementing a variety of programs and policies that complement traditional teacher recruitment methods" (p. 7). Teacher educators must master integrating multiculturalism into the curriculum in order to engage, affirm, and accept diversity within the educational context of the classroom and school environment.

A Diversity Education Model

ATE standards, especially the second, cultural competence, guides my work and area of expertise in teacher education and is especially pertinent to my teaching, research, and service. My work is also informed by Standards One: Teaching and Three: Scholarship. Teaching and scholarly work enables the heart that beats around diversity. I have developed the model below as a way of expressing how I see the landscape of diversity education.

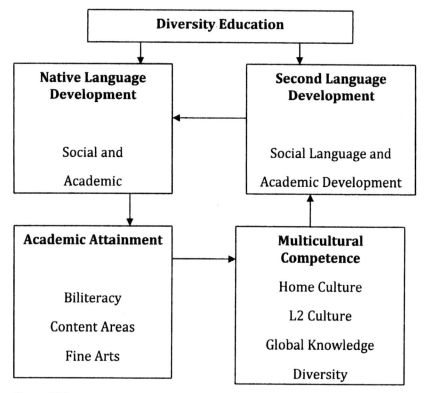

Figure 18.1.

As educators we cannot deny the diversity our students bring into our classrooms. I contend that to have successful diversity programs in school settings, teacher educators need to incorporate a theoretical framework that includes connections between native language development, multicultural competencies, and second language development. Beyond theory, with respect to implementing programs that address the needs of culturally and linguistically diverse students, Carrasquillo (2002) and Garcia (2005) proposed integrating both instructional and social services. Promoting multicultural competence enhances achievement in academic attainment.

For students to achieve academic success, teacher educators can gain a better understanding of the complexity of bicultural identity as explained by Banks (2006) in his stages of cultural identity:

- Stage 1: cultural psychological captivity
- Stage 2: cultural encapsulation

- Stage 3: cultural identity clarification
- Stage 4: biculturalism
- Stage 5: multiculturalism and reflective nationalism
- Stage 6: globalism and global competency

When educators understand the importance of biliteracy and bicultural education in the content areas, then we educators will be able to see the benefits of enhanced student achievement.

Diversity in teacher education programs is in the beginning of its transformative evolution and it needs to become a reality with completion of the standards of teachers. Appropriately, the ATE standards include cultural competence (and assess, evaluate, and monitor the progress of long term empirical research in the field) as a key standard for teacher educators. This standard helps focus attention on the need to continue the transformative evolution. The ATE standards can provide various effective research models that have been implemented throughout the country as examples to other teacher preparation programs seeking to adopt a new inclusive teacher preparation model that honors diversity.

Resistance to Diversity Education

I incorporate the ATE Standards for Teacher Educators in addition to my own diversity education model in course objectives to help my students acquire some level of cultural competence. However, there is resistance from prospective teachers who identify themselves as knowledgeable in the field but who lack the knowledge they claim to have. For example, I have heard these comments from traditional teachers: "I am not prejudiced"; "Oh my God, I have been screaming to a student thinking that he will listen"; "I love all children regardless of their background"; "Since he can't speak English, he must have a disability." When such statements are removed from their contexts, the naïve conceptions held by the speakers are not always readily evident. Nevertheless, to understand diversity, educators need to walk in the shoes of the diverse learners.

From my own perspective, confronting pre-service and in-service teachers with diversity issues is the most difficult task of teaching about diversity education. In my experience, when I challenge my students to think beyond the box of monoculturalism, they feel that I am not following curricular guidelines. For example, I have been told: "I do not need to know that"; "What is the purpose of this? If the immigrants want to live here, they should learn the American way"; or "I am not that way at all." In order to reflect on diversity, we must accept diversity.

Within the last decade, the total number of English language learners (ELL) enrolled in elementary and secondary education has increased over 105 percent nationwide. The special social and educational needs of these students have led to "increasing ELL student achievement" becoming a critical focus of the *No Child Left Behind Act of 2001* (PL 107–220). Many school systems across the United States find themselves unable to recruit and retain the teachers who are prepared to address this increasing diversity.

Eberly, Rand, and O'Connor (2007) analyzed teachers' dispositions toward diversity by investigating: (a) why do some teachers demonstrate great cultural sensitivity in their work with children while others seem mired in stereotypes, perpetuating a view of diversity as exotic or denying that race is an issue in their classrooms?; (b) why is it so difficult to change these dispositions of teachers?; and (c) what can we do in teacher education to further the cultural responsiveness we claim we want teachers to develop? The results led the authors to conclude that by understanding their students' views of multicultural issues, they could better prepare learning tools to coincide with these developmental levels.

REFLECTION ON TEACHER EDUCATION

Since court mandates and legislation have established the rights of culturally and linguistically diverse (CLD) students to equal educational opportunity and an appropriate education, the preparation of sufficient numbers of certified teachers and related personnel able to meet the educational and language-cultural needs of these children becomes both an educational imperative and a far-reaching challenge. According to federal law, these students need programs that meet both their academic and language program needs. As stated by Hollins (1996) "you cannot learn all you need to know about the students you will teach from university courses, but you can learn a process for acquiring, interpreting, and transforming knowledge about students for pedagogical practice" (p. 78).

Teacher education programs should follow the conceptualization of diversity pedagogy (Hernandez-Sheets, 2005) that links culture, cognition, and schooling. Therefore, as an institution of higher education and as faculty of teacher preparation programs, we need to prepare in-service and pre-service teachers to face the challenges of teaching children and youth from diverse backgrounds. It is imperative to have the indicators of the ATE cultural competence standard guide our work to better serve all students.

Emphases on Standards

Institutions of higher education struggle to incorporate standards for implementing diversity coursework into their certification or endorsement for teacher preparation programs (Morrier, Irving, Dandy, Dmitriyev, & Ukeje, 2007). School failure for such students has traditionally been attributed to their "deprived" or "disadvantaged" backgrounds. Educators have argued that it is not the students who have failed, but the schools, in part because they continue to use teaching approaches that do not take into consideration the cultural backgrounds and language experiences of the students.

Schools have "traditionally reinforced the ambivalence and insecurity that many minority students tend to feel with regard to their own cultural identity" (Cummins, 1989, p. 111). If the needs of this population are to be met, teachers must be sensitive to students' cultural and socioeconomic differences and have the knowledge and skills to adapt their educational practices to students' individual needs (Burstsein, Ceballo, & Hamman, 1993).

How can we prevent school failure for all children? This is a complex issue with multiple answers. We cannot do this alone. We have to work with community leaders, school districts, families, school boards and teacher preparation programs to address the underlying systemic problems in families and in communities.

As the United States becomes increasingly more culturally and ethnically diverse, the need for teachers prepared with cultural competence to serve culturally and linguistically diverse students also increases. As a result, the need for dynamic and effective programs to prepare these teachers intensifies. Understanding diversity must be an integral component of teacher education programs. Can either an ATE standard or an amendment to the U.S. Constitution bring about a culturally pluralistic society? Teacher educators must accept that our American society is culturally pluralistic and that the voices of diversity should become embedded in our minds.

The earlier teacher educators recognize the importance of integrating dynamic and effective diversity education in the curriculum, the sooner students from diverse backgrounds will benefit academically. The ATE Standards for Teacher Educators can potentially serve as an important guide in the preparation and training of culturally competent teachers.

REFERENCES

Artiles, A. J., & Kozleski, E. B. (2007). Beyond convictions: Interrogating culture, history, and power in inclusive education. *Language Arts*, *84*(4) 357–365.

Association of Teacher Educators (2008). *Standards for Teacher Educators*. Manassas, VA: Author.

Banks, J. (2006). *Cultural diversity and education: Foundations, curriculum, and teaching* (5th ed.). Boston, MA: Pearson.

Burstein, N., Cebello, B., & Hamann, J. (1993). Teacher preparation & culturally diverse students. *Teacher Education and Special Education*, *16*(1) 1–13.

Carrasquillo, A. L., & Rodriguez, V. (2002). *Language minority students in the mainstream classroom* (2nd ed.). Clevedon, England: Multilingual Matters.

Cochran-Smith, M. (2004). Taking stock in 2004: Teacher education in dangerous times. *Journal of Teacher Education*, *55*(3) 3–7.

Cummins, J. (1989). A theoretical framework for bilingual special education. *Exceptional Children*, *56* (2) 111–19.

Eberly, J. L., Rand, M. K, & O'Connor, T. (2007). Analyzing teachers' dispositions towards diversity: Using adult development theory. *Multicultural Education*, *14*(4), 31–36.

Garcia, E. (2005). *Teaching and learning in two languages: Bilingualism and schooling in the United States*. New York: Teachers College Press.

Gay, G. (2000). *Culturally responsive teaching: Theory, research, and practice*. New York: Teachers College Press.

Gay, G., & Kirkland, K. (2003). Developing cultural critical consciousness and self-reflection in pre-service teacher education. *Theory into Practice*, *42*(3), 181–187.

Gollnick, D. M., & Chinn, P. C. (2002). *Multicultural education in a pluralistic society* (6th ed.). Upper Saddle River, NJ: Pearson Merrill Prentice Hall.

Hernandez-Sheets, R. (2005). *Diversity pedagogy: Examining the role of culture in the teaching-learning process.* Boston, MA: Pearson.

Higbee, J. L., Siaka, K., & Bruch, P. L. (2007). Assessing our commitment to multiculturalism: Student Perspectives. *Journal of College Reading and Learning, 37*(2) 8–25.

Hollins, E. R. (1996). *Culture in school learning: Revealing the deep meaning.* Mahwah, NJ: Lawrence Erlbaum Associates Publishers.

Irvine, J. J. (2003). *Educating teachers for a diverse society: Seeing with the cultural eye.* New York, NY: Teachers College Press.

Kea, C., Campbell-Whatley, G. & Richards, H. (2004). *Becoming culturally responsive educators: Rethinking teacher education pedagogy.* Practitioner Brief. NCCREST

Ladson-Billings, G. (1995). Toward a theory of culturally relevant pedagogy. *American Educational Researcher Journal, 32*(3) 465–491.

Morrier, M. J., Irving, M. A., Dandy, E., Dmitriyev, G., & Ukeje, I. C. (2007). Teaching and learning within and across cultures: Educator requirements across the United States. *Multicultural Education, 14*(3) 32–40.

National Collaborative on Diversity in the Teaching Force (2004). *Assessment of diversity in American's teaching force: A call to action.* Washington, DC: National Education Association.

Nieto, S. (2000). *Affirming diversity: The sociopolitical context of multicultural education* (3rd ed.). New York: Longman.

Strasser, J., & Seplocha, H. (2005). How can university professors help their students understand issues of diversity through interpersonal and intrapersonal intelligences? *Multicultural Education, 12*(4) 20–24.

CHAPTER 19

ATE Standards as a Guide for the Evolution of a Music Educator

Lili M. Levinowitz, Rowan University

My friends and colleagues often hear "I love my life" when they ask me how I am doing. My profession is a large part of why I love my life; the Association of Teacher Educators (ATE) Standards for Teacher Educators serves as a framework to guide my professional work. The use of the ATE standards became important for my professional life because of the two professional guiding questions that have been with me since my early career: Who am I? What do I stand for? With hope, this diary transmits to the reader more about "how" the ATE standards evolved to a place of importance for me and "why" I use them as a guide for my professional life.

A richly textured, finely woven piece of fabric comprising strands from a satisfying personal life and strands from a rich and engaging professional life best defines me. I am currently a professor of music education at Rowan University where I am jointly appointed to both the College of Fine and Performing Arts and the College of Education. I also serve as the director of research for the Center for Music and Young Children (CMYC). This organization is the developer of *Music Together*, for which I am coauthor. These two strands of my professional life compliment each other and provide continuous opportunities for professional practice, development, scholarship, and reflection. Together these shape my identity as a teacher educator and strengthen my commitment to the Standards for Teacher Educators.

This identity as a teacher educator, defined by the ATE Standards for Teacher Educators, is a newly found one based on an evolutionary career path. I take very seriously that I am a model for the pre-service teachers with whom I work. Therefore, it is important for me to have a respected set of guidelines to serve as a rudder for my practice.

Even though I do not refer to the specifics of indicators set forth in the ATE standards on a daily basis, I have been able to internalize the nine standards in a manner that is useful for my reflective practice, which is a vital part of my professional life. Each semester, when I complete my grading, I reflect on the completed term. My process is to identify a standard from ATE and journal what exactly occurred during the semester that indicates progress toward it or indicators that I actually met or where I have holes to fill. In essence, the nine ATE standards have become my rubric for disciplined reflection and a beacon for future work I endeavor to do in the coming semester.

EVOLUTIONARY BEGINNINGS

In the early part of my collegiate career, I considered myself *only* a teacher educator of musicians. It did not occur to me that teacher education in music had so much in common with teacher education in other subjects. This attitude had its roots in my initial undergraduate training at the conservatory, Westminster Choir College. There music education was embedded in a strong performance environment. Although the major, music education, was offered as a four-year undergraduate degree, the tacit emphasis was on the applied performance. This is where choirs were prepared to sing choral works with major symphony orchestras, such as the Philadelphia Orchestra, New York Philharmonic, and the Boston Symphony. These performance experiences were not only exciting, but were preparatory for the teaching of my subject matter, vocal music.

At the time, I was not aware of the ATE standards. I am now cognizant that these undergraduate performance experiences were essential background for me to "demonstrate appropriate subject matter content," an indicator for ATE Standard One. In particular, knowing that I must exhibit outstanding musicianship has helped me to understand and embrace the distinction between music and music education, which is often hazy among music education students (Colwell & Wing, 2004).

Once my degree in music education was conferred, I entered the field as a secondary school music teacher responsible for developing choral activities at Shady Side Academy. The answers to my career-guiding questions were as follows: 1) I am a choral music educator; and

2) I stand for excellence in performance ensembles. My performance and strong pedagogical background developed at Westminster Choir College prepared me well for the subject matter required of this position. The choir conductors there served as powerful models for me. In Standard One, importance of effective modeling is recognized as the heart of successful teacher education programs. I believe as I entered music education at the secondary level, I became acutely aware that I borrowed heavily, imitated, and applied in my choir rehearsals the repertoire of behaviors that my models demonstrated.

However, I was not prepared for feelings of isolation to which many music and other educators are prone. There was no one with whom I could talk about music and performance at the depth discussed during my undergraduate program. This was my first recollection of the importance of professional conversation. I had appreciated the music talk about issues such as how to move a choir to a beautiful sound and quality performance. In my college days, these discussions were invigorating and necessary to my growth.

At this point in my evolution as a music educator, I was unaware of the importance of the entire educational landscape and how I fit in to it based on my music education point of view. It did not occur to me that I shared the commonality of pedagogy with teachers in other subject areas. The ATE Standard Three: Scholarship, and Standard Four: Professional Development, reflect the importance of professional dialogue. If only I had been disposed to seek such professional dialogue with my colleagues at Shady Side, I may have discovered a sense of belonging within the school culture more quickly and may not have sought employment elsewhere.

It was in my second position as an elementary general music teacher at Chestnut Hill Academy (CHA) that I discovered music as a core part of the overall curriculum for all students. This was an important evolution for me. As part of the school faculty who were responsible for the education of pre-kindergarten through fifth grade boys, I was included in informal discussions in the faculty room and formal discussions before student conferences. My input about student performance in the music classroom was valued and sought out. I was placed on the Back to School Night program to introduce and briefly explicate to the parents the goals and objectives for the music program. In fact, I was given one half-hour to speak to my curriculum, which affirmed the importance of music at CHA.

It was becoming evident to me that music education was not isolated from the other general education curricula as I had previously thought. It was essential to the core curriculum. My answers to my guiding questions changed to "I am a music teacher in a larger community of caring professional" and "I stand for pedagogical excellence that creates quality music making with my students."

During this time I also fell in love with the young child and developed an interest in understanding how children learn music. Consequently, I enrolled in a Master of Music/Doctor of Philosophy program in the psychology of music to begin to answer some of my burning questions. The ATE Standards One: Teaching; Three: Scholarship; Four: Professional Development; and Eight: Teacher Education Profession are certainly connected to the decision to return to school, even though at that time I was unaware that I would 1) become a music teacher educator or 2) embrace the ATE standards at a later date.

The completion of these degrees qualified me to teach at the university level and I secured a position at Rowan University. Here my identification with the ATE Standards for Teacher Educators evolved greatly. Through my cross-disciplinary work in graduate school combined with my experiences at CHA, I concluded that engagement with professionals outside of music was crucial to my understanding the answers to my initial questions of "Who am I?" and "What do I stand for?"

For that reason, I sought out thoughtful, caring professionals at the Faculty Center for Teaching Excellence at Rowan University and opened conversations with College of Education professors. I mostly focused on those who were responsible for the education of the early childhood and elementary teachers. It was through these teacher education professionals that I was introduced to the Association of Teacher Educators, became a member, and copresented at an ATE Conference.

EVOLUTION TOWARD IDENTIFYING WITH THE ATE STANDARDS

At Rowan, I am primarily responsible for teaching sophomore and junior level undergraduate courses and supervising senior student teachers in their clinical practice semester. These courses are specific to the Bachelor of Music Education program in the College of Fine and Performing Arts and are coordinated with the College of Education. Because my appointment in 1989 was to the College of Fine and Performing Arts and *not* to the College of Education, I was again isolated from my education colleagues in other disciplines. This was compounded by my attendance at conferences targeting music educators and my involvement in the Society for Music Teacher Education, which does not have standards for music teacher educators as does the ATE.

As my colleagues in the College of Education grew to know my work and my work ethic, collaborations began. My job responsibilities at Rowan, too, were evolving. I became an integral contributor to the education of pre-service educators in general, not just music educators specifically. I was asked to teach graduate courses in research methods for the Master of Science in Teaching program and to guide exit projects therein. Thankfully, and essential for me, more dialogue and collaboration ensued with my education colleagues who directed me to new professional associations like the American Association of Colleges for Teacher Education, the National Association for the Education of Young Children, the Association for Childhood Education International, and the Association of Teacher Educators.

I immersed myself in new literature and attended conferences that offered new perspectives on education generally and the role of music education in general education. This new literature reflects for me, specifically, ATE Standard Four: Professional Development. Concurrently, I was modeling for my pre-service music education students the importance of grounding my professional practice in research that is related to education and teacher education in general, rather than just music education in particular. This modeling points to a specific indicator of Standard One: Teaching.

More recently, I have engaged in an exciting collaborative process among members of the College of Education, College of Fine and Performing Arts, and Liberal Arts and Sciences that embodied Standard Six: Collaboration. This collaboration culminated in the introduction of a new curriculum for the Bachelor of Arts in Education. Together, as members of the program development team, we participated in a process that included joint decision making about teacher education that contributed to the improvement of our teacher education program at Rowan. As a contributor to the program development team that created a new curriculum sequence, I helped design and develop a teacher education program based on theory, research, and best practice, all of which are indicators of Standard Five: Program Development.

I felt that I had *finally* found a voice for the music education program as distinct from yet similar to the larger teacher education context. The education of a Rowan University music education student in this new program would not remain isolated in music education as I was at Westminster Choir College. Some of the early coursework and the general education courses would transpire within a community of pre-service teachers from many disciplines. This is designed to contribute to a music education student's identity as a teacher in an education ecosystem (Colwell & Wing, 2004), a concept emphasized in the first music education specific course following the initial general education courses. This underscores the importance of music education to the overall curriculum, helping students to make a critical connection that affirms the relevance of previous coursework rather than discredits it as superfluous to music education.

In the new program, the foundational courses in the sequence make connections earlier to the specifics of the discipline of music education than in the previous program. The initial courses provide an understanding of successful and caring learning communities that are now applied specifically to the music classroom. This and subsequent coursework contribute to our students identifying with music education as distinct within the teacher education curriculum.

During this collaborative process, I identified a desire to continue my work with the professionals in the College of Education. The seed for a joint appointment between my home College of Fine and Performing Arts (FPA) and the College of Education was planted. I believed that, with a joint appointment, I would be modeling that "arts education is a core component of the overall curriculum" that P–12 students experience during their student years. This joint appointment, formalized in February 2006, would potentially deepen the understanding and involvement in interdisciplinary teaching practices.

Since my joint appointment, I have been able to serve the College of Education in a more formal and concrete manner. I am currently a facilitator for a core course in the education program, *Teaching in the Learning Community-II*. This core course has a general focus for all pre-service teachers, but is also offered in specific domains such as art, music, and physical education. Because I have developed to embrace and practice the ATE standards by using them to continually help me to answer those original guiding questions, "Who am I?" and "What do I stand for?", I believe that I am well suited to facilitate this broad-based course. Based on my own evolution to understand the importance of special subjects as integral to the education of students, I believe that I bring a perspective of collaboration among all the professionals teaching this course.

I share a responsibility for active service among my teacher education colleagues, which exemplifies Standard Eight: Teacher Education Profession. I have an opportunity to reinforce the importance of arts education by modeling collaboration among the diverse faculty who teach in this cross-curricular endeavor. I believe that modeling of collaboration among faculty of different subject areas encourages students to foster professional relationships with other educators in the schools, rather than teach in isolation.

Standard Two: Cultural Competence, and Standard Three: Scholarship, both inform and provide guidance and vision for my work at the Center for Music and Young Children (CMYC). This is illustrated in my coordination of multiple quantitative research projects and engagement in action research that utilizes *Music Together* as a core component of the curriculum.[1] My interest in early childhood music and research has placed me in working relationships with not only the parents and children I serve, but with local, state, and national education leaders, policy makers, and arts organizations as well.

One current example is my role as part of a team comprising a local arts organization (Trenton Community Music School), an urban school district (Trenton Public Schools), and the external evaluators (Education Resources Group) that designed, implemented, and prepared the final report for the three-year Arts in Education grant project (Clark, Levinowitz, & Ragen, 2008). The outcomes for this federally funded project were as follows:

- comprehensive, early music experiences affecting music skills and literacy achievement
- the development of classroom teachers' skills and inclination to integrate music and movement into daily routines

- increasing the level of engagement of parents in their children's musical education

I was able to participate professionally by creating workshops for classroom professionals who would administer the music instruction. The classroom teachers would use that music instruction holistically throughout the week to support other curricular goals. To design these workshops, I researched the culture of the students who attended the Trenton Public Schools and drew on my experiences of providing music instruction to a preschool that was a Trenton community provider. These experiences embody many of the indicators in Standard Two: Cultural Competence.

Moreover, Rowan University music students were used as judges for the music evaluation piece of the project. This measurement took place directly in the classroom. Therefore I needed to inform and help these students, who were so important to the external evaluation, connect with these diverse students. The stakes were high: if my students were unsuccessful with these live measurements, the music piece of the outcomes would have failed!

Once these results are disseminated to colleagues in the teacher education community, they will contribute new knowledge to existing contexts in early literacy education. They will bring a more focused perspective on the effects of music on early literacy learning, which is reflected in the spirit of Standard Three: Scholarship. Through systematically assessing the learning goals and outcomes of the Trenton project, I provide depth and breadth from the arts perspective and contribute as a team member for the music component in a newly funded project (through the Connecticut Assembly and the federal government) in the Bridgeport Public Schools. I am anxiously awaiting the preliminary outcomes in spring 2008.

The action research component of my work at CMYC is the balance for my professional life. On a weekly basis, I teach early childhood family music classes where I work with children, birth through five years of age, and their parents. I also teach in a preschool for native Spanish speaking children. This CMYC outreach project, that I developed and acquired funding for, has enabled me to professionally participate and develop ways to connect music instruction to students' families in a culture different from my own. Furthermore, because the children are largely progeny of undocumented Latino parents, I had to investigate and understand the differences in their culture to deliver culturally responsive pedagogy, which is embedded in all indicators for Standard Two: Cultural Competence.

This action research utilizing my *Music Together* curriculum is integral to the development of that program but also to certification programs at Rowan University. I realized that my practical and scholarly experience with music and young children could serve as a resource that would contribute to improving the teacher education program. This would create another opportunity for me to practice the essence of both Standard Eight: Teacher Education Profession and Standard Five: Program Development. Students in our program need choices in their general education. My epiphany was, why not put together a course where students could learn about music and begin to bridge the gap between music education and general education right here at Rowan?

Therefore, my most recent project, informed by Standard Eight and Standard Five, was the creation of a course entitled *Music and the Child*, which launched in the Spring 2008 semester. This course, designed for pre-service elementary and early childhood teachers, focuses on music as a way of knowing and an important facilitator of knowing in other subject areas. One of the advantages of using the ATE Standards for Teacher Educators in my work is that they helped me to see that the development of this course affirms, yet again, the importance of the circle of learning that *should* occur between one's content and his or her collaborations with other professionals.

I am also hoping that the practice of talking about the ATE standards and advocating for music education as core to the curriculum could bring me the courage to engage more with local policy makers. As can be seen by examining this diary, I have only documented a few indicators for Standard Seven: Public Advocacy. In the past, the decision makers have always been the ones to ask for help, which set up an opportunity to inform and educate those policy makers. I did not, however, seek them out and, therefore, I may have missed ripe opportunities to address policy issues which affect the education profession in general and/or the music education profession specifically. Certainly, I believe this to be important, yet challenging, to begin.

MATURITY AND EVOLUTION

Through my reflection as I prepared this book chapter, I have found that, in fact, I have begun. Because of my excitement about having real standards to guide my work, since the Society for Music Teacher Education (SMTE) has none, I have spoken with my new music education colleague about ATE and the Standards for Teacher Educators. I see myself as a mentor to this new colleague and wish for him a workplace of immediate collaboration with our teacher education colleagues rather than of isolation as I once had.

Sharing the examples of how I now document my work in relation to these standards has helped him understand their importance to me personally and to music education generally. I believe that my new role as mentor to new faculty is beginning to shape a vision that focuses on educational change in the music education community. This is particularly characteristic of actively participating in learning communities that focus on educational change as seen in Standard Nine.

It seems that it is time to bridge ATE and SMTE ideals; to execute this agenda. I, or perhaps leaders in ATE, must consider reaching out to these other professional organizations in arts education. Perhaps, a special focus conference or symposia could be created and held at Rowan. In the *Handbook of Research on Music Teaching and Learning* (1992) Verrastro and Leglar comment that "as a whole, research in music teacher education is unfocused, methodologically uncertain, and not clearly conceptualized, and that the individual studies fail to form a cohesive body of knowledge."

I believe that this could provide the foundation for a meaningful agenda where leaders from both organizations could gather to share what each knows about the pedagogy and scholarship of teacher education. Music teacher education may begin to mitigate for some of the aforementioned concerns. Furthermore, I believe that a discussion about the manner in which arts educators think about and engage in their content and pedagogy would deepen the ATE standards and create new ways to think about documenting them. Accordingly, through dialogue I believe each group would discover what I have—how much we have in common with each other and how much we can learn from each other.

Although reflection has always been at the core of my professional practice, considering the guiding questions for this book chapter has been one of the most exciting processes for me in recent years. To produce an artifact that documents this practice is deeply meaningful to me because it has been through my teacher education colleagues that I was invited to write this book chapter. That is, as I was evolving toward ATE and its standards, the leaders in the organization were embracing and valuing what I could contribute as a music educator—a completed circle of learning!

Because I have spent an entire semester reflecting on a tentative outline for this chapter before setting any words on paper, I have examined under a microscope how I think about my work and what content and processes, in my work, are most important to me. Moreover, I have revisited, clarified and redefined my guiding professional questions, "Who am I?" and "What do I stand for?"

In conclusion, I have enjoyed taking a trip down memory lane and writing about "how" my evolution toward identifying with the ATE standards has occurred. Even more important to me, however, is how I discovered "why" through a deep reflective process that the ATE standards are a bulwark in my professional life.

NOTES

1. Music Together is a music and movement approach to early childhood music development for infant, toddler, preschool, and kindergarten children and their parents, teachers, and other primary caregivers. Originally offered to the public in 1987, it pioneered the concept of research-based, developmentally appropriate early childhood music curriculum that strongly emphasizes and facilitates adult involvement.

REFERENCES

Clark, T., Levinowitz, L., & Ragen, R. (2008). Music for the very young: Music, movement, literacy. U.S. Department of Education Grant Performance Report (ED 524B).

Colwell, R., & Wing, L. B. (2004). *An orientation to music education: Structural knowledge for teaching music*. Upper Saddle River, NJ: Pearson/Prentice Hall.

Verrastro, R., & Leglar, M. (1992). Music teacher education. In Colwell, R. (Ed.), *Handbook of Research on Music Teaching and Learning* (p. 676). Reston: Music Educators National Conference.

CHAPTER 20

Roles and Perspectives of State Directors of Teacher Education

Theodore E. Andrews

PERSPECTIVES

In this paper, I consider the proposed ATE standards as they might be applied to persons serving in the roles of state directors of teacher education. I am guided in the following analysis of the Association of Teacher Educators' (ATE) standards by two perspectives. First, I view the standards through my personal experience as a state director of teacher education for twenty-five years in New York and Washington and as a member of the National Association of State Directors of Teacher Education and Certification (NASDTEC). Second, I draw on the reactions of current state directors to the ATE standards.

Personal Perspective

Following six years of public school teaching and four years as an assistant professor at the State University of New York at Albany, I served as an associate in the office of Professional Education and Certification in the New York State Department. During my nine years in the New York office, I participated in more than 200 state site visits as well as National Council for Accreditation of Teacher Education (NCATE) visits to New York institutions and to out-of-state programs in Massachusetts. During that time, I established the *Performance-Based Teacher Education Consortium* consisting of the state offices of teacher education from Washington, Oregon, Minnesota, Utah, Florida, Texas, Arizona, Vermont, and New York.

In 1975, I moved to Reston, Virginia, near Washington, D.C. where I did consulting for eight years. Among my many clients were NASDTEC, where I served as its first executive secretary, and state agencies in Michigan, Georgia, California, West Virginia, and New Jersey.

In 1983, I became the director of professional education in the state of Washington and six years later became the director of professional education and certification. During that time I was elected to NASDTEC's Executive Committee and became the NASDTEC President from 1991–1992. As part of my continuing role with NASDTEC, I have coedited three editions of *The NASDTEC Manual on Certification.*

My experience with standards for teacher education include serving on the committees that developed the Interstate New Teacher Assessment and Support Consortium (INTASC) standards and two revisions of the NCATE standards while serving as a member of its Unit Accreditation Board (UAB). Prior to retiring in 1998, I participated in several revisions of the Washington state standards, including the development of a performance-based model for practicing teachers who wished to receive a professional certificate. My contributions were recognized with an honorary membership in NASDTEC. For the past seven years, I have sponsored the Western States Certification Conference (WSCC) that provides an opportunity to remain involved with issues related to teacher education and certification.

State Directors' Perspective

On January 8, 2008, a meeting of the NASDTEC western states directors was held in Palm Springs, California. Representatives of seven western states (Washington, Montana, Idaho, California, Oregon, Alaska, and Nevada) attended. I explained the purpose of the ATE teacher educator standards and asked participants to voice their perspectives on the standards. To understand the SDTE's perspective, the political scenes in which SDTEs function and their responsibilities are summarized in the following section.

STATE DIRECTORS OF TEACHER EDUCATION

While most states have one SDTE, almost every state has a different organizational pattern. Large states, New York for example, may have forty or more staff in the offices of teacher education with an administrator as chief of teacher education and an administrator as chief of certification with another administrator who is over all of the staff with a title such as "director of teacher education and certification." Smaller state agencies may have one person who administers both functions.

Some states, such as California and Oregon, have professional standards boards, which stand alone as administrative agencies. Other states, like Washington, have professional standards boards where the state agency is the administrative arm of the standards board. In most states, however, teacher education and certification programs are administered by state education agencies. This reality makes it very difficult to make general statements about all state directors of teacher education.

I assume that all state agency personnel who work in offices of teacher education and certification and/or serve on professional standards boards are included in the ATE definition of state directors of teacher education (SDTE). For purposes here, a SDTE is a political person, someone who can work with a wide range of people and ideologies, someone who is flexible while working in a changing institution (governors, cabinet officers, etc.—all appointed or elected and politically oriented—thinking about their own image, not the SDTE), and one who needs a working definition of professional education, but not necessarily an in-depth understanding of specific aspects of the profession. While all SDTEs would not meet this definition, most would, and it appears fair to consider this definition in determining the extent to which SDTEs would find the ATE standards appropriate for their state role.

State department staff members are integral to a political process that depends on changes in personnel and regulations. In order to promote change in any organization, it is almost always essential that the individual promoting the change has sufficient experience in the organization to understand fully all of the special interest groups that can deter any proposed change.

While it is true that some NASDTEC representatives have long careers in their agencies (I was the Director of Professional Education in Washington for sixteen years), the majority of NASDTEC representatives have relatively short careers in that role. They leave for various reasons: moving with their spouses to other communities, finding positions with other agencies, receiving promotions within or outside the state education agencies, and/or being replaced by incoming chief state school officers (a common occurrence in states that elect their chief state school officers, but possible even with appointed chief state school officers).

The movement of staff in and out of SDTE offices is clearly reflected in the longevity pattern in Washington. Washington had three directors of teacher education between 1948 and 1998—fifty years. Since January 1, 1999, Washington has had three directors of teacher education and the third left that office the last week in January, three in less than nine years. At the 2008 Western States Certification Conference (WSCC), when putting together a panel of experienced NASDTEC directors, I had to select two directors who had been in their positions for only four years to serve as the "experienced" NASDTEC representatives.

The extent of influence of state directors of teacher education is directly related to the extent that they can impact state policy through a close relationship with the chief state school office and/or state board of education, and/or professional standards board. Depending upon the size of the state agency, the director of teacher education may or may not have a direct and/or personal relationship with the chief state school officer. While serving in the New York State Education Department for nine years, I never entered the chief's office. In Washington, I was interviewed by the chief state school officer before I was hired (in the chief's office) and, after being hired, was in that office countless times as professional education issues were discussed by the chief and his administrative staff members.

Those state directors of teacher education who are appointed by chiefs comprising about a quarter of chief state school officers who are elected by a statewide vote. These individuals often have the advantage of personal contact and support through working for the prospective chief during the election period, which is, at least, part of the reason I became the director of professional education and certification in Washington. On the other hand, these persons are often the first to go when a different chief is elected.

THE ATE STANDARDS AND STATE DIRECTORS OF TEACHER EDUCATION

With this overview of the tenure, independence, and power of state directors of teacher education as perspective, let us now consider each of the ATE standards. Because they are extensively discussed in other parts of the book, the specific standard is not listed.

Standard One: Teaching

SDTEs are not hired to be, nor are they expected to serve as, formal teachers or teacher educators. While they often have the responsibility for working with various groups to explain evolving state policies, a form of teaching, they are not being paid to teach. A review of the Standard One indicators and artifacts clarifies that this standard applies to persons in teaching roles. Thus, Standard One: Teaching is not relevant to SDTEs as a tool for studying teaching.

Standard Two: Cultural Competence

While Standard Two is far more relevant to SDTEs than Standard One, again the focus is on teaching. For example, the ATE descriptions designed to clarify the meaning of this standard include words that I italicized, which are appropriate for teacher educators, not SDTEs: "To develop capacity among culturally, socially, and linguistically diverse *students*, *teachers* first need to know their own cultures. They also need to hold high expectations for all *students*, understand developmental levels and what is common and unique among different groups, reach out to families and communities to learn about their cultures, select *curriculum* materials that are inclusive, use a range of assessment methods, and be proficient in a variety of *pedagogical methods* that facilitate the acquisition of content knowledge for all *learners*" (ATE, 2008).

The artifacts are even more clearly designed for the traditional teacher educator: Course syllabi, instructional materials, evidence of involvement in schools and other organizations with diverse populations, video and/or audiotapes of teaching, course assignments, student work samples, evidence of involvement in school-based projects and/or service learning, evidence of providing professional development to others at all levels, philosophical statements that reflect underlying attention to diversity, and assessment tools appropriate for use with diverse learners. Of the ten proposed artifacts, eight are clearly designed for the teacher educator. While the SDTE is concerned with cultural diversity as a part of his/her responsibility to all children and youth in the state, it is not directly as a teacher educator. Therefore, Standard Two: Cultural Competence is not relevant to SDTEs in ways that it may be for teacher educators.

Standard Three: Scholarship

While Standard Three is still focused, in part, on teaching, it is approached in a broad enough fashion to encompass many of the roles of SDTEs. For example, the indicators include the study of theoretical and practical problems of teacher education, pursuit of new knowledge and connecting new understandings to existing contexts and perspectives, conducting program evaluation, applying research to current programs and state requirements, engaging in research and development grants, and disseminating research findings to the broader community. All of these indicators would be evident over time in the best of SDTEs. Only three of the artifacts are inappropriate for SDTEs: evidence of improved teaching practice, evidence of increased student learning, and National Board Certification. Each of these assumes the person who demonstrates Standard Three is a teacher.

In Standard Three, ATE, has, nonetheless, identified many essential qualities for a SDTE. Standard Three: Scholarship is, for the most part, appropriate for SDTEs as they examine their role as scholars.

Standard Four: Professional Development

The indicators and artifacts for Standard Four could apply to SDTEs. However, I, based on personal experience, doubt that the state agency personnel who supervise the SDTE would place a high priority on supporting activities that would give the SDTE these skills. For example, funds for travel are often limited. State directors of teacher education often obtain ideas and support from other directors by attending meetings and conferences where they can learn about activities in other states. When state funds are limited, out-of-state travel is restricted, with the number of persons allowed to attend meetings reduced or in some cases eliminated.

State directors, in any given year, have the opportunity and in many cases are expected to attend the national NASDTEC conference, regional NASDTEC meetings, the national Alternative Certification conference, the NCATE state partnership meeting, and INTASC meetings. In addition, national associations such as American Association of Colleges for Teacher Education (AACTE), American Education Research Association (AERA), and ATE hold annual conferences. Specialty organizations such as the National Council of Teachers of English, National Council for the Social Studies, International Reading Association, etc., also hold national conferences.

Actually, the reality is that even if money were available, there is often not time for a state director of teacher education to attend all of the appropriate meetings or conferences. This reality makes it difficult for a SDTE to engage fully in professional development. This time issue is a problem inherent in the role of SDTEs, not in the ATE standards.

All of the indicators and artifacts could be demonstrated by SDTEs. However, as previously noted, opportunities to do so may be limited. Standard Four: Professional Development is certainly appropriate, but sometimes impractical, for SDTEs.

Standard Five: Program Development

This standard describes almost perfectly the "leadership" role of the SDTE. "Accomplished teacher educators (SDTEs) are regular contributors to and often leaders in the development, refinement, and revision of programs and portions of programs focused on initial teacher preparation and on-going teacher professional development" (ATE, 2008). In many ways, this standard could be used as a job description for a SDTE. All of the indicators and most of the artifacts are perfect matches for the job responsibilities of the SDTE. For example, the indicators identified below highlight importantly the responsibilities and obligations of SDTEs:

- Design, develop, or modify teacher education programs based on theory, research, and best practice
- Provide leadership in obtaining approval or accreditation for new or modified teacher education programs
- Lead or actively contribute to the ongoing assessment of teacher education courses or programs
- Provide leadership that focuses on establishing standards for teacher education programs or on developing, approving, and accrediting

teacher education programs at the local, state, national, or international level

- Contribute to research that focuses on effective teacher education programs

Standard Five: Program Development is certainly very appropriate for SDTEs.

Standard Six: Collaboration

This standard also captures another essential element of a successful SDTE. "Professional relationships foster a community of collaboration in which teacher educators make explicit their work and increase self-learning and knowledge. Collaboration is often formalized in partnerships that join individuals and institutions to work together on a long term basis" (ATE, 2008). These formal collaborative relationships exist in most states through advisory committees or professional standards boards. The indicators and artifacts are excellent choices for the SDTE role as collaborator. For example, the indicators include:

- Engage in cross-institutional and cross-college partnerships
- Support teacher education in the P–12 school environment
- Participate in joint decision making about teacher education
- Foster cross-disciplinary endeavors
- Engage in reciprocal relationships in teacher education
- Initiate collaborative projects that contribute to improved teacher education
- Acquire financial support for teacher education innovation to support collaboration

Standard Six: Collaboration, with all of its indicators, is also very appropriate for SDTEs.

Standard Seven: Public Advocacy

The ATE description for "public advocacy" begins, "Teacher educators advocate both within and outside of the profession for high quality education for all students at all levels. Influencing decision makers and promoting changes to laws and other government policies to advance the mission of a high quality education for all is paramount to the profession" (ATE, 2008). My experience recognizes that an SDTE's role in advocating policy is limited to supporting the views of the chief state school officer or professional standards board. He or she is not free to advocate any position that he or she personally supports. The national debate over the *No Child Left Behind* law (NCLB) is a good example of the limitations placed upon SDTEs. If the state (the governor, chief state school officer, professional standards board) supports or opposes NCLB, then the SDTE would also, or would soon be available for a different line of work.

ATE appears to believe that "teacher educators" have autonomy in their support of issues. Teacher educators may have, but SDTEs do not, making the indicators and artifacts for Standard Seven much less relevant for SDTEs.

Standard Eight: Teacher Education Profession

In Standard Eight, I have substituted SDTE for "teacher educators" in the description following the standard. "Through a visionary and collaborative approach, accomplished SDTEs accept responsibility for improving their profession . . . SDTEs share a responsibility for active service as members of local, state, and national professional organizations. These affiliations offer a venue for professional identification and support to improve the teacher education profession. Collective membership in professional organizations contributes to the strength of teacher education" (ATE, 2008). This is an excellent description of the effective SDTE.

While the indicators have several criteria focused on recruiting which few SDTEs would be able to demonstrate, the artifacts are all appropriate: evidence of active participation in professional organizations, conference programs, and proceedings; books/monographs/periodicals edited or reviewed; testimonials; evidence of support of student organizations; reports and evaluations of projects/advancement programs; and records of awards/recognition for excellence in teacher education. Standard Eight: Teacher Education Profession is certainly relevant for analyzing the role and effectiveness of SDTEs.

Standard Nine: Vision

While Standard Nine: Vision appears appropriate for SDTEs, a review of the artifacts implies that again the focus is on the teacher educator: for example, course syllabi, student work samples, evidence of using new and evolving technologies or content in teaching and learning. While SDTEs provide leadership in teacher education, they often are constrained by their peers who do not want or seek change. When SDTEs are too insistent on promoting change, they often have the opportunity for early retirements. Standard Nine: Vision is not relevant for SDTEs.

SUMMARY

In this chapter, I have reviewed the ATE standards from the perspective of a state director of teacher education by considering the extent to which the standards reflect the roles and responsibilities of SDTEs.

Indeed, it has been concluded above that some of the ATE standards are much more relevant to the role of SDTEs than are others. The teaching, cultural competence, public advocacy, and vision standards do not have the relevancy for SDTEs that the scholarship, professional development, and teacher education profession standards have.

The two standards that have the most relevance for SDTEs are program development and collaboration. Certainly, ATE should not view these conclusions as a criticism but rather as a compliment. To my knowledge, based on forty-one years of involvement with SDTEs, there are no standards for SDTEs. Now there is a beginning.

REFERENCES

Association of Teacher Educators. (2008). *National standards for teacher educators (revised)*. Manassas Park, VA: Association of Teacher Educators.

CHAPTER 21

Association of Teacher Educators' Standards for Teacher Educators: A Tool to Clarify and Inform Teacher Educators' Professional Goals

Arthur E. Wise and Jane A. Leibbrand, National Council for Accreditation of Teacher Education

We thank the editors and the Association of Teacher Educators (ATE) for this opportunity to reflect on the ATE Standards for Teacher Educators. Certainly these aspirational standards are poised to serve teacher educators well. They help clarify teacher educators' professional missions and inform their professional goals. As all standards, these are dynamic, not static. They continue to evolve as research continues to shape professional practice and as the profession advances. At the National Council for Accreditation of Teacher Education (NCATE), our professional life is much taken up with standards for schools of education, while for ATE, standards are but one facet of an organizational mission of your professional association. Thus, we ask your indulgence as we applaud you for developing these standards while providing some suggestions for your consideration when you engage in a regular revision process.

The ATE Standards for Teacher Educators serve as a conceptual framework by which teacher educators can analyze their own practice. NCATE's definition of a conceptual framework is "the shared vision for . . . efforts in preparing educators to work in P–12 schools . . . that provides direction for programs, courses, teaching, candidate performance, scholarship, service, and . . . accountability" (NCATE, 2008). The ATE standards provide such a framework for teacher educators.

STRENGTHENING THE ATE STANDARDS

Standard One: Teaching

"Accomplished teacher educators model teaching that demonstrates content and professional knowledge, skills, and dispositions reflecting research, proficiency with technology and assessment, and accepted best practices in teacher education" maps well onto NCATE Standard One. Both expect teacher educators and candidates, respectively, to model teaching that "demonstrates content and professional knowledge, skills, and dispositions." The ATE standard further ensures that teacher educators reflect research, proficiency with technology and assessment, and accepted best practices. Preparing candidates to use technology and assessment effectively, likewise, are interwoven throughout the NCATE standards.

One difference between NCATE's Standard One on Candidate Knowledge, Skills, and Professional Dispositions and ATE's Standard One on Teaching lies in the area of student (candidate) outcomes. NCATE's Standard One concludes, "teachers . . . demonstrate the content, pedagogical, and professional knowledge, skills, and professional dispositions *necessary to help all students learn"* (NCATE, 2008).

The supporting explanation of the ATE standard notes that teacher educators must model appropriate behaviors in order for them to be replicated and applied appropriately to learners, but neither the ATE standard itself nor the explanation requires teacher educators to provide evidence of student (candidate) learning. Certainly videos and testimonials could provide evidence of student learning, but the expectation is not explicit. The indicators for the ATE standard on teaching, such as "demonstrate appropriate subject matter content" or "demonstrate a variety of instruction and assessment methods including use of technology" do not require the teacher educator to show that students (candidates) have learned as a result of the teacher educator's efforts.

Standard Two: Cultural Competence

"Accomplished teacher educators apply cultural competence and promote social justice in teacher education" gets closer to student (candidate) outcomes, as the supporting explanation says that teacher educators "share the responsibility of helping pre-service and in-service teachers to understand these concepts and to apply them successfully in their classrooms. . . . they . . . clearly demonstrate how those concepts are applied in their own teaching and in that of their students." This phrasing could be incorporated into ATE Standard One: Teaching as it relates to professional knowledge, skills, and professional dispositions to make a clearer link between practices of teacher educators and candidate learning.

This ATE standard has distinct similarities to NCATE's Standard Four on Diversity. ATE is to be commended for including cultural competence in the standards for teacher educators. Developing instruction responsive to students' cultures and backgrounds, which helps students relate to what is being taught, is culturally responsive pedagogy.

ATE Standard Two is composed of two phrases, one on cultural competence and one on promoting social justice in teacher education. Promoting social justice, as noted in the supporting explanation, is a concept which teacher educators should help candidates to "understand and . . . apply . . . successfully in their classrooms" according to ATE standards. However, a definition of social justice is not found in the supporting explanation. 'Social justice' is a concept that has very disparate meanings to different audiences. To some audiences, it may mean redistribution of wealth, while to other audiences, it may mean equality of opportunity — or any number of other connotations.

NCATE previously listed the phrase 'social justice' in the glossary to the NCATE standards manual as an example of a disposition that institutions might advance, along with honesty, fairness, and others. Critics outside the education profession seized the phrase and interpreted it as an ideology, which NCATE sanctioned. ATE is asking teacher educators to help candidates understand and apply social justice in their classrooms. We would caution ATE to define the phrase 'social justice' in the ATE standards, so that readers are clear as to the specific meaning assigned to it in relation to the standards. Another option would be to simply use the phrase 'cultural competence' in ATE Standard Two.

In addition, in this ATE standard, no clear connection is made between the two concepts of cultural competence and social justice. Connecting them in the actual standard implies relationship, but it is not explained in the supporting paragraph. Only cultural competence is defined.

Again, the indicators do not provide clarification as to what is meant by social justice. One indicator is 'engage in activities that promote social justice.' This would mean to some that the teacher has a particular ideological or political agenda that is fostered in the classroom. The first indicator, "instruction that meets the needs of society," is so broad and vague as to be meaningless in operational terms. If social justice is defined by some of the indicators (i.e., foster a positive regard for individual students and their families regardless of differences such as culture, religion, etc.) this definition should be noted in the supporting explanation of the standard where cultural competence is defined.

Standard Three: Scholarship

ATE Standard Three on Scholarship is an excellent contribution to the standards literature. It should foster an expectation for teacher educators to engage in grounded inquiry, which focuses on teaching, learning, and teacher education practice. Results can be shared with the broader community. It would have been more optimal for the supporting explanation to include language connecting inquiry on teaching and learning to P–12 student learning. Working with P–12 educators on action-research projects on student learning could be an additional indicator under this ATE standard. Merging theory and inquiry with P–12 practice has been missing in much research in teacher education.

NCATE's professional development school (PDS) standards bring these two concepts together, as the PDS is conceptually about inquiry into teaching and learning, and connecting the results to P–12 student learning. Focused inquiry into teaching and learning is one of the four purposes of a professional development school; it is an integral part of the mission and the culture. Roles of teacher educator and teacher are often combined, as teacher educators consult and teach classes on-site and sometimes work with P–12 teachers on inquiry projects. NCATE has advocated that professional development schools should become the norm in teaching because of their fourfold mission: (1) the preparation of new teachers, (2) faculty development, (3) inquiry directed at the improvement of practice, and (4) enhanced student achievement (NCATE, 2001).

Professional development schools bring together theory and practice in a way that heightens the effectiveness of the preparation experience. Research indicates that it benefits P–12 student learning, the ultimate outcome of teacher preparation (Cochran-Smith & Zeichner, 2005). NCATE advocates professional development schools become widely available so that teacher candidates and beginning teachers have access to them.

Standard Four: Professional Development

The ATE standard on professional development certainly encourages the link between teacher educators and P–12 teachers as it notes that "accomplished teacher educators help . . . in-service teachers with professional development and reflection. . . ." However, the supporting explanation does not explicitly state that teacher educators should engage in continued formal professional development experiences, although the second indicator does. Perhaps the language in the second (engage in purposeful professional development focused on professional learning goals) and third indicators (develop and maintain a philosophy of teaching and learning that is continuously reviewed based on a deepening understanding of research and practice) could be moved to the supporting explanation of the standard, to provide a more substantive explanation. Currently, the explanation focuses on examining beliefs, reflection, and collaboration.

Standard Six: Collaboration

Standard Six: Collaboration is certainly grounded in research. It could be strengthened with the addition of some key concepts that are contained in NCATE's professional development school standard on collaboration, as follows:

PDS partners and partner institutions systematically move from independent to interdependent practice by committing themselves and committing to each other to engage in joint work focused on implementing the PDS mission. They collaboratively design roles and structures to support the PDS work and individual and institutional parity. PDS partners use their shared work to improve outcomes for P–12 students, candidates, faculty, and other professionals. The PDS partnership systematically recognizes and celebrates their joint work and the contributions of each partner (NCATE, 2001).

While the ATE standard would not "parrot" this standard, it could weave in certain language (i.e., partners use their shared work to improve outcomes for P–12 students, candidates, faculty, and other professionals; move from independent to interdependent practice by committing themselves and committing to each other to engage in joint work; collaboratively design roles and structures to support teacher education, teaching and learning) and acknowledging the NCATE PDS standards as the source.

In addition, the following could be included as indicators for the ATE collaboration standard

- partners select and prepare school and university faculty to mentor and supervise candidates
- arts and sciences, school, and university faculty together plan for and implement the candidates' curriculum and instruction
- systematically recognize and celebrate joint work and contributions of each partner (NCATE, 2001)

with an acknowledgement that these phrases were borrowed from the NCATE PDS standard on collaboration.

Standard Seven: Public Advocacy

Standard Seven: Public Advocacy is a key to helping teaching become a profession. Educating legislators and policy makers on the local, state, and national levels as to the necessity of high quality teacher preparation is an ongoing challenge in America today. We applaud ATE for including advocacy as a standard. To their detriment, some teacher educators do not see advocacy as a part of their role or the profession. But the day is past when higher education professionals can shun the political and economic landscape and believe themselves insulated from it.

The Spellings Commission is the latest evidence that university educators must maintain awareness of the external environment and the ongoing necessity for advocacy of high quality educator preparation. Legislators and policy makers have put in place policies limiting teacher preparation in some states, have questioned the effectiveness of educator preparation, and have demanded evidence that P–12 students are learning. Teacher educators must engage in a proactive advocacy role by communicating with and informing policy makers on a regular basis, not simply in response to a negative report. NCATE's Standard Five on Faculty Qualifications, Performance, and Development borrows language from ATE Standard Seven on Advocacy in its supporting explanation: "[Faculty] serve as advocates for high quality education for all students, public understanding of educational issues, and excellence and diversity in the education profession" (NCATE, 2008).

Standard Eight: Teacher Education

ATE Standard Eight, like the advocacy standard, is a positive benchmark, encouraging teacher educator involvement in professional associations, scholarship, new publication development, mentoring newer professional colleagues, and supporting high standards. Again, the supporting explanation to NCATE's Standard Five:

[Faculty] also contribute to improving the teacher education profession. Faculty are actively involved in professional associations as shown through their provision of education-related service and leadership at the local, state, national, and international levels (NCATE, 2008).

borrows from ATE's Standard Eight.

Standard Nine: Vision

On Standard Nine, we also salute the openness to new technology and the acknowledgement of the impact of globalization. We would suggest including language that contains caveats about becoming uncritical adopters of new configurations of learning, or adding to existing language in the supporting explanation that adoption of new configurations of learning must be based on solid research. We recall the open classroom phenomenon of the 1970s, which was a "new configuration of learning" that did not work. The term "change agents" might best be explained. Otherwise, the term could lead to a similar public relations problem as the "social justice"'phrase caused for NCATE.

CONCLUSION

In conclusion, NCATE salutes ATE for developing and promoting these teacher educator standards as benchmarks to which all teacher educators can aspire and by which they can measure their practice. The ATE standards cover not only the content and substance of their job descriptions, they also incorporate the elements of vision and advocacy to help advance the profession in the twenty-first century. Preparing the nation's teachers is and should be a top priority of policy makers today, and ATE is to be saluted for its efforts to advance the teaching profession.

REFERENCES

Association of Teacher Educators. (2008). *Standards for teacher educators (revised)*. Manassas, VA: Author.

Cochran-Smith, M., & Zeichner, K. M. (Eds.). (2005). *Studying teacher education: The report of the AERA panel on research and teacher education*. Mahwah, NJ: Lawrence Erlbaum Associates.

National Council for Accreditation of Teacher Education. (2001). *Standards for professional development schools*. Washington, DC: Author.

National Council for Accreditation of Teacher Education. (2008). *Professional standards for accreditation of teacher preparation institutions*. Washington, DC: Author.

Part IV

PERSPECTIVES ON STANDARDS

The Role of Standards on the Educational Landscape: Perspectives on Standards for Teacher Educators

Scott R. Imig, University of North Carolina, Wilmington
David G. Imig, University of Maryland, College Park

The dignity and power of the independent professional scholar should be as much a trait of the state's servant as of any private worker, and while in preparing teachers to serve a carefully controlled and measured need, he must be allowed to do it with vitality and free responsibility of a genuine educator. (Learned et al., 1920, p. 348)

A dozen years ago, one of the authors of this chapter had the opportunity to listen to a state superintendent for public instruction in a western state addressing a group of teacher education faculty and deans. The state had recently added to the list of mandated courses and program specifications for teacher education programs and the state superintendent was besieged by an audience hostile to what they perceived as further state intrusion into program conduct. In a passionate response to one inquiry, the chief state school officer asserted, "you are state employees, accountable to the Department of Public Instruction, no different than anyone else who works for me." Her assertion left the audience fuming but raised a fundamental question about the "obligations" of teacher educators to the state's agendas for staffing the schools of a particular state.

INTRODUCTION

This chapter examines the "surround" of competing pressures and expectations on teacher educators that make the Association of Teacher Educators (ATE) standards-based initiative for teacher education so significant. While it failed to gain traction in the mid-1990s, for a host of reasons to be described later, the reassertion of this policy proposal is timely and can contribute to the discourse regarding the future of teacher education.

Our approach to describing the role of standards for teacher educators is to consider the way that professional standards can resolve the often competing claims on the intellect and obligation of teacher educators. We use the word "obligation" to explore these claims and argue that teacher educators have duties and responsibilities to fulfill the expectations of their host campus, their profession, and the state which sets the boundaries for their performance.

The act of announcing that one is a teacher educator, we contend, binds oneself to a course of action set by the host institution, the education profession, and the particular state in which one works. We argue that this sense of obligation (or responsibility or duty) is opaque, at best, to most teacher educators. However, it is the basis for claiming professional autonomy and achieving professional status. Absent such autonomy to enable teacher educators to use professional judgment, teacher education will continue to be both minimized and further marginalized. We contend that such autonomy, which is a prerequisite for professional practice, can only be claimed if there is an understanding of the obligations that teacher educators have to their students, professional colleagues, and the state.[1] The ATE standards are a bold statement of professional identification to provide clear and reasoned direction for the future.

The *professional project* is the effort to gain recognition for teaching as the equivalent of medicine or law or other established professions. The acknowledgement of teaching and teacher education as professional work and the professionalization of all aspects of teaching and teacher education is the goal. Robert Houston, Robert Fisher, and their ATE colleagues have advanced a set of teacher education standards intended to contribute to the *professional project* that has occupied teacher educators for more than a century (Gitlin & Labaree, 1996; Labaree, 2004). Much has been written about the ways that traditional or true professions gain recognition and the *professional project* in education draws upon those ideas and projects a way for teacher educators to assert a positive role for themselves and for their contributions to professionalism.

That teacher education is an integral part of a profession of education was asserted in *Educating a Profession* (Howsam, Corrigan, Denemark, & Nash, 1976) with claims that teacher education was the "training and research arm of the profession." That statement focused on identifying the features of a profession and claimed a set of normative notions including the use of a theoretical knowledge base, reliance on protracted academic preparation, adherence to a code of professional conduct oriented towards the "public good", and dependence on a powerful professional organization as the criteria of a profession. Appealing to the "traditional or mature professions" of law and medicine, *Educating a Profession* sought to move teaching from what it described as its "semi-professional status" to "full professional status."

It furthered the *professional project* in education and prompted a long line of reports on the status and condition of teaching and teacher education. The Carnegie Forum on Education and the Economy (Tucker, 1986) embraced these themes as did the Holmes Group (2007) and the Education of Educators initiative (Goodlad, 1990) with scholars such as Shulman (1987) and Darling-Hammond (1996) leading the movement to describe a profession of education in an era of standards and accountability.

Over the past twenty-five years there have been repeated efforts to convey to the public and to policy makers that teachers should be accorded professional status and reward because they:

- Place the good of the learner above the immediate interest of the teacher
- Understand growing bodies of knowledge, research and practice
- Have extensive training and formal qualification
- Have mastered technical skills and practices and are able to apply them in classrooms and schools and other learning environments
- Make worthy judgments under uncertainty
- Learn from experience, error and others
- Are members of a professional community that has laws, principles, ethics and other conventions and monitors their quality and practice (Shulman, 2007)

Efforts by the Association of Teacher Educators to ensure that teacher educators meet those same high qualifications and abide by those same ethical standards are an important contribution to the *professional project*. Those standards, as described in this volume, are a powerful assertion of professional rights and a claim to special status for teacher educators. The ATE standards implicitly rebut the claims of "state" sovereignty over teacher education and challenge the "powerful force-field of institutional life" on the practice of education. They appeal "to the core values" of "professional identity and integrity of their fields" as Parker Palmer (2007) so aptly described the goal for professional education. ATE is to be commended for its leadership in articulating a vision of professorial responsibility at a time when teacher education was diminished in policy circles and besieged by demands from both the state and the academy.

This chapter examines the competing pressures on teacher education over time and the way the *professional project*, as it came to be articulated by professional interest groups, teacher organizations, and others, stimulated dialogue and conversation. We describe the often conflicting accountability expectations for teacher education. This chapter concludes with our vision of both obligation and responsibility at a time when the concept of professionalism is being reexamined and reframed by ethicists, legal scholars, policy makers, and others.

The Obligation to the Campus

We live in a time of heightened accountability. For most teacher educators, there is little debate about to whom we are accountable. We are immersed in the day-to-day responsibilities of teaching pre-service candidates and providing professional development to practicing teachers. It is to them we feel our greatest accountability. Teaching loads and research expectations, committee assignments and advisement responsibilities, and student teacher supervision and professional development school (PDS) commitments shape the lives of teacher educators. Finding time to write, meet with students, spend time in PDSs, and interact with colleagues all must be carefully wrapped around that obligation to our students. The lives of tenure-track faculty (a rapidly declining proportion of education school faculty) are shaped by departmental expectations and collegial interactions, all of which are primarily campus based.

Letters of appointment tell us to whom we report and the terms and conditions of our employment. Faculty handbooks specify the rules for teaching, advisement, research, and service. Promotion and tenure policies call for excellence in teaching with appropriate integration of technology and attention to diversity. The expectations include effectiveness as an advisor, engagement in professional development, and the conduct of significant research resulting in articles in refereed and professional journals, conference proceedings, book chapters, books, and receipt of competitive grants. There are also well-stated service expectations that include active participation in professional organizations, reasonable amounts of service on the campus, and consultative roles to educational institutions and other agencies.

So-called "union shops" may be far more specific about these terms and conditions, but on the whole, teacher educators see their obligations being to students, their faculty colleagues, and, with begrudging acknowledgement, to chairs and deans. Conditions for retention are known and promotion and tenure policies are well stated in the handbooks and other policy documents that guide university life. Faculty prerogatives are widely understood to be based on seniority and accomplishment (in that order). Principles of academic freedom are enshrined in the work we do. Therefore, teacher educators aspire to be recognized and rewarded in the way that colleagues in the arts and sciences are recognized and rewarded.

Terms of appointment vary widely across the spectrum of the more than 1150 teacher education programs that are campus based (with different teaching loads and research expectations). Course loads can range from two to five courses per semester with the number of advisees and student teaching supervisions varying greatly. Most teacher educators recognize these differences and at the annual meetings of the Association of Teacher Educators or the American Association of Colleges for Teacher Education (AACTE) or the American Educational Research Association (AERA), hallway conversations are often punctuated by lots of "my gosh, I had no idea that you had such a load." Despite this and the fact that they often hold the lowest status and the least well-paid academic jobs on the campus, teacher educators do their work earnestly and with much fulfillment (NCES, 1997, p. 31).

Universities and colleges rarely ask faculty to teach in a particular way or to instruct students in a particular doctrine—although there have been attempts to do so in some sectarian institutions over the past twenty-five years. When such attempts to constrain faculty prerogative are made, cries of academic freedom are invoked and the administrators and trustees generally accede to the rights of the faculty and the tenets of that freedom. Faculty then reclaim their prerogatives to set the curriculum and to teach the content in which they hold particular expertise. Unlike colleagues in the arts and sciences, however, teacher educators have responsibilities and obligations that extend beyond the campus, most particularly to novice teachers and interns in PDSs and other public or parochial schools.

On most campuses, teacher educators teach in a climate where their freedom to teach is unconstrained. In the United States, academic freedom is defined by the "1940 Statement of Principles on Academic Freedom and Tenure," jointly authored by the American Association of University Professors (AAUP) and the Association of American Colleges (AAC— now the Association of American Colleges and Universities). These principles state that "Teachers are entitled to freedom in the classroom in discussing their subject." The statement also permits institutions to impose "limitations on academic freedom because of religious or other aims," so long as they are "clearly stated in writing at the time of the appointment."

Most teacher educators recognize that their right to teach a particular subject is circumscribed by the agenda of the state and the needs of local education agencies, and the need for their students to both complete a course of study prescribed by the state and to prepare for teaching examinations set by the state. Others on the campus (and elsewhere in the education school) have much greater latitude to choose their courses and to set the syllabi.

We pride ourselves on teacher education's membership in the wider academic community. At the University of California–Berkeley, this is described in their handbook as "membership in the academic community [that] imposes on students, faculty members, administrators, and Regents an obligation to respect the dignity of others, to acknowledge their right to express differing opinions, and to foster and defend intellectual honesty, freedom of inquiry and instruction, and free expression on and off the campus." (University of California, Berkeley *Faculty Handbook, 2007–08.*) Consequently, it is to the college or university that the first loyalty of teacher education faculty is due.

Despite the enormous expectations for teacher education faculty in most colleges and universities, there is an affinity to the host institution (and an often expressed sentiment that this is far better than the teaching job one held in an elementary or secondary school not so many years ago). There is also a ready desire to be accepted and acknowledged as part of the intellectual life or community of scholars that inhabit the particular college or university.

The Professional Obligation

Over the past twenty-five years, teacher educators have led the efforts to claim that teaching or education should be recognized as a true profession—no different than the recognition accorded to the established professions. Seemingly, every decade there is a report by a distinguished group of educators and policy makers, politicians and foundation leaders, academics and media representatives that asserts that teaching is a profession. While the reports always stop short of defining the education profession (or acknowledging the role and significance of the organized profession of teacher advocates and union organizers), there is the assumption that a profession of education exists and teacher educators only need to "connect" with that profession to realize even greater benefits for their students and the students whom they eventually teach.

As Lanier and Little (1986) pointed out two decades ago, teaching is a "mass profession" with more than 3.7 million P–12 teachers and another 2.5 million teaching in degree-granting institutions. Finding common cause across that mass profession remains a challenge today, as it has been since the earliest days of formal schooling in America. Despite this, most teacher educators readily ascribe to the notion of a teaching profession and perceive themselves connected to that community of professionals in a variety of ways. Most teacher educators recognize the role of professional accreditation and certification as setting standards for professional practice. Most teacher educators acknowledge that they have responsibilities and obligations to the education profession just as faculty in other professional schools on their campus have responsibilities to their particular societies, accreditation practices, and colleagues.

For teacher educators this is made more difficult because the sense of responsibility is most often to the discipline-based teaching organization to which they affiliated when they were classroom teachers (e.g., National Council of Teachers of Mathematics, International Reading Association, National Council for the Social Studies, National Council of Teachers of English) and not to organizations of teacher educators. These professional connections are primarily with P–12 teaching organizations and not with the professional societies of mathematicians or linguists, historians or physicists.

In contrast to faculties who teach in other professional schools and who are more clearly identified with academic endeavors and derive benefit for being part of professional communities, teacher educators derive little benefit from being identified with P–12 teaching or the organizations that represent teachers. This has been a longstanding issue for teacher educators and for others in education schools (Clifford & Guthrie, 1988; Conant, 1963; Judge, 1982; Labaree, 2004).

In professional schools, promotion and tenure policies drive faculty work, recognition, and reward. Faculty are assessed and promoted on the basis of contributions to their profession and for work in professional endeavors. They are obligated to both draw from and contribute to a professional knowledge base about their field of study and to abide by the ethics and values that are hallmarks of practice. If one reads about the preparation of medical doctors or lawyers, the clergy or accountants, the "community of scholars" concept in professional schools is much more narrowly drawn than for the university as a whole with the first obligation of those faculties to professional practice.

Teacher education has never been able to achieve such professional school status in the university, in part because there are too many good undergraduate programs that prepare teachers well, but also because teacher education has always sought to emulate the arts and sciences at both the undergraduate and graduate level rather than to create rigorous professional preparation programs. Only when teacher education becomes a graduate level endeavor and is governed like other professional schools within the university can we dispel the notion that teacher education is not professional education.

For twenty-five years, we have avoided the uncomfortable debate of where teacher education should be situated—at the baccalaureate or graduate school level—as part of the undergraduate curriculum or in specially designated professional schools of education—with the consequence that alternative providers are now challenging policy makers to consider that it can be done anywhere (Gordon, Kane, & Stager, 2006; Hess, 2001; Paige, 2002).

The serious work of building a profession of education might begin with serious engagement of faculty and teachers in building a professional curriculum for teacher education. While there is a seeming sameness to the professional curriculum in other fields of study, teacher education remains, as Darling-Hammond asserts, "quite idiosyncratic to the state, college, and program" (Darling-Hammond, 2000). "Unlike other professions where the professional curriculum is reasonably common across institutions and has some substantive coherence, the curriculum of teacher education is often idiosyncratic to the professors who teach whatever courses are required, which are different from place to place" (Darling-Hammond & Ball, 1997).

Teacher education seems to lack a sense of professional commitment that extends beyond the local public school, the embrace of nearby P–12 teachers, or the obligation to more than the subfield or discipline to which they contribute. The result is that teacher education programs—regardless of where they are located in the structures of universities—are under-resourced and over-committed, disconnected from the profession and marginalized in their connections to local schools.

Obligation to the State

The most contentious and often dismissed obligation that faculty have is to the state—defined by Marshall (1998) as "the distinct set of institutions that has the authority to make the rules which govern society." In the United States, this is the institution that governs teacher education. The state is the governmental unit that "recognizes" programs and "licenses" graduates. It sets the standards for admission to a preparation program and determines the criteria for graduation. It specifies the courses to be taken and the "cut-score" on the standardized assessment. The state can determine the eligibility of faculty to teach in the program and whether candidates must have a PDS experience. It can set expectations for induction and obligate teacher preparation programs to support their graduates in such experiences.

The state superintendent noted at the outset was expressing a sentiment often heard at annual gatherings of other state school superintendents. Her reaction hearkens back to comments probably expressed at the founding of public normal schools in New England in the 1830s. The public normal schools were an extension of the state mandate to support the expansion of public education in a particular state and were created by states (or local communities) to train teachers. When universities claimed the right to prepare teachers, they assumed a role and responsibility that was state controlled.

As normal schools and universities and colleges came to look alike relative to teacher education and to have similar missions relative to education, the role of the state was extended to cover all institutions—public and private—that sought to make teacher education a part of their course offerings. It would take nearly a century and the establishment of "autonomous professional standards boards" to confront the issue of faculty responsibility to the state.

For the majority of faculty members this is an obligation rarely acknowledged; indeed, Goodlad (1990) suggests that faculty often suffer from "myopia" when it comes to the role of the state. His contention was that the ascendancy of the state role in teacher education seems to have "tranquilized normal sensitivity" because so many faculty fail to see the erosion of faculty prerogative or curricular autonomy. If challenged, faculty denounce this intrusion as a violation of the most basic tenets of university life—academic freedom—but ultimately accede to the realities of state prerogatives and regulations. Goodlad asserts that "no higher education specialty approaches teacher education in the degree of influence exerted by outside agencies, particularly state agencies controlling entry into public school teaching" (p. 93).

State imposition of particular courses of study or mandates to use specific tests, requirements to send students to mandated settings or to specify particular experiences student teachers must undertake should be seen as distractions if not intrusions into the traditional privileges of faculty. More recently, the growing opposition by faculty to state-prescribed reading and mathematics curriculum (let alone to the testing mantra imposed by the federal *No Child Left Be-*

hind Act of 2001) have generated a host of journal articles and conference presentations denouncing state (or government) intrusion.
Some foundations faculty promote "civil disobedience" and critical
theorists denounce "government curriculum" while teacher educators
are left to teach students who must succeed in the public schools using curricula set by the state.

Being Accountable

There have been repeated efforts in the last quarter century to recon-
cile these seemingly irreconcilable forces that impose both obligation
and responsibility on teacher educators. However, the often competing
interests of the state, the college, and the profession have left teacher
educators with a sense of unease relative to their responsibilities, if not
obligations.

In the 1980s, faced by a persistent and profound teacher shortage and
the recognition that the Reagan Administration would do little to com-
bat it, the Council of Chief State School Officers (CCSSO) engaged its
members in articulating a new compact with the teaching profession to
both guarantee an adequate supply of beginning teachers and ensure
that those teachers were competent to teach. While that recognition led
to the reinvestment of CCSSO in the National Council for the Accreditation for Teacher Education (NCATE) and to work that led to the creation of the Interstate New Teacher Assessment and Support Consortium
(INTASC), it also ensured that campus-based teacher education would
become more of an instrument of the state.

At the national level, this compact extended to other state-based
groups (most notably the National Governors Association, National Association of State Boards of Education, the Education Commission of
the States, and the National Council of State Legislators) that forged relationships with the teaching profession regarding teacher education
and professional development. It embraced the efforts of the teacher organizations (National Education Association and the American Federa-
tion of Teachers) and groups like AACTE and ATE. It legitimized the
concept of an extra-state or national certification system for advanced
teaching practice and fostered the expansion of the federal government's role in teacher education.

Curiously, none of the reports that have been written in the past twenty-five years have examined the effort to bridge the state-- professional divide. The closest anyone has come to examining this condition has been Darling-Hammond in her reports for National Commission on Teaching and America's Future (NCTAF) that described a "three-legged stool" of professional accountability and professional autonomy with the state a beneficiary of, and supporter for, the movement.

STANDARDS-BASED REFORM AND EDUCATION

Standards were the glue to hold this professional-state partnership together. As Roth (1996) described, the motivation of the proponents of standards-based teacher education was twofold: some saw the necessity for standards for "sheer accountability" purposes, holding teacher education programs to new levels of performance, while others proposed using standards as "an efficacious strategy to create a profession." While there was division within the state-based organizations, the prevailing strategy was to use standards to define performance levels and minimal qualifications for teachers.

To accomplish this, in 1987 the Council of Chief State School Officers convened representatives of professional organizations (including both AACTE and ATE) and state agencies to develop performance-based standards for the initial licensure of teachers. Framed as INTASC, this group articulated the knowledge, skills, and dispositions that beginning teachers should possess to practice responsibly and begin their development toward accomplished, professional practice. CCSSO had for a long time operated the interstate reciprocity system that facilitated teacher mobility, and INTASC was consistent with that work. It was different, however, because now this consortium was moving to describe what all teachers would need to know and be able to do regardless of where they had been prepared.

Jean Miller and Linda Darling-Hammond led the work of INTASC (1992) that identified ten principles to guide the work of the Consortium. These principles were to lead to a common core of teaching knowledge and skill that should be gained by all teachers. These principles would, in turn, lead to specific standards for each of the core teaching areas. The core principles were:

Principle 1—Making Content Meaningful: The teacher understands the central concepts, tools of inquiry, and structures of the discipline(s) he or she teaches and creates learning experiences that make these aspects of subject matter meaningful for students.

Principle 2—Child Development and Learning Theory: The teacher understands how children learn and develop and can provide learning opportunities that support their intellectual, social, and personal development.

Principle 3—Learning Styles/Diversity: The teacher understands how students differ in their approaches to learning and creates instructional opportunities that are adapted to diverse learners.

Principle 4—Instructional Strategies/Problem Solving: The teacher understands and uses a variety of instructional strategies to encourage students' development of critical thinking, problem solving, and performance skills.

Principle 5—Motivation and Behavior: The teacher uses an understanding of individual and group motivation and behavior to create a learning environment that encourages positive social interaction, active engagements in learning, and self-motivation.

Principle 6—Communication/Knowledge: The teacher uses knowledge of effective verbal, nonverbal, and media communication techniques to foster active inquiry, collaboration, and supportive interaction in the classroom.

Principle 7—Planning for Instruction: The teacher plans instruction based upon knowledge of subject matter, students, the community, and curriculum goals.

Principle 8—Assessment: The teacher understands and uses formal and informal assessment strategies to evaluate and ensure the continuous intellectual, social, and physical development of the learner.

Principle 9—Professional Growth/Reflection: The teacher is a reflective practitioner who continually evaluates the effects of his or her choices and actions on others (students, parents, and other professionals in the learning community) and who actively seeks out opportunities to grow professionally.

Principle 10—Interpersonal Relationships: The teacher fosters relationships with school colleagues, parents, and agencies in the larger community to support students' learning and well-being.

It was envisioned that INTASC would build upon and be compatible with the National Board for Professional Teaching Standards (NBPTS). The advanced teaching standards of NBPTS were the model and helped to stimulate an important conversation about the difference between advanced and initial practice. The INTASC Task Force saw these differences in terms of the "sophistication" that experienced teachers "exhibited" in contrast to "the kind of knowledge needed" (INTASC, 1992).

INTASC foresaw the use of these standards by states and institutions for the purpose of constructing performance-based assessments for licensing and in program conducted by teacher educators. They advocated the adoption of these standards by state agencies and correctly foresaw that professional accreditation would embrace these standards and seek to determine whether teacher education programs had provided adequate "life space" to enable candidates to attain the knowledge, skills, and dispositions needed to teach.

Teacher Education Standards

While we celebrate the coming together of professional and state interests to write the INTASC standards, teacher educators had worked on standards for a very long time. In their *Brief History of Standards in Teacher Education*, Edelfelt and Raths (1999) identify events in the 1860s and 1870s that amount to the start of a standards movement for teacher education. They report, however, that these efforts had little staying power because "there were no procedures for closing down programs and institutions deemed to be substandard" (p. 2).

In the Carnegie Foundation's massive study of teacher education in the early twentieth century, there was again much consideration of the role that standards might play. The authors of that report identified key "elements" of good teaching and celebrated the fact that there was agreement to use a common set of expectations to govern all aspects of the operation of teacher education (Learned et al., 1920, p. 251). The authors of Carnegie Report #14 saw "mutually accepted standards of work" for faculty in Missouri's Normal Schools as "without exception in the direction of progress from earlier conditions and may signify an epoch-making change in the conduct of the schools." These were essentially a set of conditions for student admissions, faculty qualifications, program content, credit, and resources and facilities for program conduct (p. 355).

Not everyone was comfortable with the reliance on standards to guide the work of teacher education programs. Hunt (1933) reports that at the 1915 meeting of the National Council of Normal School Presidents and Principals (NCNSP&P) papers were presented on "The Evils of Standardization," "Standardization as it Affects the Normal Schools," and "How Are Standards Determined for the Judging of the Efficiency of the Work of Any Particular Institution and Can a Survey Report Made by People Outside the Institution be Reliable?"

A year later, according to Hunt, the NCNSP&P approved a resolution that stated that "all normal schools should survey themselves cooperatively and that not all this work should be done by the school itself" (Hunt, 1933, p. 12). In 1916, NCNSP&P "voted to cooperate in every way possible with the North Central Association" to develop standards for accreditation of normal schools, but it would take a decade (and merger of the Principals and Presidents with the American Association of Teachers Colleges) before a set of "tentative standards" was presented and the AATC would launch the first professional accreditation effort for teacher education.

The AATC approved this set of eighteen standards at their 1923 meeting. Hunt describes the standards as follows: "The power to grant degrees was required (Standard I). A standard four-year high school curriculum [was] required for admission to the college course . . . (Standard II). At least one hundred twenty semester hours of credit or its equivalent was required for graduation (Standard III)." "A reasonable ratio of students to faculty" was called for (Standard IV) and "members of the faculty of the teachers college [were required to] have a master's degree, but the desirability of a longer period of education was recognized (Standard V)."

Hunt continues, "the teaching load was to be a maximum of 16 clock hours each week (Standard VI)" and each teachers college "was required to maintain a training school under its own control as a laboratory school for observation, demonstration, and supervised teaching" with each candidate required "to take at least 90 hours of supervised teaching (Standard VII)." There were other standards, according to Hunt, that focused on facilities, financial support, enrollment, and location. By 1933, Hunt was ready to conclude that "the standards have been used to move the whole field forward" (Hunt, 1933, p. 16).

In their work, Edelfelt and Raths (1999) document the 1945 effort by the Committee on Standards and Surveys of the AATC to develop new standards for student teaching. "The intent," they surmise, "was to determine the field's readiness for improving standards and to identify the aspects of student teaching to which readiness might be applied" (p. 7). A most notable effect of this effort, according to Edelfelt and Raths, was a decision by the AATC members that "it was time to apply to professional education what was known about how learning takes place" (p. 7). This talk of a gap between research and practice is as prescient today as it was more than sixty years ago.

Growing out of the work of the National Commission on Teacher Education and Professional Standards (NCTEPS), established in 1946 by the National Education Association, was the creation of the National Council for the Accreditation of Teacher Education (NCATE). It was formed to write and enforce a national set of teacher education standards for all colleges and schools and assume responsibilities that previously had been left to the states, regional accreditation agencies, and AATC. By 1952, the NCTEPS Commission was in serious negotiation with the successor to AATC, AACTE, to transfer the list of accredited institutions and the standards for accreditation from AACTE to NCATE, and in 1954 the new professional accrediting association was launched (Haberman & Stinnett, 1973).

Almost immediately, NCATE began a process of standards revision that would see important changes in the focus of the standards and their impact on all preparation institutions. This process of the "continuous revision" of standards would result in at least eleven different set of standards during the course of the next thirty-five years (Cruickshank, McCullough, Reynolds, Troyer, & Cruz, 1991).

Faculty standards in the NCATE accreditation process would draw upon work of the original standards' setting committees dating back to the early 20th century but add new dimensions to reflect changes in the field. The matter of commitment to and evidence of inquiry activity originated in the first set of NCATE standards, to which were added requirements for continuing association with elementary and secondary schools (1960), reflection of the cultural diversity of the student population (1977), and participation in the profession (1986) (Cruickshank et al., 1991).

Today faculty are expected to be highly qualified, model best professional practices, engage in self-assessment, and collaborate with P–12 practitioners and disciplinary colleagues. There is also the need for faculty to integrate diversity and technology throughout their teaching, enable prospective teachers to adjust teaching to meet the needs of diverse learners, and introduce candidates to research and good practice "that counters myths and misperceptions about teaching and learning" (NCATE, 2007).[2]

Teacher Education Standards in the National Context

While the debates surrounding standards for teacher education date back to at least the late nineteenth century, most school reformers consider two events as providing the "momentum" for the standards movement that would shape the educational landscape for at least two decades (Cobb, 1994; Tucker & Codding, 1998). The first was the release of the curriculum standards by the National Council of Teachers of Mathematics and second, the convening of the nation's governors and the President of the United States at Charlottesville, Virginia, in 1989.

The major instrument for achieving standards-based reform of schooling in America was *Goals 2000: Educate America Act*. Drawing upon the bipartisan efforts of governors from both parties and members of the Bush and Clinton administrations, this legislation was enacted early in 1994, and signed by the president on March 31, 1994. It codified the six national educational goals adopted by the governors at Charlottesville, added new goals on professional development and parental involvement, instituted the National Goals Panel, and created a new oversight or standards' recognition board. The law placed major emphasis on creating challenging content and student performance standards for all children.

States, districts, and schools were called upon "to break with past practice by replacing minimum standards for some children with challenging standards for all." The law called upon states to develop or adopt content standards, in at least reading, language arts, and mathematics, by school year 1997–98. By that time, they were also to have performance standards for at least three levels of attainment: two high-performance levels, proficient and advanced, and a partially proficient level that could be used to determine how well children were learning the material in the state content standards.

With the enactment of *Goals 2000*, there was tremendous progress in articulating sets of national curriculum standards and designing new assessment schemes. Standards for mathematics, the arts, civics, geography, physical education, U.S. history, and world history were either complete or would soon be finalized. It was expected that standards for English, economics, foreign languages, and science standards would follow. While the release of the U.S. history standards provoked both unprecedented criticism from political and cultural conservatives and a fear that standards-based reform would be derailed, it was readily apparent that despite such opposition standards-based reform would survive and flourish as an important policy instrument (Cheney, 1994).

These efforts at developing content standards were guided by the National Council on Standards and Testing, which released its blueprint for standards development, *Raising Standards for American Education*, early in 1992. The panel also agreed to support a national voluntary assessment system to provide accountability, improve instruction, and promote student learning that triggered strong opposition from Republican members of the Congress and others. In January 1992, the National Education Goals Panel reconfigured the National Council and renamed it the National Education Standards and Assessments Council (NESAC) and assigned it the purpose of coordinating the various standards writing efforts.

With the enactment of *Goals 2000* two years later, NESAC assumed even more authority and was reconfigured as a nineteen-member panel to certify education standards that the professional associations and the states submitted. Many saw this as an ambitious reach by the federal government to create a national school board with significant authority to approve student learning expectations and to support them with coherent coordinated policies that would reach to the local school level.

These efforts at standards development were being monitored by the teacher education community and throughout the early 1990s there were "convenings" of professional educators to examine the array of standards and their potential impact on the *professional project*. Diez led one such dialogue on the role of standards and assessments in the early 1990s that is useful for understanding both the potential in the standards' movement and the nagging concerns about the potential for "standardization." It was a dialogue that included Linda Darling-Hammond, Raymond Pecheone, Diane Pullin, Lelia Vickers, among others, with Diez asserting that "the development of standards is directly related to the development of teaching as a profession" (Diez, 1998, p. 12).

In that dialogue, concerns were expressed that "there is a real lack of defined standards . . . not just in teacher preparation but in all areas of education." "If we become serious about standards and assessments, then we will find them debated, expanded, paraphrased, and used." The participants in the dialogue saw the intent of the "standards discussion" being to "spark a serious dialogue about what constitutes good teaching. In fact, that may be the most important role of standards—to lay out a vision of teaching in a public way so that all in the profession can contribute to its critique and refinement" (Diez, 1998, pp. 11–12). Participants in the dialogue also saw "dangers inherent in the standards and assessment movement" and urged vigilance as it proceeded.

So If Standards Were So Good, Why Didn't ATE's Standards for Teacher Educators Get Attention?

As noted elsewhere in this volume, in 1992 the Association of Teacher Educators launched an effort to identify standards for teacher educators with the goal of creating a certification process for master teacher educators. Led by Robert Houston, the ATE Task Force on the Teacher Educator Standards, which included an array of leading teacher educators drawn from various fields and institutions, shaped a set of ambitious standards that were presented to and adopted by the ATE membership in 1996.

The ensuing four years saw a variety of efforts undertaken by both the task force and its members to seek both confirmation for the standards and their adoption by the wider education community. Instead, there was both ambivalence and reluctance about the desirability of the standards and little agreement that they would be a useful addition to those already used by NCATE and the various discipline-based organizations. Given the national discourse underway by mid-decade, it is useful to consider why there was such reluctance or ambivalence.

The simple answer, borrowing from Yinger (1999), was that by the late-1990s there was "standards exhaustion" with "standards for learners, standards for instruction, standards for teachers, standards for curriculum, standards for teacher education, standards for teacher licensure, standards for performance, standards for testing, and even standards for standards." In addition, the Clinton administration had aggressively pursued the concept of "opportunity to learn standards" but the change in Congressional leadership in 1994 shifted the policy debate and reframed the conversation to focus on outcomes.

At the same time, the NBPTS was struggling to certify its first teachers and Congress was increasingly skeptical of the so-called *professional project* then being emphasized by the NCTAF and supported by the U.S. Education Department. A new accrediting agency, Teacher Education Accreditation Council (TEAC), challenged NCATE and an increasing advocacy for "deregulation" in state and national policy debates. The "deregulators" or "de-professionalists" brought proposals to the forefront for alternative routes to teaching and "alternative certification" with teachers to be hired irrespective of their credentials or experience.

There were internal organizational challenges for ATE and a lack of involvement of the education professoriate (particularly the leadership of Division K of AERA) in the endeavor. There was also a belated reaction to the systemic and extraordinarily ambitious reform initiatives of the Clinton administration.

Systemic Reform: Re-enforcing the State's Role in Teacher Education

Of the many factors that retarded the adoption and acceptance of the ATE standards by teacher educators, we contend it was "standards exhaustion" and a growing apprehension with systemic reform that were the major culprits. Standards-based reform had come to be interpreted (and funded) by the Clinton administration as a concept that embodied three components: a) the promotion of ambitious outcomes for all students, b) alignment of policy approaches and the actions of policy institutions to promote such outcomes, and c) restructuring the governance system to support improved achievement (Goertz, Floden, & O'Day, 1996).

Systemic reform was the "watchword" for both reformers and policy makers throughout the 1990s, and advocated by scholars and academics associated with the Clinton administration (Fuhrman, 1994). It essentially argued that all of the components of a viable, effective, and high quality school system existed and that what needed to be done was to make the several pieces work better to benefit all children. It made use of the language of capacity building and policy integration and promoted the idea that by "tightly coupling" teaching with content standards, pupil learning with assessment, and teacher training with teacher performance, significant change could be realized. Teacher education was to be an integral part of this reform agenda with both pre-service and professional development driven by the aspirations of the policy makers and reformers.

Advocates for systemic reform were most apprehensive about the capacity of teachers to deliver new and challenging content to all students and the willingness of teacher educators to prepare teachers to teach the content expected of students. Finding incentives and other ways to overcome "the traditional independence of higher education institutions, and the tradition of faculty autonomy" was cited as necessary to increase the capacity of teachers (Goertz, Floden, & O'Day, 1996). Teacher education and professional development were integral and vital components of a set of coordinated strategies that included identifying educational goals, setting high academic standards, describing academic frameworks, agreeing on core competencies, and setting benchmarks and framing new assessments for all students.

These efforts were national in scope and attempted to align federal and state policies with local school plans and practices. All the pieces were to be "tightly coupled" with common "road maps" and much oversight. The participants were supposed to work for a common end—the improvement of schooling for all children. In such a vision, the role of teacher educators was to be aligned to a larger cause, "to create a teaching force that was up-to-date in the content areas and skilled in imparting knowledge to diverse populations of students" (Corcoran, 1995).

While the challenges of coordination and alignment were enormous, some of the leading academics agreed that the American education system could be so aligned (O'Day & Smith, 1993). While the extremes of systemic reform were challenged by both liberals and conservatives, it was overwhelmingly supported by the nation's governors and, in alliance with the Clinton Education Department, was broadly endorsed by the American public. Public Agenda estimated that 80–90 percent of Americans embraced standards-based systemic reform (Stanfield, 1996). There was widespread agreement that this was the best way to transform education to enable American children to compete with their counterparts in other industrialized nations.

In this design, teacher educators were "implementers" of curricula designs and pedagogical approaches set elsewhere. Teacher education programs were "instruments" of state policies to produce sufficient numbers of beginning teachers capable of implementing state approved lessons. To ensure compliance with this design, there were extraordinary investments made in redesigning state licensure systems and program approval processes for teacher education. The 1992 amendments to the Higher Education Act called for state plans that would lead to "an integrated and coherent approach to attracting, recruiting, preparing and licensing teachers, administrators, and other educators so that there is a highly talented workforce of professional educators capable of preparing all students to reach challenging standards" (Cohen & Smith, 1993).

Opposition to systemic reform (and to the role assigned to initial teacher education and professional development) emerged from several quarters. In a Public Agenda report, *Different Drummers: How Teachers of Teachers View Public Education*, the authors contended that while policy makers and parents believed that teacher education was a vital component in the systemic reform movement and "could not operate in isolation or ignore consideration of the P–12 student standards, teacher educators held a different set of beliefs" (Farkas & Johnson, 1997).

Issued by the New York-based public interest group, the report essentially argued that teacher educators were "disconnected" from the prevailing attitudes and beliefs of the public and the policy community relative to the reform of education in this country. Particularly disconcerting was the accusation that not only were education schools disconnected but that faculty dismissed the educational concerns of nearly everyone else as being "inconsequential." The authors asserted "the disconnect between what the professors want and what most parents, teachers, and students say they need, is staggering" (Farkas & Johnson, 1997). The report would become a major source for the "findings" section of the subsequent reauthorization of the federal Higher Education

Act and lead to the accountability provisions that came to dominate teacher education programs at the end of the decade.

The Congressional elections in November 1994, with Republicans retaking both the House and Senate, led to a rethinking of systemic reform. Some argued that school change was not linear or rational but, instead, was characterized by "complexity, dynamism, and unpredictability" (Fullan, 1993). Other critics opposed systemic reform because they saw it as a threat to local control, parental rights, and academic freedom (Strike, 1997). They viewed the effort to create such a system as centralized goal formation and predicted that it would "run afoul of certain liberties beginning with the liberty of students or their parents to be free from unreasonable education coercion . . . [and] the prospect of additional centralization of educational authority" (Strike, 1997, p. 2).

The election results propelled a resurgence of local control advocates into key leadership positions in the Congress and led to a reframing of the national agenda for education. This, in turn, prompted a spirited debate about teacher professionalism and the role of "unionism" in the political dialogue about school reform (Applebome, 1995). There was also a growing antiprofessional sentiment among public policy officials, a rise in 'anticredentialism' sentiments in the wider society and growing antiunionism that had consequences for teacher education.

The enactment of a set of principles regarding teacher education by the American Association of State Colleges and Universities (AASCU), which called for states to reassert their responsibilities for licensure and program approval (and to subvert professional accreditation and credentialing), and the efforts of the Council of Independent Colleges (CIC) to establish an alternative accreditation body for teacher education, reflected the positions of many college and university leaders and reinforced the efforts of many teacher educators to disconnect from systemic reform efforts.

THE NCTAF REPORT AND THE REFRAMING OF THE PROFESSIONAL PROJECT

The dominant policy vehicle for the *professional project* during this difficult period was the NCTAF report *What Matters Most: Teaching for America's Future*. Chaired by North Carolina Governor James

Hunt, the Commission's report appeared in September 1996. It generated much attention from policy makers and the public. It promoted a set of strategies designed to achieve high quality pre-service preparation and continuous professional development for all school personnel, autonomous professional standards boards and advanced certification (NBPTS), a more robust professional accreditation body (NCATE), and new state licensing systems (INTASC). This came to be referred to as "a three-legged stool" of reform.

What was striking about the report was that it sought to align state licensing and program approval with national accreditation and advanced certification. It broke the boundaries of state-professional-campus contributions to teaching and teacher education. Whether it was "a reach too far" was a question that rose almost immediately on campuses and in policy centers (Darling-Hammond, 1996).

Nevertheless, the Clinton administration would invest $23 million in an initiative known as the National Partnership for Excellence and Accountability in Teaching (NPEAT) to provide a research base to support the implementation of the recommendations of the NCTAF report. This investment was paralleled by other contributions of public and private corporations and foundations. NCTAF became a permanent organization bringing together state and professional leaders "to create new policies and practices for dramatically improving the quality of teaching" (Darling-Hammond, 1996).

Opposition to the NCTAF agenda came from many different groups. The most aggressive of these opponents were the advocates for more market oriented competition and the deregulation of state controls over teacher education. In contrast to those who promoted the *professional project*, conservative think tanks and others called for the end of current practices for licensing teachers, the de-emphasis on program accreditation, and the promotion of alternative preparation programs. They called for states to deregulate program approval or state prescriptions of courses of study, appealed for the use of content knowledge tests to determine the suitability of those who want to teach, and urged that school principals be given much greater discretion in hiring practices. This became part of the escalating mantra for new approaches to preparing teachers and staffing America's schools (Soler, 1999; Phillips & Kanstoroom, 1999).

Ultimately, this agenda would prevail, manifested in the 1998 amendments to the *Higher Education Act* and the enactment of the *No*

Child Left Behind Act. We had come so close to the realization of the *professional project.* What had gone wrong? A powerful countermovement to the professionalism efforts was mounted in the late 1990s. For both political reasons (the teacher organizations were too influential) and for ideological reasons (many theorists saw traditional professions as too elitist, paternalistic, authoritarian, and exclusionary), a new pathway was sought for the attainment of professional recognition for teaching.

With the inauguration of George W. Bush, the *professional project* was diminished and a new era of deregulation was promoted. In a series of bruising reports on the condition of teacher education, Rod Paige, appointed as education secretary by President Bush, pointed in a direction of alternative preparation, heralded *Teach for America* as a model teacher education program, created alternative licensure and advanced certification bodies (American Board for Certification of Teacher Excellence (ABCTE)), and recast the professional discourse regarding teacher education. The most comprehensive statement of those policy proposals was contained in a seriously flawed report to the Congress by the U.S. Department of Education entitled *The Secretary's Annual Report on Teacher Quality: Meeting the Highly Qualified Teachers Challenge* (Paige, 2002). That report offered four far-reaching policy proposals:

- support the development of new models of "teacher training" that are "local," "based on the best alternative route programs of today," and "produce teachers with those skills that are in high demand"
- support state initiatives to end the "exclusive franchise" of schools of education and to curtail the "shocking number" of mandated education courses and assist state efforts to uncouple education school courses from state licensure, making "attendance at schools of education . . . optional"
- help states to "streamline" licensure requirements to place a premium on verbal ability and content knowledge, develop new and "challenging assessments" for teacher candidates, and require "content area majors"
- promote state efforts to shift authority for determining the qualifications of beginning teachers "from state certification officials to local school principals"

In such an environment, standards for teacher educators lost their potency and possibility. The reservations expressed about the ATE initiative on the part of faculties and other campus leaders led to the reconsideration of the need for such standards. Now, some five years later, there is renewed interest in the *professional project* and an insistence that teacher educators be recognized for their professional contributions. The need for teacher educators to gain the right to use their professional judgment in teaching and to be granted the autonomy necessary to practice their profession has never been greater. The pending reauthorization of the *No Child Left Behind Act* and a Congress insistent on greater accountability for teacher education makes the recognition of teacher education as a professional endeavor even more important.

THE NEW PROFESSIONAL PROJECT: WHY THE ATE STANDARDS INITIATIVE IS TIMELY

Growing opposition to *No Child Left Behind* and the calls for new forms of accountability for teachers and students has generated new consideration of the role of standards. It is also causing policy makers and others to seek new ways to recognize and reward meritorious teachers. A fundamental reconsideration of the way that teachers are granted the right to practice and then are rewarded for successful teaching is underway (Imig & Imig, 2008). It is a system in which credentials and credits are less important and performance and practice assume much greater importance. Whether local education agencies continue to invest in traditional professional development provided by local colleges and online universities is doubtful.

In such a system, traditional academic courses and advanced credentials are less valued and, instead, new forms of professional development that address real and immediate classroom problems sought. Since there are now more sophisticated ways to measure teacher instruction and to determine the value of their teaching relative to the successes of their students, performance rather than longevity and seniority likely matter. Merit pay proposals are already commonplace in many school districts. Teacher organizations and other local education agencies are negotiating new ways of compensating good teaching (Toch & Rothman, 2008).

The ATE teacher education standards recognize that teacher education occurs in many venues and that teacher educators work in both collegiate and noncollegiate settings. With alternative route teachers now constituting more than one in five new hires and new forms of teacher development available online and in other formats, the traditional conception of standards for teacher educators is under reconsideration. A parallel development is the reconsideration of the *professional project* and the definition of teacher educator as professional in a variety of settings far beyond traditional colleges and universities.

The standards provide boundaries and expectations for that practice but ultimately their success will be measured not by attainment of credentials but rather by the success of those they prepare, or "in-service." In such an environment, the obligations teacher educators have to their students is more carefully drawn and the need for professional autonomy and the right to practice more critical for successful practice.

The terrain of teacher professionalism is highly contested; for example, between 'the state' and teachers, between teacher unions and local boards of education, between parents' groups and teachers, between communities and schools. With little certainty about who should 'control' the agenda related to teacher's work, it seems that we are headed into a time of greater uncertainty in where and how teaching and teacher education take place. The redefinition of schools and schooling—with greater consideration of "advanced distributed learning" beyond the traditional boundaries of P–12 schools—portends changes in every aspect of education (Fletcher, Tobias, & Wisher, 2007). The balance between obligation and autonomy is more vigorously challenged in an environment in which the traditional boundaries are more permeable and unconstrained.

Teacher education has experienced profound changes over the past twenty-five years in terms of both content and structure, delivery and focus. The field has become more and more school based (with the advent of the PDS) and now offers a more practical-based form of preparation with the aim of helping candidates attain competencies set by the state and fulfilling obligations to more diverse students. Teacher education has been reshaped by both efforts of the federal government (particularly in literacy or reading) to set a 'national curriculum' for teaching and by rules and regulations set by the "state"—with Title II of the Higher Education Act offering a most "intrusive" set of reporting requirements.

In his recent contribution to the definition of the "new professional," Parker Palmer (2007) exhorts teacher educators to be, "in but not of 'their' institutions." He contends an "allegiance to the core values of their fields" enables them to "resist the institutional diminishment of those values." To the teacher educator drowning in layers of often competing university, state, and professional requirements, Palmer's words may seem like an idyllic battle cry for another day. But, turning back to what we do best—preparing and supporting teachers to serve all children and expanding our understanding of effective educational practices—is what we must do to reestablish the profession's place at the table.

Darling-Hammond and Bransford (2005) conclude their book, *Preparing Teachers for a Changing World*, with the admonition that policy makers must understand "that, if American public education is to meet the aspirations this nation has assigned to it, the preparation of excellent teachers is the central commitment without which other reforms are unlikely to succeed" (p. 479). The ATE standards for teacher educators can provide direction for such work. They offer teacher educators the way to engage in the policy discourse on preparation—we can not quietly let this moment pass.

NOTES

1. L.S. Shulman (1983) contributed an important chapter to the *Handbook on Teaching and Policy* entitled Autonomy and Obligation: The Remote Control of Teaching. Using the metaphor of "nightmares," Shulman describes the chasm between teachers and policy makers. We are drawing from that chapter to argue that autonomy can only be achieved on the basis of obligation.

2. Similar faculty standards exist in the alternative teacher education accreditation agency. The Teacher Education Accreditation Council asserts that "the program faculty must be qualified to teach the courses in the program to which they are assigned as evidenced by advanced degrees held, scholarship, contributions to the field, and professional experience."

REFERENCES

Applebome, P. (1995, September 4). GOP efforts put teachers' unions on the defensive. *The New York Times*, p. 1.

Cheney, L. (1994, October 20). The end of history. *The Wall Street Journal.*

Clifford, G. J., & Guthrie, J. W. (1988). *Ed school: A brief for professional education.* Chicago: The University of Chicago Press.

Cobb, N. (Ed.). (1994). *The future of education: Perspectives on national standards in America.* New York: The College Board.

Conant, J. B. (1963). *The education of American teachers.* New York: McGraw-Hill.

Corcoran, T. (1995). Helping teachers teach well: Transforming professional development. *CPRE Policy Briefs.* (RB-16-June).

Cruickshank, D. R., McCullough, J. D., Reynolds, R. T., Troyer, M. B., & Cruz, J. (1991). *The legacy of NCATE: An analysis of standards and criteria for compliance since 1957.* Washington, DC: ERIC Clearinghouse on Teacher Education.

Darling-Hammond, L., (1996). *What matters most: Teaching for America's future.* New York: Teachers College.

Darling-Hammond, L., & Bransford, E. (Eds.). (2005). Preparing teachers for a changing world: What teachers should learn and be able to do. San Francisco, CA: Jossey-Bass.

Darling-Hammond, L., & Ball, D. L. (1997). *Teaching for high standards: What policymakers need to know and be able to do.* Washington, DC: The National Education Goals Panel.

Darling-Hammond, L., Wise, A. E., & Klein, S. P. (1997). *A license to teach: Building a profession for 21st-century schooling.* Boulder, CO: Westview.

Diez, M. E. (Ed.) (1998). *Changing the practice of teacher education: Standards and assessments as a lever for change.* Washington, DC: American Association of Colleges for Teacher Education.

Edelfelt, R. A., & Raths, J. D. (1999). *A brief history of standards in teacher education.* Reston, VA: Association of Teacher Educators.

Farkas, S., & Johnson, J. (1997). *Different drummers: How teachers of teachers view public education.* New York: Public Agenda.

Fletcher, J. S., Tobias, S., & Wisher, R. A. (2007). Learning anytime, anywhere: Advanced distributed learning and the changing face of education. *Educational Researcher, 36*(2), 96–102.

Fuhrman, S. H. (1994). Politics and systemic education reform. (*CPRE Policy Briefs*). New Brunswick, NJ: Consortium for Policy Research in Education.

Gitlin, A., & Labaree, D. (1996). Historical notes on the barriers to the professionalization of American teachers: The influence of markets and patriarchy. In I. Goodson & A. Hargreaves (Eds.), *Teachers' professional lives,* (pp. 88–108). New York: Routledge.

Goodlad, J. I. (1990). *Teachers for our nation's schools*. San Francisco, CA: Jossey-Bass.

Gordon, R., Kane, T., & Stager, D. O. (2006). *Identifying effective teachers using performance on the job*. Washington, DC: The Brookings Institution.

Hess, F. M. (2001). *Tear down this wall: The case for a radical overhaul of teacher certification*. Washington, DC: Progressive Policy Institute.

Holmes Partnership. (2007). *Triology: Tomorrow's teachers, tomorrow's schools, tomorrow's schools of education*. New York: Peter Lang.

Howsam, R. B., Corrigan, D. C., Denemark, G. W., & Nash, R. J. (1976). Educating a profession. *Report of the Bicentennial Commission on Education for the Profession of Teaching of the American Association of Colleges for Teacher Education*. Washington, D.C.

Hunt, C. W. (1933). The development of standards in the teachers college. Reprint January. *Educational Administration and Supervision*.

Imig, D., & Imig, S. (2008). From traditional certification to competitive certification: A twenty-five year retrospective. In M. Cochran-Smith, S. Feiman-Nemser, D. McIntyre, & K. Demers (Eds.), *Handbook of research on teacher education: Enduring questions in changing contexts* (3rd ed., pp. 886–907). Mahwah, NJ: Taylor & Francis Publishing.

Interstate New Teacher Assessment and Support Consortium. (1992). *Model standards for beginning teacher licensing, assessment and development: A resource for state dialogue*. Washington, DC: Council of Chief State School Officers.

Labaree, D. F. (2004). *The trouble with ed schools*. New Haven, CT: Yale University Press.

Lanier, J., & Little, J. (1986). Research on teacher education, in M. C. Wittrock (Ed.), *The Handbook of research on teaching* (pp. 527–569). New York: Macmillan.

Learned, W. S., Bagley, W. C., McMurry, C. A., Strayer, G. D., Dearborn, W. F., Kandel, L., & Josselyn, H. W. (1920). *The professional preparation of teachers for American public schools: A study based upon an examination of tax-supported normal schools in the state of Missouri* (Bulletin no. 14). New York: Carnegie Foundation for the Advancement of Teaching.

National Council for the Accreditation of Teacher Education. (2000). *NCATE 2000 Unit Standards*. Washington, DC: Author.

O'Day, J., & Smith, M. (1993). Systemic reform and educational opportunity, in Susan Fuhrman (Ed.), *Designing coherent education policy* (pp. 250–312). San Francisco: Jossey-Bass.

No Child Left Behind Act of 2001, Pub. L. No. 107–110, 115 Stat. 1425.

Paige, R. (2002). *Meeting the highly qualified teacher challenge, The Secretary's annual report on teacher quality.* Washington, DC: Department of Education.

Palmer, P. (2007). A new professional: The aims of education revisited. *Change,* November-December. Retrieved December 30, 2007 from www.carnegiefoundation.org/

Roth, R. A. (1996). Standards for certification, licensure and accreditation, in J. Sikula, T. Buttery, & E. Guyton (Eds.), *Handbook of research on teacher education* (2nd ed., pp. 242–278). New York: Macmillan.

Shulman, L. S. (1987). Knowledge and teaching: Foundations of the new reform. *Harvard Educational Review, 57*(1), 114–135.

Shulman, L. S. (2007). *Scholarships of practice and the practices of scholarship: Education among the doctorates; Observations on the varieties of doctoral education.* A Paper Presented at the Annual Meeting of the Council of Graduate Schools. Seattle, WA.

Soler, S. (1999). *Teacher quality is job one.* Washington, DC: Progressive Policy Institute.

Stanfield, R. (1996). Schoolhouse politics. *National Journal, 28*(12), 673.

Strike, K. (1997). Centralized goal formation and systemic reform: Reflections on liberty, localism and pluralism. *Education Policy Analysis Archives, 5*(11), 1–35.

Toch, T., & Rothman, R. (2008). *Rush to judgment: Teacher evaluation in public education.* Washington, DC: Education Sector.

Tucker, M. (1986). *A nation prepared: Teachers for the 21st century.* New York: Carnegie Forum on Education and the Economy.

Tucker, M. S., & Codding, J. B. (1998). *Standards for our schools: How to set them, measure them, and reach them.* San Francisco, CA: Jossey-Bass.

Yinger, R. (1999). The role of standards in teaching and teacher education, in G. A. Griffin (Ed.), *The Education of Teachers* (pp. 85–114). Chicago, IL: University of Chicago Press.

CHAPTER 23

What Can Standards Do for Teacher Educators?

Roy A. Edelfelt

The Standards for Teacher Educators of the Association of Teachers Educators (ATE) (2008) bring to mind a number of issues that members need to think about in this new era in ATE's history:

- The definition of teacher educator
- The lessons of the history of standards
- The effect of the standards on criticisms of teacher educators
- Urgent next steps for teacher educators

THE DEFINITION OF TEACHER EDUCATOR

There are probably several definitions of teacher educator. For the purposes of this chapter, I think that the qualities and competencies in the standards describe senior-level professionals involved in the preparation and continuing development of teachers. These people have extensive experience in education. They have successfully completed advanced graduate study. They work in high-level positions in teacher education institutions and agencies involved in the initial preparation and continuing development of teachers and other school personnel. They may also be involved in monitoring teacher education programs.

Teachers who supervise student teachers, mentor new teachers, or are involved in other phases of teacher education may not be full-fledged teacher educators as described in the standards unless they can demonstrate or model the competencies described by the standards. However, such personnel can benefit from, try to practice, and demonstrate some of the standards. Because there is currently no demarcation or assessment process to distinguish teacher educators from other personnel involved in teacher education, the fundamental questions that must be answered are: How will the distinction be made, and who will make it?

Deciding who is a teacher educator may be down the road a bit. So let me not dwell on that issue ahead of other preliminary questions.

THE LESSONS OF THE HISTORY OF STANDARDS

A review of the history of establishing standards in teacher education can be helpful in planning how the ATE standards can become something more than rhetoric. Even though times have changed, considering how and why teacher education progressed to its current stage may make it possible to avoid stumbling blocks to implementation. For example, it may be instructive to review protocols and procedures that facilitated or have been essential to change, recognize circumstances in which resistance has been greatest, be reminded of the legal barriers that must be managed, and acknowledge the changes in prestige and hierarchy of personnel that raising standards creates.

The promulgation of these standards is encouraging because it signals that progress is under way in teacher education. Progress has been a long journey (Charters & Waples, 1929; Edelfelt & Raths, 1999; Evenden, 1935; Learned et al., 1920). In the twentieth century (NCTEPS, 1964), progress was phenomenal. Preparation increased from one or two years of college to four. By 1960, most states required a bachelor's degree for certification (Edelfelt & Johnson, 1980).

In the process, normal schools became state teachers colleges (AATC, 1948). Practice teaching in laboratory schools (often part-time) became student teaching in public schools (full-time). Selected practicing teachers were enticed, encouraged, helped, trained, and sometimes forced to become cooperating teachers to guide and counsel student teachers.

For teacher training institutions, becoming departments and schools in universities, particularly in private academies, was not easy. It was less difficult in public universities because many of them, having been state colleges, had already been preparing elementary school teachers. Public universities also had long experience in preparing secondary school teachers.

Getting professional, public, and legal acceptance of higher standards was slow and difficult (NEA, 1967). Equally difficult but important was getting public support and state legislation requiring schoolteachers to be licensed. The research, promotion, and politicking involved were mind-boggling but significant.

Some university entities still do not accept teacher educators as equal partners in higher education. Shedding the image of the normal school, where scholarship was lacking, research largely unknown, and scholarship poorly respected, has not been easy.

Reviewing the work of study groups, committees, commissions, conferences, and the like provides illustrations of how consensus, legislation, and financing can be achieved in setting and applying higher standards, and how many and various roles evolve.

THE EFFECT OF THE STANDARDS ON CRITICISMS OF TEACHER EDUCATORS

Skepticism about teacher educators and complaints about the prevailing norms in teacher education are rampant. The ATE standards address some of the criticisms directly. Also, they can help bring attention to what teacher educators need to know and be able to do, and the roles they should play.

Looking at Arthur Levine's (2006) criticism of teacher education faculty provides an example. He claims, "teacher education faculty mirror the historical conflicts and confusions of the profession. They are disconnected from the schools. They are disconnected from the arts and sciences. They engage in research disconnected from policy, practice, and the academy" (p. 45).

The ATE standards clearly respond to Levine's criticisms. Below I have juxtaposed selected quotes from the Levine study and the ATE standards that address those criticisms:

- "Most of the professors had no idea of what was going on in today's classroom" (p. 45).
  —Standard One: Teaching

(continued)

- "Professors were not sufficiently involved with schools" (p. 46).
  —Standard Six: Collaboration

- "The more senior faculty members become, the more likely they are to withdraw from clinical activities" (p. 47).
  —Standards One and Six: Teaching and Collaboration

- "The status differences between the academic and clinical faculties are profound. Joint program planning is the exception rather than the rule" (p. 47).
  —Standard Four: Professional Development

- "Arts and sciences faculty complain that education research is simplistic, that education students are among the weakest on campus, that course work in education lacks rigor" (p. 48).
  —Standard Three: Scholarship

- "The low status of education schools on most campuses leads to what can be an almost unbridgeable chasm between the arts and sciences and the education faculties" (p. 48).
  —Standard Six: Collaboration

- "Practitioners—school administrators and teachers—have little or no voice in determining the content and organization of education school programs" (p. 50).
  —Standard Six: Collaboration

- "A lack of continuity from one course to the next and insufficient integration between course work and field work resulted in a fractured curriculum" (p. 50).
  —Standard Four: Professional Development

- "80 percent of teacher education professors . . . had been denied tenure owing to their minimal publications records and the low quality of their work" (p. 51).
  —Standard Eight: Teacher Education Profession

- "There is a consistent complaint that teacher education research is subjective, obscure, faddish, impractical, out of touch, inbred, and politically correct, and that it fails to address the burning problems of the nation's schools" (p. 52).
  —Standard Three: Scholarship

URGENT NEXT STEPS FOR TEACHER EDUCATORS

Approval of the standards by the ATE governance signifies that the Association's membership approves and endorses the concepts and positions presented. The approval is an affirmation of an attempt to raise standards. But a pronouncement is not enough. Action is required for the standards to become policy and practice.

The standards could be practiced voluntarily by ATE members and become their credo for professional behavior. Such action would be admirable, but would hardly make much of an impact on teacher education in the United States. My assumption is that ATE's intention is a much broader application of the standards.

How can the standards become policy and be implemented in practice? Getting them accepted and implemented will be difficult. It is not a task that ATE should undertake alone. It is much too large a project, and it affects many more teacher educators than members of ATE.

Following are a few questions that ATE must consider as first steps in adoption of the standards:

- Will promotion and application be strictly an ATE project, or will ATE need to collaborate with other associations and organizations, and the public? (Lindsey, 1961)
- To what associations and organizations will the standards be disseminated?
- How should dissemination take place?
- By what means should ATE promote discussion of the standards in professional and public forums, the media, etc.?
- How can other associations and organizations be enlisted to join in developing the standards further and in implementing them? (AATC, 1948; NCTEPS, 1953; NEA, 1954)
- Is a national effort or endeavor (a commission or a board) needed to provide leadership to accelerate and support the progression of standards from policy to action?
- How can a project of this magnitude be financed?
- By what means will ATE, the profession in general, and the public monitor and assess progress?

ATE should make clear whom the standards are intended to cover. Earlier I suggested that they apply at least in part to all personnel engaged in some way in the education of teachers. Aspects of the standards could be applied to cooperating teachers, to teachers who team-teach with professors, and to teachers who help prepare teachers in professional development schools (Darling-Hammond, 1994). Similarly, aspects could be applied to schoolteachers who serve as mentors to beginning teachers in school-university partnerships (Reiman, 2000). Of course, the main group to which the standards should apply is the professionals at the top rung of the ladder of teacher educators.

As it becomes clearer which of the people involved in teacher education must meet all or some of the ATE standards, additional questions to be addressed are these:

- Will the standards be applied to individual practitioners or to teacher educators as a group?
- Will elements of the standards be adapted to apply to teachers and other personnel in schools and colleges working in teacher education? (Reiman, 1999, 2000)

History suggests that many of the difficulties in raising standards can be anticipated. Experience in teacher education over the years provides some guidance in moving ahead. Studies, reports, and journals from the twentieth century (for descriptions and references, see Edelfelt & Johnson, 1980; Edelfelt & Raths, 1999) are instructive. Notable examples of a successful implementation of standards are (1) the standards developed by the Association for Student Teaching (ATE's former name) for student teaching, which through negotiations became the National Council on Accreditation of Teacher Education's Standard Six (currently Standard Three), and (2) the postbachelor's national professional certification for individual teachers, established by the National Board for Professional Teaching Standards (NBPTS) as a result of wide participation from teachers, teacher education associations, and other groups. To date, the NBPTS has certified more than 50,000 teachers. Important to note is that the NBPTS received major funding from the U.S. Congress.

The experience of other professions is also instructive. Numerous ones (mostly in medical and allied health fields) have established postdoctoral diplomates and board certifications for individual practitioners (see, for example, APA, 2004; Batalden, Leach, Swing, Dreyfus, & Dreyfus, 2002; Brown et al., 2004; Exstrom, 2001; Madewell, 2004; Rhodes, 2007).

Several major universities have already established doctoral programs with requirements similar to the new ATE standards. If the standards were adopted by teacher education accreditation agencies, the distance between the doctoral degree and a certificate as a teacher educator would be minimal.

A huge effort, widespread professional commitment and support from all or most of the stakeholders in teacher education, and adequate financial resources could bring implementation of these standards within reach. The accompanying competence, prestige, and status would be a giant step in bringing many current teacher preparation programs to a level high enough to ensure that most new teachers are well prepared.

The ATE Standards for Teacher Educators also can help the teaching profession advance along the road of professionalizing itself. Doing so is particularly important at this time in history, when a well-educated citizenry is required to make democracy work better (see Gallagher, 2008; Garrison, 2008; Neumann, 2008).

REFERENCES

American Association of Teachers Colleges, Subcommittee of the Standards and Surveys Committee. (1948). *School and community laboratory experiences in teacher education*. Oneonta, NY: AATC.

American Psychological Association, Board of Educational Affairs. (2004). *Developing and evaluating standards and guidelines related to education and training in psychology: Context, procedures, criteria, and format*. Washington, DC: Author. Retrieved February 20, 2007, from www.apa.org/ed/graduate/beaguidelines_04Final.pdf

Association of Teacher Educators. (1991). *Restructuring the education of teachers: Report of the Commission on the Education of Teachers into the 21st Century*. Reston, VA: Author.

Association of Teacher Educators. (1996). *Certification of master teacher educators: Final report of the Task Force on the Certification of Teacher Educators*. Reston, VA: Author.

Association of Teacher Educators. (1996). *National standards for teacher educators: Report of the Task Force on the Certification of Teacher Educators*. Reston, VA: Author

Association of Teacher Educators. (2008). *Standards for teacher educators (revised)*. Reston, VA: Author.

Batalden, P., Leach, D., Swing, S., Dreyfus, H., & Dreyfus, S. (2002). General competencies and accreditation in graduate medical education. *Health Affairs*, *21*, 103–111.

Brown, D. T., Benson, A. J., Walker, N. W., Sternberger, L. G., Lung, D. S., & Kassinove, H. (2004). A systemic view of higher education and professional psychology: Implications of the Combined-Integrated model of doctoral training. *Journal of Clinical Psychology*, *60*, 1091–1108.

Charters, W. W., & Waples, D. (1929). *The Commonwealth Teacher-Training Study*. Chicago: University of Chicago Press.

Darling-Hammond, L. (Ed.) (1994). *Professional development schools: Schools for developing a profession*. New York: Teachers College Press.

Edelfelt, R. A. (1969). *Redesigning the education profession*. Washington, DC: National Commission on Teacher Education and Professional Standards.

Edelfelt, R. A. (1972). The reform of education and teacher education: A complex task. *Journal of Teacher Education*, *23*, 117–125.

Edelfelt, R. A., & Johnson, M. (1980). A history of the professional development of teachers. In C. E. Feistritzer & C. Dobson (Eds.), *1981 Report on Educational Personnel Development* (pp. 1–76). Washington, DC: Feistritzer Publications.

Edelfelt, R. A., & Raths, J. D. (1999). *A brief history of standards in teacher education*. Reston, VA: Association of Teacher Educators.

Evenden, E. S. (1935). *National survey of the education of teachers: Vol. 6, summary and interpretations*. (Bulletin 1933, no. 10). Washington, DC: Government Printing Office.

Exstrom, S. M. (2001). The state board of nursing and its role in continued competency. *Journal of Continuing Education in Nursing*, *32*, 118–125.

Gallagher, C. W. (2008). Democratic policy making and the arts of engagement. *Phi Delta Kappan*, *89*, 340–346.

Garrison, W. H. (2008). Democracy and education: Empowering students to make sense of their world. *Phi Delta Kappan*, *89*, 347–348.

Learned, W. S., Bagley, W. C., McMurry, C. A., Strayer, G. D., Dearborn, W. F., Kandel, I. I., & Jossalyn, H. W. (1920). *The professional preparation of teachers for American public schools: A study based upon an examination of tax-supported normal schools in the state of Missouri*. (Bulletin no. 14). New York: Carnegie Foundation for the Advancement of Teaching

Levine, A. (2006). *Educating school teachers*. Princeton, NJ: Education Schools Project.

Lindsey, M. (Ed.). (1961). *New horizons for the teaching profession*. Washington, DC: National Commission on Teacher Education and Professional Standards.

Madewell, J. E. (2004). Lifelong learning and the maintenance of certification. *Journal of the American College of Radiology*, *1*, 199–203.

National Commission on Teacher Education and Professional Standards. (1953). *Teacher education: The decade ahead.* Washington, DC: Author.

National Commission on Teacher Education and Professional Standards. (1964). *Milestones in teacher education and professional standards.* Washington, DC: Author.

National Education Association, National Commission on Teacher Education and Professional Standards. (1954). *Competent teachers for America's schools: Lay-professional action programs to secure and retain quality teachers.* Washington, DC: Author.

National Education Association, National Commission on Teacher Education and Professional Standards. (1967). *Remaking the world of the career teacher.* Washington, DC: Author.

Neumann, R. (2008). American democracy at risk. *Phi Delta Kappan*, *89*, 328–339.

Reiman, A. J. (1999). The role of the university in teacher learning and development: Present work and future possibilities. In R. A. Roth (Ed.), *The role of the university in the preparation of teachers* (pp. 241–260). New York: Falmer Press.

Reiman, A. J. (2000). Designing coherent and effective teacher education internships. In J. Milner (Ed.), *Promising practices in teacher education.* New York: Corwin Press.

Rhodes, R. S. (2007). Maintenance of certification. *American Surgeon*, *73*, 143–147.

BIBLIOGRAPHY

Applebome, P. (1995, September 4). GOP efforts put teachers, unions on the defensive. *The New York Times*, p. 1.

Association of Teacher Educators. (1991). *Restructuring the education of teachers: Report of the Commission on the Education of Teachers into the 21st Century.* Reston, VA: Author.

Association of Teacher Educators. (1996). *Certification of master teacher educators: Final Report of the Task Force on the Certification of Teacher Educators.* Reston, VA: Author.

Association of Teacher Educators. (1996). *Standards for teacher educators: Report of the Task Force on the Certification of Teacher Educators.* Reston, VA: Author.

Holmes Group. (1995). *Tomorrow's schools of education*. East Lansing, MI: Author.

Howsam, R. B., Corrigan, D. C., Denemark, G. W., & Nash, R. J. (1976). *Educating a profession*. Washington, DC: AACTE.

Lortie, D. (1995). *Schoolteacher: A sociological study*. Chicago: University of Chicago Press.

Milner, J. O., Edelfelt, R. A., & Wilbur, P. T. (Eds.) (2001). *Developing teachers: Fifth year programs for outstanding students*. Lanham, MD: University Press of America.

National Commission on Teacher Education and Professional Standards. (1963). *A position paper on teacher education and professional standards: Axioms and goals, selected recommendations, questions, and issues*. Washington, DC: Author.

National Commission on Teaching and America's Future. (1996). *What matters most: Teaching for America's future*. Washington, DC: Author.

National Education Association, Research Division. (2003). *Status of the American public school teacher 2000–2001*. Washington, DC: Author.

Smith, B. O., Cohen, S. B., & Pearl, A. (1969). *Teachers for the real world*. Washington, DC: American Association of Colleges for Teacher Education.

Smith, B. O., Silverman, S., Borg, J. A., & Fry, B. V. (1980). *A design for a school of pedagogy*. Washington, DC: Department of Education.

Washington State Board of Education. (1985). *Continuity and progress: The State Board of Education's report on teacher education in Washington*. Olympia, WA: Author.

CHAPTER 24

The Teacher Educator Standards as a Foundation for Professional Self-Study

Emily Lin and Cari L. Klecka
University of Nevada, Las Vegas

There is general and widespread agreement from the reform literature and public policy arena that teacher education preparation programs are one of the important factors for meeting the challenges and demands of preparing quality teachers and increasing student achievement (Cochran-Smith & Fries, 2005; Darling-Hammond, 2006; Darling-Hammond & Bransford, 2005; National Commission on Teaching and America's Future, 1996; 1997). If the quality of the classroom teacher is vital to improving student learning, then the quality of teacher educators—the teachers of teachers—may also be fundamental to improving education.

Yet, there exists an inattention to the preparation and professional development of teacher educators and to research about teacher educators. Little is known about the nature and impact of their work across varying institutional and state policy contexts (Cochran-Smith, 2003; Zeichner, 2005).

The development and revision of the Association of Teacher Educators' (ATE) Standards for Teacher Educators brings much needed attention to the nature of the professional work of teacher educators. The standards communicate a clear, shared vision of the core purposes and responsibilities of teacher educators. They provide a framework through which teacher educators could assess their professional performance within the local teacher education context and beyond. Ultimately, these standards strive to define what it means to be an accomplished teacher educator.

Given this, there are several questions posed. How could the revised standards for teacher educators be conceptualized into a working framework to help teacher educators better understand the socially transformative nature, scope, and objectives of their role? How can these standards be enacted into the practical teaching realities of teacher educators' work? Consideration of these questions focuses the discussion on the values and societal expectations for teacher educators' work.

In this chapter, it is argued that the standards provide a language of possibility to articulate the values and social participation objectives for teacher educators. To accomplish this, a working theoretical framework grounded in the standards is proposed as a pedagogical self-study framework that can potentially guide teacher educators in their reflections on their work and the profession. This is followed by a discussion of the methodologies and methodological considerations associated with using the standards as a framework for self-study. This chapter concludes with the sharing of a project as an example of how the standards have been used as a basis for reflection and collaboration among teacher educators and its connections to the framework proposed.

INTERPRETING THE STANDARDS INTO A WORKING FRAMEWORK

The ATE standards clarify the type of knowledge, values, attitudes, commitments, skills, and participation that characterize professional teacher educators. Similar to the new paradigm of teacher learning (Cochran-Smith, 2005; Darling-Hammond, 1997), the standards acknowledge and address the importance of different facets of teacher educators' knowledge and exemplary practices, and emphasize the continuing professional development of teacher educators in a complex system.

Several of the standards facilitate an inquiry-based approach that encourages teacher educators to adopt a research stance toward their own practice. This invites them to document and critically reflect on their own work, which can generate meaningful collaborations to resolve problems in the profession. The standards support the promising trend for teacher educators to work simultaneously within and against the larger education system as "critical friends." The standards support teacher educators' commitments to be active change agents and challenge inequities embedded in practices and policies in schools and society.

Darling-Hammond (1997) asserted that teachers learn best "by studying, doing, and reflecting; by collaborating with other teachers; by looking closely at students and their work; and by sharing what they see" (p. 319). Situated within this paradigm, the standards can be conceptualized as a working framework that allows teacher educators to adopt a new language to *learn about*, *learn within* and *learn for* teacher education. This may result in the adoption of new patterns of thinking for individuals and groups of teacher educators.

The implied three types of learning goals (*about*, *within*, and *for* teacher education) offer teacher educators a way to deliberately think about the nature of their work, guide their practice, and empower themselves to transform the profession. Each type of essential learning by teacher educators is briefly described below to illustrate the contrasting and formative needs reflected in the standards with this transformative endeavor.

Learning *about* Teacher Education

Learning *about* teacher education implies that teacher educators must first become knowledgeable and aware of the nine newly revised standards and all the necessary knowledge, values, skills, and dispositions conveyed within them. For example, in Standard One: Teaching, accomplished teacher educators are knowledgeable about research-based practices and how to best model the appropriate behaviors in preparing teachers before actual application can occur. Similarly, in Standard Two: Cultural Competence, teacher educators are first knowledgeable about themselves, their own attitudes and beliefs, the cultures of others, and the pedagogical methods and their application before any integration or change can occur.

In other words, learning *about* teacher education connotes a clear cognitive goal of teacher educators' understanding of the nine standards in relation to the nature of their work, their professional selves, and their context. Learning about teaching assumes the intellectual and technical skills necessary for examining the nature of their roles.

Learning *within* Teacher Education

Learning *within* teacher education is characterized by teacher educators adopting ways of thinking and behaving that emphasize continual reflective inquiry, research and reflection into their local context, their subject area, and their interaction and relationship to the social and political world. This type of learning is especially reflected in standards three, four, five, six, eight, and nine where the context in which teacher educators' work can influence others, offering opportunities to develop analytical, reflective, research, and collaborative competencies that provide a purposeful, systematic route to becoming an accomplished teacher educator.

In developing these competencies, teacher educators recognize that teaching and learning are contextual as they prepare prospective and in-service teachers as models for their P–12 students. The reflective capabilities of observation, analysis, interpretation, and decision making (Duckworth, 1987; Richardson, 1989; Zeichner & Liston, 1987) are necessary for making sense of the complexities of the teaching and learning profession. Teacher educators strive to imprint the inquiry-reflection cycle as a foundation for practice. This develops within and models for their students the attitudes and dispositions essential for reflection: open-mindedness, responsiveness, and wholeheartedness (Dewey, 1933) within their working context.

Learning *for* Teacher Education

Learning *for* teacher education implies that teacher educators develop the understanding, attitudes, critical thinking abilities, and political know-how to participate in action to improve the profession and teacher education in general. This action orientation emphasizes the need for educators to be advocates who critique the educational values and assumptions that inform teacher education resources, policies, and practices. In critically examining and understanding the interests of various stakeholders in teacher education, teacher educators reflect their own professional beliefs and practices and empower themselves to make constructive social changes across various programs and social systems (Giroux & Freire, 1987).

Teacher educators actively undertake the challenges of determining educational policies and practices (Cochran-Smith, 2006) that will address the structures of inequalities in schools, communities, and the larger society (Apple, 1995). It is expected that teacher educators possess "not only the knowledge of how the economic and social system operates to maintain a repressive status quo but also commitment and actions to change the world, to change the distributions of power and resources" (McDiarmid & Clevenger-Bright, 2008, p. 142).

The goals of learning for teacher education are especially evident in standards five, six, seven, eight and nine. Rather than exhibiting a language of pessimism, these standards provide a language of possibility, which highlights the values and social participation objectives for teacher educators.

ENACTING THE STANDARDS THROUGH SELF-STUDY RESEARCH

Enacting the standards into the working realities of teacher educators begins with an approach nested within the framework of learning *about*, *within*, and *for* teacher education. The standards advocate a purposeful and systematic way of examining the dynamic complexities of the relationship between teaching and learning, and learning about teaching (Loughran, 2007). Self-study research methodology holds the key to a deeper understanding of teaching and learning for teacher educators to advance the profession practically and theoretically. Using the standards as a foundation for teacher educators to engage in self-study is proposed to further develop learning *about*, *within*, and *for* teacher education.

Self-study research became more visible in the published literature in teacher education in the early 1990s with teacher educators studying their own practice (Lunenberg & Willemse, 2006; Zeichner, 1999). Zeichner (1999) defines 'self-study' by teacher educators as the "disciplined and systematic inquiry into one's own teaching practice" (p. 11). Although the term "self-study" may connote individualism in studying how an individual thinks and acts in reframing one's practice (Schon, 1983), there is also an expectation that self-study may be a vehicle to positively change teaching and teacher education practices within the profession.

Self-study can serve as a compelling method for professional development and also contribute to a broader knowledge base in teacher education (Cochran-Smith, 2003; Cochran-Smith & Lytle, 1992; Loughran, 2007; Zeichner, 2005; 2007). Operationalizing the standards as a framework for self-study directly links the articulated accomplished practices to the potential of research to influence practice (and improvement of practice) of teacher educators. As Hamilton and Pinnegar (1998) note,

> research on teaching practice by teachers holds invaluable promise for developing new understandings and producing new knowledge about teaching and learning. Formalizing such study of practice through self-study is imperative...The value of self-study depends on the researcher/teacher providing convincing evidence that they know what they claim to know (p. 243).

Conducting and engaging in self-study research that is shared and built upon, between, and within a network of researcher-practitioner partnerships may provide the genesis for building a more coherent picture of teacher education research (Zeichner, 2005; 2007). This promising advance of self-study research supports the ATE standards in reconceptualizing the role of teacher educators.

Teacher educators who embark on self-study often are motivated by the notion of improving their practice. In her analysis of the literature, Berry (2004) noted that the primary reasons for teacher educators engaging in self-studies include: (1) examining varying components of practice; (2) scrutinizing the alignment of teaching philosophies, practices, and beliefs; (3) fostering a model for reflecting critically; and (4) considering and creating a reframed perspective of institutional evaluations. As Harfitt and Tavares (2004) emphasize:

> teachers themselves are the primary initiators of their own development. The spirit of enquiry, the wish to reflect on one's own teaching, perhaps to explore other paths, comes from within the practitioner; it cannot be imposed from outside . . . teachers cannot be given a purpose, because purposes must come from within . . . teaching lies within the control of teachers. It is something that we can study and improve (p. 344).

Positioning the ATE Standards for Teacher Educators as a basis for self-study and a catalyst for inquiry frames this self-improvement.

Zeichner (2005) reported on the outcome of self-study and mentioned that "many teacher educators who conduct research on their own courses and programs argue that they benefit greatly from these inquiries and that this visible commitment to self-inquiry provides a model for their students. They also argue that improvements in their work as teacher educators and their programs result from these self-studies" (p. 750). Teacher educators enacting the new ATE standards through self-study research suggests a blossoming potential for furthering the discourse about the nature and values of teacher education. This research specific to better understanding teacher educators' work in relation to the standards provides a vision for our profession.

Self-Study Methodology

Although the embryonic development of self-study research lacks a clear consensus on its use in professional practice, many researchers/practitioners have outlined several key principles considered important (Laboskey, 2004; Loughran, 2006a; 2006b; 2007; Mishler, 1990; Pinnegar, 1998; Russell, 2006). Self-study allows for the documentation and dissemination of learning and serves as a pedagogy of teacher education (Loughran, 2006a; 2006b). Further, it builds the knowledge, skills, and dispositions of teacher educators to meet the socially transformative nature of their objectives.

The following approaches suggest ways to enact the ATE standards and consider their relationship to teaching, learning, and research. Loughran (2006a) describes three levels of self-study, "personal (oneself); collaborative; and institutions" (p. 50), that provide a useful framework for using the ATE standards in such an endeavor.

Personal self-study centers on inquiry into an individual's practice with the intent to better understand the development of one's knowledge of practice. These studies tend to stem from one's issues and predicaments of teaching about teaching.

Collaborative self-study seeks to understand practice not only from an individual's perspective but also by engaging others so that new, shared meanings may be generated. The opportunity for diverse critical views allows for making explicit commonly held assumptions.

Educational/institutional self-study critically examines policies and practices at the institutional programmatic level rather than the daily actions found in individual classroom contexts. These studies provide a broad view of challenging existing program assumptions and resistance to change in institutional practices.

Loughran (2006b, pp. 46–47) further categorized the three levels of self-study described above to include specific research lenses for teacher educators to conduct self-studies. They are included here as they make specific connections to how self-study could be considered utilizing the standards as a framework.

- *Learning about self:* This assumes that a better understanding of one's practice and students begins with the initial deep understanding of oneself and one's self-perceptions. The standards provide a foundation for examination into one's professional role in relation to what is defined as accomplished in the profession.

- *Learning with and through critical friends:* This entails the practice of habitual reflection through the perspectives of "critical friends" for deepened understanding of teaching practices. Involving "critical friends", a collaborative process of group self-study and analysis, permits teacher educators to interpret the standards and apply them to practice and shifts the sense of self from working individually to engaging with others. Collaborative "critical friends" may include other faculty, teachers, graduate students, pre-service teachers, etc.

- *Learning by observing practice from students' perspective:* This includes a shift from a teacher-centered perspective to a learner-centered perspective of teaching. This enhances the ability to conceptualize the philosophical foundations of one's own practice. Studying practice in this manner affords the unfolding of teaching to encompass more than simply teaching content to consideration of student experiences and backgrounds.

- *Learning by the teacher educator through the student-teacher:* Teacher educators gain insights into their own practice as they examine the experiences of prospective and in-service teachers who are developing their own knowledge and skills. Teachers are frequently asked to reflect on the standards in relation to practice. Teacher educator participation in this activity grounded in their own standards provides insight into what is required of teacher education students and how teachers construct the standards grounded in practice (Klecka, Donovan, & Fisher, 2007).

- *Learning by teacher educator through school experiences:* As teacher educators engage teachers and administrators in the workplace, they gain a greater understanding for the implications of their own instruction and research. Examining self in relation to standards (e.g., Standard Seven: Public Advocacy, and Standard Eight: Teacher Education Profession) further push teacher educators' thinking about their role and implications for their work.

- *Learning by teacher educator as school teacher.* When teacher educators explore their practice while actually teaching pre-K-12 students, their own research and teaching is enhanced. This practice encourages teacher educators to reformulate their roles and unpack the tacit knowledge and values of experiential learning in the classroom.

Features of Self-Study Methodology

Self-study research, as introduced in this document, encourages teachers and teacher educators to engage in practitioner inquiry in their context to build their professional knowledge. This has resulted in a flurry of published self-study research conducted by teacher educators in recent times (Lunenberg & Willemse, 2006; Zeichner, 1999). There is also stinging criticism and, at times, outright dismissal of this type of research by the larger educational research community (Cochran-Smith, 2005; Loughran, 2007; Zeichner, 2007). The debate related to issues of trustworthiness and problems of bias and subjectivity contribute to questions about the legitimacy and broader significance of self-study research.

Teacher educators may minimize these criticisms by embracing the interpretive nature of this type of research. This includes utilizing the traditions of clearly articulated research questions and providing rigorous and explicit descriptions of data collection and analysis techniques to document and report their findings. At the same time, teacher educators should not lose sight of the central goal of self-study research, which is to "provoke, challenge, and illuminate rather than confirm or settle" (Bullough & Pinnegar, 2001, p. 20). Teacher educators may maintain this fundamental purpose and yet still uphold the traditions of good research by following LaBoskey's (2004) four key features of self-study methodology. They include the:

- requirement of evidence of reframing and transformation of practice.
- need for interactions with colleagues, students, educational literature (and the researcher's previous work) to continually question developing understandings in order to question assumptions and values.
- competent use of multiple methods to provide opportunities to gain different, and thus more comprehensive, perspectives on the educational processes under investigation

- demand that self-study work is formalized so that it is available to the professional community for deliberation, further testing and judgment (Loughran, 2007, p. 15).

In this way, future self-studies may extend previous works to accrue a professional knowledge base for teachers and teacher educators. Conducting self-study using the ATE standards as a framework would further this endeavor.

CONCEPTUALIZING SELF-STUDY GROUNDED IN STANDARDS FOR TEACHER EDUCATORS

Taking into consideration the key features of self-study discussed in the previous section, this section highlights one project as an illustration in which the ATE Standards for Teacher Educators could be used as a framework for self-study. Although this project was not initially conceptualized as self-study research, this example is one way that the standards have been operationalized within a project and provides some possibilities of how the standards could be used.

Teacher Educator Standards Cohort (TESC)

TESC was a project of the Commission on the Assessment of the Teacher Educator Standards designed to provide a foundation on which the original version of the standards (ATE, 1996) could be evaluated. To this end, in 2005 the commission recruited teacher educators to engage in a collaborative project in which they would create standards-based portfolios showcasing their work in relation to the standards. Fourteen teacher educators from across the country and in various roles took part in the year-long project (see Klecka, Donovan, & Fisher, 2007 or Klecka, Donovan, Venditti, & Short, 2008). These teacher educators created their portfolios demonstrating how they addressed each of the original standards within their practice. To accomplish this, they collected artifacts such as syllabi and student work as evidence of the standards.

For some, involvement in TESC provided a framework for self-study in that they examined the process from the students' perspective (Klecka, Donovan, & Fisher, 2007). These teacher educators engaged in TESC to examine their own work grounded in standards just as they ask their students to do the same. Through this examination, the standards acted as a unit on which they based their electronic portfolio development. The teacher educators focused on learning about the standards-based portfolio development process. This provided a purposeful grounding for self-study in the process of developing an electronic portfolio based on the standards.

For others, TESC evolved as a self-study in that participants collaborated as "critical friends" who questioned, commented, and pushed one another's thinking. This was evidenced in the teacher educators sharing their electronic portfolios grounded in the standards and soliciting feedback on how to enhance their articulation, reflection, and representation of their work. Much of this discussion shaped their end products and extended their views about themselves as teacher educators in relation to the standards.

Using TESC as a basis for considering how to use the standards themselves as a framework for self-study, it may be more beneficial to move beyond examination of the standards as a unit, and rather individually focus on different standards in relation to an aspect of a teacher educator's practice. In looking at individual standards in relation to practice, a teacher educator could select a standard on which to focus and examine his or her work. As mentioned earlier, the initial TESC project was not conceptualized as a self-study, and therefore did not infuse multiple methods and sources of data to explore questions grounded in the standards. To frame examination into the nature of our work through the standards requires framing research questions grounded in the standards and drawing on multiple methods to better understand and answer the set research questions.

In the end, it is essential to move beyond the self to make more explicit connections to teaching and learning, and learning about teaching to extend learning beyond the individual to the profession (Loughran, 2007). As a collaborative framework, TESC involved constant interrogation of one another's assumptions, assertions, and interpretations on their own work and that of the articulated standards. Through this, a reconceptualization not only of self as a teacher educator can occur but also the nature of work within the profession. With a project like TESC, teacher educators analyze their own practices to provide insight and to broaden interpretation not only of their practice and context, but also to extend the conversation to the standards. Considering projects like TESC, or different forms of self-study, contributes to our understanding of the nature of work and social participation of teacher educators. Engagement in this work provides an opportunity to carve out a path for the profession grounded in research and development of common vision. It is for this purpose that using the teacher educator standards as a framework for self-study is intended.

REFERENCES

Apple, M. W. (1995). *Education and power* (2nd ed.). New York: Routledge.

Association of Teacher Educators. (1996). *National standards for teacher educators*. Reston, VA: Association of Teacher Educators.

Berry, A. (2004). Self-study in teaching about teaching. In J. Loughran, M. L. Hamilton, V. LaBoskey, & T. Russell (Eds.). *International handbook of self-study of teaching and teacher education practices*. (Vol. 2, pp. 1295–1332). Dordrecht, The Netherlands: Kluwer Academic.

Bullough, R., & Pinnegar, S. (2001). Guidelines for quality in autobiographical forms of self-study research. *Educational Researcher, 30*(3), 13–21.

Cochran-Smith, M. (2003). Learning and unlearning: The education of teacher educators. *Teaching and Teacher Education, 19*, 5–28.

Cochran-Smith, M. (2005). Teacher educators as researchers: Multiple perspectives. *Teaching and Teacher Education, 21*, 219–225.

Cochran-Smith, M. (2006). *Policy, practice, and politics in teacher education*. Thousand Oaks, CA: Corwin Press.

Cochran-Smith, M., & Fries, K. (2005). Researching teacher education in changing times: Politics and paradigms. In M. Cochran-Smith and K. Zeichner (Eds.), *Studying teacher education* (pp. 69–109). Mahwah, NJ: Lawrence Erlbaum.

Cochran-Smith, M., & Lytle, S. L. (1992). Communities for teacher research: Fringe or forefront? *American Journal of Education, 100*(1), 298–324.

Darling-Hammond, L. (2006). *Powerful teaching education: Lessons from exemplary programs*. San Francisco: Jossey-Bass.

Darling-Hammond, L. (1997). *The right to learn: A blueprint for creating schools that work*. San Francisco, CA: Jossey-Bass Publishers.

Darling-Hammond, L., & Bransford, J. (2005). (Eds.). *Preparing teachers for a changing world*. San Francisco: Jossey-Bass.

Duckworth, E. (1987). *The having of wonderful ideas*. New York: Teachers College Press.

Giroux, H. A., & Freire, P. (1987). Series introduction. In D. W. Livingston, *Critical Pedagogy and Cultural Power*, South Hadley, MA: Bergin and Garvey.

Hamilton, M. L., & Pinnegar, S. (1998). The value and promise of self-study. In M. L. Hamilton et al. (Eds.), *Reconceptualizing teacher practice: Self-study in teacher education* (pp. 235–246). London: Falmer Press.

Harfitt, G. J., & Tavares, N. J. (2004). Obstacles as opportunities in the promotion of teachers' learning. *International Journal of Educational Research, 41*, 353–366.

Klecka, C. L., Donovan, L., & Fisher, R. (2007). In their shoes: Reframing portfolio development from the students' perspective. *Journal of Computing in Teacher Education, 24*(1), 31–36.

Klecka, C. L., Donovan, L., Venditti, K, & Short, B. (2008). Who is a teacher educator? Enactment of teacher educator identity through electronic portfolio development. *Action in Teacher Education, 29*(4), 83–91.

Laboskey, V. K. (2004). A history and context of self-study and its theoretical underpinnings. In J. Loughran, M. L. Hamilton, V. LaBoskey, & T. Russell (Eds.). *International handbook of self-study of teaching and teacher education practices*. (Vol. 2, pp. 817–869). Dordrecht, The Netherlands: Kluwer Academic.

Loughran, J. (2006a). A response to 'reflecting on the self.' *Reflective Practice, 7*(1), 43–53.

Loughran, J. (2006b). *Developing a pedagogy of teacher education: Understanding teaching and learning about teaching*. New York: Routledge.

Loughran, J. (2007). Researching teacher education practice: Responding to the challenges, demands and expectations of self-study. *Journal of Teacher Education, 58*(1), 12–20.

Lunenberg, M., & Willemse, M. (2006). Research and professional development of teacher educators. *European Journal of Teacher Education, 29*(1), 81–98.

McDiarmid, G. W., & Clevenger-Bright, M. C. (2008). Rethinking teacher capacity. In M. Cochran-Smith, S. Feiman-Nemser, D. J. McIntrye, & K. Demers (Eds.). *Handbook of research on teacher education: Enduring questions in changing contexts* (3rd ed., pp. 134–156) New York: Routledge.

Mishler, E. (1990). Validation in inquiry-guided research: The role of exemplars in narrative studies. *Harvard Educational Review, 60*(4), 415–442.

National Commission on Teaching and America's Future (1996). *What matters most: Teaching for America's future*. New York: NCTAF.

National Commission on Teaching and America's Future (1997). *Doing what matters most: Investing in quality teaching.* New York: NCTAF.

Pinnegar, S. (1998). Methodological perspectives: Introduction. In M. L. Hamilton (Ed.), *Reconceptualizing teaching practice: Self-study in teacher education* (pp. 31–22). London: Falmer.

Richardson, V. (1989). The evolution of reflective teaching and teacher education. In R. Clift, W. R. Houston, & M. Pugach (Eds.), *Encouraging reflective practice: An examination of issues and exemplars.* New York: Teacher College Press.

Russell, T. (2006). How 20 years of self-study changed my teaching. In C. Kosnik, C. Beck, a. R. Freese, & a. P. Samaras (Eds.), *Making a difference in teacher education through self-study: Studies of personal, professional and program renewal* (pp. 3–18). Dordrecht, The Netherlands: Springer.

Schon, D. A. (1983). *The reflective practitioner: How professionals think in action.* New York: Basic Books.

Zeichner, K. (1999). The new scholarship in teacher education. *Educational Researcher, 29*(9), 4–15.

Zeichner, K. (2005). A research agenda for teacher education. In M. Cochran-Smith and K. M. Zeichner (Eds.), *Studying teacher education* (pp. 737–761). Mahwah, NJ: Lawrence Erlbaum.

Zeichner, K. (2007). Accumulating knowledge across self-studies in teacher education. *Journal of Teacher Education, 58*(1), 36–46.

Zeichner, K. & Liston (1987). Teaching student teacher to reflect. *Harvard Educational Review, 57*(1), 23–48.

CHAPTER 25

Be Careful of What You Ask For: Do We Really Want or Need Standards for Teacher Educators?

Renée Tipton Clift, University of Illinois at Urbana-Champaign

The term "standards" is one that cannot be understood outside of other, relational concepts, outside of contexts, or outside of value orientations. For example, the terms *high standards* versus *minimal standards* versus *no standards* in relation to one another convey a continuum of quality and a judgment—without established standards a person, institution, or organization is somehow derelict. The terms *program standards* versus *individual standards* convey a locus of responsibility, the former holding an institution or curriculum accountable for meeting criteria, the latter interrogating actions by people independent of context.

I was asked to write this chapter, in part, because when the Association of Teacher Educators (ATE) first surveyed members concerning standards, my response was quite negative. I elaborated on my concerns in a 2007 session at the Association of Teacher Educators Annual Meeting (following their adoption by the ATE Board of Directors and prior to adoption by the ATE General Assembly), raising several questions about the intended and unintended consequences of setting individual standards for teacher educators—questions that now form the base for this chapter.

In the first section I discuss some concerns with standards and the accompanying assessments that are currently driving education practice. In the second section I discuss my concerns with ATE's decision to adopt individual standards, particularly as they may impact beginning teacher educators. In the third and final section I discuss what we have learned from research on beginning teachers and how that might better inform what we do as teacher educators. My argument is simple. ATE has defined the individual as the target or the locus for change.

This decision, one that is made over and over again in all facets of education, is shortsighted and highly unlikely to lead to improving teaching or teacher education (Fullan, 2007).

WHAT WE HAVE LEARNED ABOUT STANDARDS AND HIGH STAKES TESTING

When the standards movement in education began it seemed, to many people, to be a reasonable, practical, and long overdue concept. What do we want students—children and adolescents—to know and be able to do? The publication of *A Nation at Risk* (1983) called for tougher educational standards, particularly in mathematics and science, and in 1989 the National Council of Teachers of Mathematics (NCTM) released *Curriculum and Evaluation Standards for School Mathematics*, which set curriculum standards for K–12 education. In 1991, NCTM published *Professional Standards for Teaching Mathematics* and, in 1995, *Assessment Standards for School Mathematics* completed the trilogy. The NCTM Standards 2000 project updated the earlier work, noting in the introduction that:

> Attaining the vision laid out in Principles and Standards will not be easy, but the task is critically important. We must provide our students with the best mathematics education possible, one that enables them to fulfill personal ambitions and career goals in an ever changing world. (http://standards.nctm.org/document/chapter1/index.htm)

It is difficult to argue with the language in this statement. Providing students with the best education possible and focusing on personal and career goals is something to which all educators should aspire. It is positive, forward looking, student oriented, and as Schoenfeld's (2002) review stated, somewhat effective. "The fact is that reform curricula (curricula aligned with the *Standards*) can be made to work as hoped. When teachers are well supported in teaching for understanding and have good curricular materials to use, children really do learn, and racial differences in performance diminish" (p. 19).

At the same time, Schoenfeld also cautioned that there was considerable evidence that it was not easy to implement standards-based curricula well, and, even more troubling:

In the current climate of accountability, teachers are increasingly being de-professionalized. Many of the current high-stakes accountability measures focus on skills. Given the stakes, many teachers feel that they deviate from skills-based instruction at their (and their students') peril. Partly because there are (real and perceived) weaknesses in the teaching force, a number of widely used skills-oriented curricula (in reading as well as in mathematics) are so prescriptive that little teacher discretion is allowed. This can lead to a downward spiral, since neither the curricula nor the work conditions under which most teachers operate provide opportunities for professional growth. It may contribute to high attrition rates, which contribute to teacher shortages, which result in the hiring of under-prepared teachers, who (in this way of thinking) would then need even more prescriptive teaching materials. (p. 22)

As other curriculum standards have become institutionalized, put into practice, and assessed with high stakes testing, researchers have argued that they have become restrictive, oppressive, and even harmful to children, adolescents, and their teachers. For example, Au (2007) reported on a qualitative metasynthesis on the impact high stakes testing has had on narrowing curriculum content and on fragmenting knowledge. Heilig and Darling-Hammond (2008) found a long-term impact of the accountability system in a large, urban school district in Texas using a mixed-methods approach. They found considerable evidence of "gaming" the system. For example, some schools encouraged students to skip tenth grade and some excluded low-scoring students from testing. Other schools pushed adolescents out of high school altogether. In concluding their article they noted:

Schools were forced to organize their resources around snap-shot accountability measures based on test scores and reported drop-out rates instead of a long-term measure of student learning and success in completing school. From an institutional theory perspective, this macro-level policy sought to build public confidence in education based on student achievement on standardized tests. As test scores improved, the state and the district gained confidence from the media and political system. However, when students did not show test score improvement, the onus of accountability fell on them and their schools, instead of the state. Although many schools and students were handicapped by capacity and resource constraints, the state was able to transfer the consequences of failure to them. Improvements in the educational quality for the least advantaged students did not materialize. (p. 107)

It is entirely probable that the authors of the curriculum standards did not foresee the translation of standards into high stakes testing, nor did educators in general foresee what impact assessing the proliferation of standards, across many content areas, has done to inhibit creative teaching, to restrict students' curricular choices, or increase the general perception that public education in the United States is broken and is getting worse. As teacher educators, however, we have the benefit of knowing what has happened in the past. We know that well-meaning policies have unintended and problematic consequences.

DO WE NEED TEACHER EDUCATOR STANDARDS? WHAT FOR?

Houston's (2009) chapter in this volume locates the development of teacher standards in the behaviorist tradition and the movement toward competency-based education. He argues that "Standards have become the indicator of quality in products, professionals, services, and organizations. They form the basis for the school curriculum, for teacher licenses, and for the organization of schools and universities" (p. 49). On the ATE Web site there is a document that also provides a brief history and justification for the standards for teacher educators, claiming that "There is a groundswell of activity under way to ensure the preparation and maintenance of more relevant and effective teacher educators. A more systemic orchestrated approach to selection, preparation, and renewal of teacher educators is needed." (www.ate1.org/pubs/Revised_Standards_.cfm).

What do these statements mean? One plausible interpretation is that quality in teacher education is a skill set, a series of quantifiable and measurable indicators on which teacher preparation curriculum and individual teacher educators can be assessed. Is this the case? Do we have a base for developing a skill set? Many recent research publications would suggest that we do not. For example, in the American Educational Research Association's book on the impact of pre-service teacher education (Cochran-Smith & Zeichner, 2005), the chapter authors all concluded that we do not have much research that links teacher education practice with short-term impact on prospective teachers and almost no research on long-term impact.

An additional, plausible interpretation is that by adopting and implementing standards, teacher education and teacher educators will be validated and accorded greater status. Edelfelt's (2009) chapter in this volume supports this interpretation and the one above:

> Some university entities still do not accept teacher educators as equal partners in higher education. Shedding the image of the normal school, where scholarship was lacking, research largely unknown, and scholarship poorly respected, has not been easy (Edelfelt, 2009, p. 277).

He argues that standards will provide teacher educators with a base for their practice and for moving the profession forward:

> Skepticism about teacher educators and complaints about the prevailing norms in teacher education are rampant. The ATE standards address some of the criticisms directly. Also, they can help bring attention to what teacher educators need to know and be able to do, and the roles they should play (Edelfelt, 2009, p. 277).

Labaree's (2004) thoughtful discussion of the low status of education schools in general and teacher education in particular describes the market forces that work against high social and academic value for the products that education produces both in terms of labor and research:

> Pressures came from two sources—employers (pressuring ed schools to meet social efficiency demands) and consumers (pressuring them to meet social mobility demands). The result was an institution that was part teacher factory and part people's college. (pp. 13–14)

And:

> Disdain for education professors is near universal and studies of this group do not paint a pretty picture. We don't show up well in the criteria that matter within the academic status order: research productivity; focusing on hard and pure knowledge; producing exchange value; and association with elite students and professions. One way we adapt is by internally stratifying the education professoriate, as those who do research

and teach doctoral students at major universities try to distance themselves from those who do teacher preparation at former normal schools. But these efforts are largely for naught. (p. 15)

It is highly unlikely that teacher educator standards—even if mandated and applied rigorously and widely—will impact the culture of the university or society. Indeed, the standards may only serve to reinforce the low status of teacher educators. Recall the Heilig and Darling-Hammond (2008) conclusion cited above that the individual bore the brunt of blame for failure to achieve. In many ways, we may be setting our colleagues and ourselves up for the same outcomes as they described. We need to be mindful of unintended and negative possibilities.

Three chapters in this volume provide us with a cautionary perspective on using the standards. Grant and Gibson's (2009) chapter elaborates on three of the standards—teaching, cultural competence, and public advocacy—in order to examine the ways standards can encourage stronger links between multicultural and teacher education. They remind us that having a set of standards is far from sufficient if we wish to continue to improve our practice as teacher educators:

However, while the standards are well researched, inclusive, and comprehensive, they strike us as functioning still as rhetoric. There is certainly no argument about their validity and importance, but what happens now that these standards have been added to the teacher education discourse? How well will they accomplish what they set out to, and how will we evaluate and measure our progress? Where is the language moving towards action, and then where are the tools of adjudication to measure this action? (Grant & Gibson, p. 134).

Heiden's (2009) chapter gives us an example of how one literacy teacher educator felt about how working with both the ATE standards and the International Reading Association's (IRA) standards. She notes that she cannot think of herself as a generic teacher educator, but rather she must also think of herself as a literacy educator as well:

As a literacy teacher educator, I believe that the best uses of the ATE standards have included fostering reflection and goal setting, stimulating shared conversations with my colleagues, and modeling those habits of mind for my students (p. 166).

Heiden's work with the standards was entirely voluntary, and she enables us to see how she used the standards in a context that was supportive of her doing so. She echoes Lin & Klecka's (2009) belief that the standards are for individual use and as a stimulus for self-study.

The chapter by Imig & Imig (2009) documents the ways in which the state can transform intriguing ideas into policy mandates and the volume of stakeholders who compete for control of education:

> The terrain of teacher professionalism is highly contested; e.g., between 'the state' and teachers, between teacher unions and local boards of education, between parent's groups and teachers, between communities and schools. With little certainty about who should 'control' the agenda related to teacher's work, it seems that we are headed into a time of greater uncertainty in where and how teaching and teacher education take place (p. 269).

So what might happen if the ATE standards were to become widely adopted by state accrediting agencies? I have argued so far that the standards promote individual accountability, that they suggest that we can quantify teacher education quality, and that they are unlikely to impact teacher education's status in a positive way. I now argue that if teacher education policy held teacher educators accountable for creating portfolios, presumably demonstrating proficiency in the standards, we would face negative and punitive consequences on teacher educator career development.

SOME POSSIBLE CONSEQUENCES

In this section I elaborate on three areas in which it is possible that holding teacher educators accountable for meeting the teacher educator standards is neutral at best and will lead to a mass exodus from the field at worst. The first area concerns those who will and will not be impacted by such accountability. There are approximately fifty-six institutions in my home state of Illinois that prepare teachers and approximately 1200 in the United States. The contexts for preparing teachers range from online programs, to two-year colleges, to four-year institutions, to universities that vary in the degree to which they have high research activity. Some of the people working in any one of these programs were prepared in research intensive institutions and think of themselves as scholars who study art history, learning, economic policy, string theory, postcolonial theory, second language acquisition, virtual learning environments, etc. Although they may teach key courses for prospective teachers in colleges of education and in colleges other than education (especially when instructing prospective secondary and fine arts teachers), they do not consider themselves to be teacher educators, and the study of teacher education is something they have no wish to pursue. They did not obtain a doctorate to be teacher educators, they may not have even been hired (originally) to work in teacher education, they do not affiliate with ATE or AACTE, and they may not even know about the existence of such organizations.

Bob Fisher's (2009) chapter reminds us that there are many, many people who are, in fact, teacher educators:

Institutions other than those in higher education frequently conduct alternative teacher education programs. In both of these instances, personnel in schools and other agencies play a significant role in the initial and/or continuing education of teachers. Using this view of teacher educator, individuals fall into the following categories:

- Faculty in higher education who provide coursework and conduct research described by NCATE as *professional studies*, including clinical experiences
- Personnel in schools and higher education institutions who provide instruction or supervision of clinical experiences of prospective teachers
- Personnel in schools and higher education institutions who administer or conduct instructional activities designed to provide advanced professional study for teachers
- Personnel from other agencies who design, implement, and evaluate professional study for teachers (e.g., state department certification officers, U.S. Department of Education personnel, researchers in research and development centers, and professional association leaders (pp. 32–33).

These people may be professors who did or did not prepare for a career in research; they may be practitioners serving as clinical faculty; graduate students from within or outside of the United States; full time teachers; intermediate service providers; or school administrators.

Some of these teacher educators may have prepared for their roles. They may have completed programs in which the study of teacher education, teacher learning, and teacher development was the norm. More likely, however, they did not. Does accountability mean that professors and others who are new to the academy or new to working with prospective teachers need to complete some type of program before or after being hired as faculty members to prepare them to be teacher educators? In other words, should one's first position at a college or university include a teacher education induction program, based on the standards, with sanctions for failure to satisfactorily meet beginning level proficiency? Does this hold for all faculty and all school personnel who work with prospective teachers?

The second area relates to the consequences, both process and outcome, of determining who does and who does not meet standards. As noted earlier, many of the advocates for standards see them as a useful tool, a set of guidelines that promote self-study and continuous improvement for volunteers who choose to work with this tool. But just as the INTASC standards were transformed into the Illinois Professional Teaching Standards (one of three sets of standards that all state-accredited teacher education institution graduates must meet in order to be recommended for certification [www.isbe.state.il.us/profprep/pcstandardrules.htm]), it is a distinct possibility that a state or a national accrediting body might similarly transform the teacher educator standards.

If this were to happen, and if all who work with prospective teachers (defined broadly) were to prepare standards related documents, what could we envision about that process? In the University of Illinois at Urbana-Champaign elementary and secondary teacher preparation programs, students prepare electronic portfolios in which they present artifacts from teaching and from coursework that document their proficiency in the standards. They work on these portfolios across semesters and across courses. Preparing the portfolio is time and labor intensive, but because it is embedded in coursework it is more palatable than if it were a stand-alone project.

For faculty and staff based at institutions that require annual reports, one could envision that the task of maintaining a standards-based portfolio might become a part of one's annual review. The question then becomes how large a role should it play in determining individual history, educational foundations, elementary education, salary increase, promotion, or tenure decisions? What training would be necessary for the peers and administrators who review the portfolios? If one does not meet standards, but fulfills all other expected roles, what are the consequences? And, is this a useful and helpful intensification of professors' work? Will moving the task from "voluntary" to "mandatory" enhance the quality of teacher education or will it become an onerous task that dissuades professors from interacting with prospective teachers?

For P–12 school administrators and teachers, there is no current structure in which performance is documented by portfolio, other than when one decides to apply for certification by the National Board for Professional Teaching Standards. All of the questions raised above can be raised within the P–12 sector, which is already under a great deal of pressure. The possibility that teachers and administrators would continue to welcome student teachers and to allow themselves to be held accountable for doing so through a time and labor intensive process is almost nonexistent.

The third area relates to the locus of responsibility on the individual as opposed to the institutional culture. Controversial as they may be, Arthur Levine's (2005; 2006; 2007) critiques of colleges of education are useful in that he lays out three criteria for conceptualizing the preparation of education professionals. Whether preparing administrators, teachers, or educational researchers, purpose, curricular coherence, and curricular balance are three important components in preparing education professionals at all levels.

There is considerable variation in the degree to which colleges and universities implement programs, and, therefore, program delivery is often incomplete, seldom monitored, and understudied. Note the emphasis here on the word *program*. The assumption in Levine's reports is that quality of impact is much less a function of individual achievement and more a function of capable individuals working in a cohesive culture that promotes their success. This observation is one that has empirical support from a related area of research—studies of new teachers who do and do not remain in their original schools and in teaching.

WHAT CAN WE LEARN FROM STUDIES OF NEW TEACHERS?

There is a growing body of qualitative and quantitative research on teacher retention, particularly the retention of new teachers. In the 1990s Bullough and Baughman (1997) documented Baughman's progression from novice to experienced teacher to feeling like a novice again. After six years of teaching she moved from a school in which she had established herself as a strong teacher and a good colleague to one that was closer to her home and in which she would make more money.

The challenges presented by the new environment were very difficult in that she needed to learn how to work with a different population with no support from her administration, no help from her colleagues, and no training. In other words, her prior successful experiences as a teacher did not transfer into a very different setting. And so, even though her second year in the new school was an improvement, she decided to switch careers and leave teaching. "Part of Kerrie's story is a gradual wearing down" (p. 134).

School context matters. This finding holds across time and across studies. For example, Shen's (1997) analysis of the 1990–91 Schools and Staffing Survey and the 1991–92 Teacher Follow-up Survey indicated that teachers who left the profession or moved to a different school were more apt to be in a school with a higher percentage of teachers with less than three years of teaching experience, more students receiving free and reduced lunch, and a lower salary for teachers with master's degrees and twenty years of teaching experience.

The data indicated that the presence of a mentoring program seemed to have a positive impact on teachers remaining in the profession and in the same school and that those who stayed in teaching tended to believe that they have more influence over school- and teaching-related policies. Shen concluded that there appeared to be a positive correlation between teachers' appreciation of the intrinsic merits of teaching, their ability to influence school, and teaching policies and teacher retention.

Smith and Ingersoll (2004) found that 15 percent of first-time teachers changed schools (movers) and that 15 percent left teaching (leavers), and that these percentages were higher in high poverty schools. Having a mentor in one's field of study, however, lowered the probability of leaving the profession by 30 percent and having additional support available (such as collaboration with other teachers, common planning time, an external network of teachers, supportive administration) lowered the probability of leaving or moving even more.

Susan Moore Johnson and her colleagues (2004) have provided us with a series of cases, compiled over four years, which tell us more about what supportive conditions encouraged the fifty teachers in her study to remain in the profession. She concluded that:

> The greatest responsibility for the induction of new teachers also rests with the school, and it takes resources, planning, and good will to do it right. . . . Schools that attend to the development of new teachers initially provide them with some shelter—a less demanding assignment or slightly reduced load, additional help, staged expectations—so that they can gradually gain instructional competence and professional confidence. . . . In many schools this support comes in the form of an assigned mentor. . . . Another way to attend to the development of new teachers is to provide them with adequate curricular supports. Giving new teachers difficult teaching assignments is bad enough; giving them difficult assignments with little or no curriculum is irresponsible. (pp. 259–261)

Across the sources there is a growing body of evidence that suggests that teaching assignment in one's field, having one or more mentors to assist in the transition from student to teacher, professional development that is specific to one's job and location, and support and encouragement are all important contributing factors. The culture of the workplace is one of the strongest and most important forces for encouraging new teachers to remain in their buildings and to thrive in the workplace.

Granted, new professors in education have different needs and work in very different situations from those of beginning P–12 teachers, but it seems reasonable to at least consider whether what we are learning about educators in transition might inform beginning teacher educators. If we were to do so, then the onus of accountability would be on the institutional culture, not on the individual.

One of the first things institutions would need to do is ensure a fit between what the teacher educator is to teach and the prior experience and education she or he has had. We would provide the new professor with a syllabus, with materials, and with an experienced colleague who has taught the same course. We would not expect new professors to take leadership roles in developing or implementing new programs; we would not expect them to teach the teacher education programs more experienced faculty no longer wanted to teach.

We would also provide a supportive and encouraging environment that rewards excellence in teaching. But that is not the norm in many colleges and universities. In Illinois, I am privileged to work with a number of educators from disparate institutions across the state. All of the institutions are sending the same messages: get grants, conduct research, publish. And yet, my teaching workload is lower than theirs and the resources I have available to me are far greater in number. But still, the three of us (experienced professors all) work in environments in which we are critiqued for our individual accomplishments by our peers and we are expected to conduct research and publish our results in top tier, peer refereed journals.

In summary, I am arguing that if our goal is to encourage continuous improvement and to work toward excellence in teacher education, administrative nurturing matters, mentoring matters, support, sufficient resources, and encouragement matter. I am arguing that all of the above are only possible if the departments, schools, colleges, and universities begin to transform themselves into professional learning cultures— something that may be very hard for us to do, given that we work in often entrepreneurial, competitive environments.

The Association of Teacher Educators' adoption of Teacher Educator Standards is a done deal. Many thoughtful and well-meaning educators have contributed to the conceptualization, drafting, redrafting, vetting, and working with the standards. We don't know what will happen to them in the future. They may simply exist as placeholders on the ATE Web site; they may serve as a useful guide to those who wish to engage in self-study; they may become institutionalized in several or many teacher education programs, or they may become mandates in what is already an overly regulated higher education enterprise. What are the authors in this book asking for? Will they get it? Or will there be an unintended and catastrophic consequence as more and more talented young professors decline to engage in preparing the next generation of teachers?

REFERENCES

Association of Teacher Educators. (2008). *National standards for teacher educators (revised).* Manassas Park, VA: Association of Teacher Educators.

Au, W. (2007). High-stakes testing and curricular control: A qualitative metasynthesis. *Educational Researcher, 36*(5), 258–267.

Bullough, R. V., & Baughman, K. (1997). *"First-year teacher" eight years later: An inquiry into teacher development.* New York: Teachers College Press.

Cochran-Smith, M., & Zeichner, K. (Eds). (2005). *Studying teacher education: The report of the AERA Panel on Research and Teacher Education.* Mahwah, NJ: Lawrence Erlbaum.

Edelfelt, R. A. (2009). What Can Standards Do for Teacher Educators? In C. L. Klecka, S. J. Odell, W. R. Houston & R. McBee (Eds.). *Visions for teacher educators.* Lanham, MD: Rowman & Littlefield Education.

Fullan, M. (2007). *The new meaning of educational change.* New York: Teachers College Press.

Fisher, R. L. (2009). Who is a teacher educator? In C. L. Klecka, S. J. Odell, W. R. Houston & R. McBee (Eds.). *Visions for teacher educators.* Lanham, MD: Rowman & Littlefield Education.

Grant, C. A., & Gibson, M. (2009). A Multicultural Approach to ATE's Standards for Teacher Educators. In C. L. Klecka, S. J. Odell, W. R. Houston & R. McBee (Eds.). *Visions for teacher educators.* Lanham, MD: Rowman & Littlefield Education.

Heiden, D. (2009). Perspectives on Standards from a Teacher Educator of Literacy. In C. L. Klecka, S. J. Odell, W. R. Houston & R. McBee (Eds.). *Visions for teacher educators.* Lanham, MD: Rowman & Littlefield Education.

Heilig, J. V., & Darling-Hammond, L. (2008). Accountability Texas-style: The progress and learning of urban minority students in a high stakes testing context. *Educational Evaluation and Policy Analysis, 30*(2), 75–110.

Houston, R. (2009). Conceptualizing, developing, and testing standards for teacher educators. In C. L. Klecka, S. J. Odell, W. R. Houston & R. McBee (Eds.). *Visions for teacher educators.* Lanham, MD: Rowman & Littlefield Education.

Illinois State Board of Education. (2002). *Illinois Professional Teaching Standards.* Retrieved on October 9, 2008, from http://www.isbe.state.il.us/profprep/pcstandardrules.htm

Imig, S. R., & Imig, D. G. (2009). The role of standards on the educational landscape: Perspectives on standards for teacher educators. In C. L. Klecka, S. J. Odell, W. R. Houston & R. McBee (Eds.). *Visions for teacher educators*. Lanham, MD: Rowman & Littlefield Education.

Johnson, S. M., & the Project on the Next Generation of Teachers. (2004). *Finders and keepers: Helping new teachers survive and thrive in our schools*. San Francisco: Jossey-Bass.

Labaree, D. F. (2004). *The trouble with ed schools*. New Haven: Yale University Press.

Levine, A. (2006). *Educating school teachers*. Washington, DC: The Education Schools Project.

Levine, A. (2005). *Educating school leaders*. New York: The Education Schools Project.

Levine, A. (2007). *Educating researchers*. Washington, DC: The Education Schools Project.

Lin, E., & Klecka, C. L. (2009). Interpreting the teacher educator standards: Establishing a foundation for self study. In C. L. Klecka, S. J. Odell, W. R. Houston & R. McBee (Eds.). *Visions for teacher educators*. Lanham, MD: Rowman & Littlefield Education.

National Commission on Excellence in Education. (1983). *A nation at risk: The imperative for educational reform*. Washington, DC: U.S. Government Printing Office.

National Council of Teachers of Mathematics. (1989). *Curriculum and evaluation standards for school mathematics*. Reston, VA: Author.

National Council of Teachers of Mathematics. (1991). *Professional standards for teaching mathematics*. Reston, VA: Author.

National Council of Teachers of Mathematics. (1995). *Professional standards for teaching mathematics*. Reston, VA: Author.

National Council of Teachers of Mathematics (2000). *Principles and standards for school mathematics*. Retrieved on June 27, 2008, from http://standards.nctm.org/document/chapter1/index.htm.

Schoenfeld, A. H. (2002). Making mathematics work for all children: Issues of standards, testing, and equity. *Educational Researcher*, *31*(1), 13–25.

Shen, J. (1997). Teacher retention and attrition in public schools: Evidence from SASS91. *Journal of Educational Research, 91(2)*, 81–88.

Smith, T. M., & Ingersoll, R. M. (2004). What are the effects of induction and mentoring on beginning teacher turnover? *American Educational Research Journal, 41(3)*, 681–714.

Afterword

Cari L. Klecka, Sandra J. Odell, W. Robert Houston,
and Robin Haskell McBee, Editors

In the final chapter preceding this afterword, Renée Clift poses the question to the authors of this book regarding their intentions for the Standards for Teacher Educators and, essentially, for what are we asking? As the editors of this book, we wrote this afterword in response to her question, but also to articulate our intentions for this book and for the continued work of the Commission on the Assessment of the Teacher Educator Standards.

By providing this edited volume, the four editors intended to highlight the work and visions of the National Commission on Teacher Educator Standards and the later Commission on the Assessment of the Teacher Educator Standards. Our goal was to disseminate the ideas, conceptions, and intentions of the original development and subsequent revision of the Standards for Teacher Educators. We also aimed to unearth questions and issues about these conceptualizations. We feel that the authors of the individual chapters have helped us realize this goal.

In the pages of this book, a cross section of teacher educators have contextualized the history of the Standards for Teacher Educators, conceptualized the standards as visions for teacher educators, and provided a variety of perspectives on these standards and their place and influence on the educational landscape. These chapters have confirmed what we believe not only about the profession and standards for teacher educators, but have also raised questions about their interpretation and implementation.

Several authors recommended that the standards provide a vehicle for establishing a vision and further define that vision of a teacher educator.

The term *teacher educator* casts a wide net encompassing an array of roles and responsibilities in which we engage. Our interpretation is that these standards contribute to how those in and outside of teacher education understand the complexities involved with being a teacher educator. The intent is not to have these standards narrowly define what a teacher educator does but rather to provide a lens that broadens the definition and interpretation of our work. The goal is to be inclusive, but also specific about what we think it means to be an accomplished teacher educator. This set of standards provides a vision for the professional role of the teacher educator that encompasses the multiple layers of our work. It is grounded in a commitment to students, as noted by Imig and Imig in their chapter, while embracing the multifaceted responsibilities from teaching to research and beyond.

In her chapter, Clift makes the explicit connection between high stakes accountability measures and the establishment of Standards for Teacher Educators. It is not the intention of the editors to endorse the future development of an accountability structure grounded in these standards. Rather, as suggested in the title of this book, it is our intent to envision what's possible through the standards. We call on the profession to unify and use this book as a basis to discuss the complexity of our roles that not only entails involvement with schools, but also the generation of new knowledge around that involvement with the end goal of improving teaching and learning for all students. These standards are intended for teacher educators to use in goal setting and self-study as we develop and evolve in our careers. They are not intended for beginning teacher educators to demonstrate proficiency, but rather to provide a vision for how to develop one's research and practice over time toward being an accomplished teacher educator.

About the Editors

Cari L. Klecka is an assistant professor of curriculum and instruction at the University of Nevada, Las Vegas and Associate Editor of the *Journal of Teacher Education.* She teaches courses in research on teaching, curriculum, and action research. Her professional interests center on development of communities to support teacher education and action research. Dr. Klecka works in collaboration with the Clark County School District on the Initiative on National Board Certification, which focuses on candidate recruitment and professional development.

Sandra J. Odell is professor and chair of the Department of Curriculum and Instruction, University of Nevada, Las Vegas and Editor of the *Journal of Teacher Education.* She has maintained a career-long research interest in teacher development and teacher induction and mentoring in collaborative university/school district programs. She has chaired and served on several ATE National Commissions related to mentoring, induction, and teacher development. Dr. Odell was the recipient of the ATE *Distinguished Teacher Educator* award in 1999.

W. Robert Houston, John and Rebecca Moores Professor of Education, University of Houston, has authored or edited forty-five books including the first edition of the *Handbook of Research on Teacher Education.* He served as ATE president in 1985–1986, and has received numerous honors, including being the first recipient of ATE's *Distinguished Teacher Educator* award in 1997 and the 2000 *Edward C. Pomeroy Award for Distinguished Contributions to Teacher Education,* presented by the American Association of Colleges for Teacher Education.

Robin Haskell McBee is a professor in the teacher education department at Rowan University. Her areas of interest include caring in schools, curriculum integration, multicultural education, and social studies education.